The
ALTERNATIVE PRESS
ANNUAL, 1984

Edited by

PATRICIA J. CASE

With the assistance of librarians, scholars, activists, and alternative press people

Temple University Press · Philadelphia

Temple University Press, Philadelphia 19122
© 1985 by Temple University. All rights reserved.
Published 1985
Printed in the United States of America

ISSN 0748-9463
ISBN 87722-392-0

Alternative Cataloging in Publication Data

The alternative press annual. 1983–
  Philadelphia, PA: Temple University Press.

  Editor: 1983–   Patricia J. Case.
  "News items, essays, poetry, songs, cartoons,
and graphics published in alternative press magazines
and newspapers." Includes directory.
    1. Alternative press publications—Excerpts.
  2. Alternative press—Directories.   3. Radicalism.
  4. Social change.   5. Grassroots movement.   6. Corporate
  power. I. Case, Patricia J., editor.

081 or 301.23

"All the news they never print."
    Radioactive Times

"What happens to the news that doesn't get printed anyway?"
    Tuli Kupferberg, *Working Classes*

"Most of the news I need most, *The New York Times* doesn't see fit
    to print."
    Daniel Ellsberg, *In These Times*

"All the fits that's news to print."
    Madness Network News

"News NOT in the News."
    CounterSpy: The Magazine for People Who Need to Know

"All the News that Fitz Won't Print."
    Convoy Dispatch, Teamsters for a Democratic Union

"All the News to Give You Fits."
    Multnomah Monthly Magazine

"All the Dirt That's Fit to Print."
    Grub

"If all you know is what you read in the papers, you're missing most
    of the world."
    Sojourners

"All the truth that's fit to think."
    Dick Gregory

"If It Moves Print It."
    Rolling Stock

CONTENTS

Preface

Section 1: ORWELL WASN'T ALL WRONG

Section 2: IGNORANCE IS NOT STRENGTH

Section 3: WAR IS NOT PEACE

Section 4: FREEDOM IS NOT SLAVERY

Section 5: WATCH OUT, BIG BROTHER!

Postscript

Directory

Index

Preface

As 1984 approached, the commercial press bombarded us with George Orwell's predictions, although they were never intended as such but were reflections on 1948, the year in which he wrote 1984. Television commentators and journalists toyed with examples of Newspeak and left no bush unbeaten in a search to find out whether Orwell's metaphors had become reality. Then they breathed a sigh of relief concluding that Orwell was wrong: 1984 was not the year that Big Brother assumes power.

The alternative press, on the other hand, did little to hype Orwell. Instead, it continued to chronicle the slow deterioration of our freedoms and civil rights that has been proceeding for more than a decade. Following its lead, this year's Alternative Press Annual takes a close look at the impact government agencies, multinational corporations, and professional associations are having on our lives, liberty, and pursuit of happiness. We have reprinted here, for example, a tally of this year's worst Supreme Court decisions compiled for the American Civil Liberties Union and published in their newspaper, Civil Liberties. An article from Not Man Apart shows us that the Food and Drug Administration, having failed to protect us from pesticides in our food, is now worrying about how to overcome our customary reluctance to accept new technology as it moves toward introducing irradiation as a means of preserving food. Other articles focus on AT&T, the American Medical Association, and Nuclear Regulatory Commission.

This year's Annual brings you messages from people you didn't hear from in 1984. Tomas Borge of Nicaragua Libre talks about his country and living under the threat of a U.S. invasion. He had been invited to speak to organizations and university audiences across the United States, but he was denied entry here. No speeches, no press conferences. And Sonia Johnson, who was big news when she was excommunicated from the Mormon Church during the ERA battles, was not news this year when she ran for president, in spite of the fact that she was the first third-party candidate ever to qualify for federal matching funds. She received over $150,000 in federal matching funds for the Citizens Party ticket and campaigned from coast to coast.

The alternative press also addressed topics that the commercial press didn't touch such as the collapse of the health-care system in Grenada in the aftermath of the U.S. invasion, homophobia, a plan to reduce the cost of housing by 90 percent, and the potential dangers of immunizing children. Millions of us watched Nestlé officials and boycotters chomp on Nestlé

Crunch Bars to celebrate the end of the boycott and Nestlé's agreement to stop the deceptive marketing of infant formula in the Third World, but how many of us know that it was the most successful boycott of the decade, that it was conducted worldwide for more than ten years by a loosely knit network of women's, religious, and pacifist groups? Nor do most people know of the massive resistance movement that has been organized to protest the expected invasion of Nicaragua.

If you read the commercial press, you probably know that instances of rape are increasing even in localities where the overall crime rate is declining. Yet journalists and society at large still have yet to learn what rape really is, what feminist groups and rape crisis centers have been teaching police, medical, and emergency personnel for the last decade; that rape is an act of premeditated violence, not a crime of uncontrolled passion. Yet the commercial press still serves us the same old myths and innuendos. It ignores the pain and the reality that no woman asks to be raped, no woman wants to be raped—any more than a man wants to be robbed or beaten. We are dedicating a section to rape and other forms of violence against women, because only in the alternative press, especially in feminist and lesbian publications, are women writing about what it means to live in fear, how they can defend themselves, and how to sort the sex from the violence. In the light of all that women have suffered and continue to suffer, it is enraging that the Minneapolis Pornography Ordinance was not taken more seriously as an attempt to defend the civil rights of women—our right to walk the streets without harassment, our right to live free of pornographic images, our right to live without fear.

Once again we are trying to rewrite history as we select the news and opinions that don't have the megabucks behind them to reach every American living room every evening, or to get on the library shelves. The opinions, issues, and events compiled in this volume are significantly different from those the commercial press published in 1984 and will be different from the history that will survive and be recorded in history books.

The small sampling of articles, poetry, cartoons, photographs, signs, and line drawings that is reprinted here, in the second volume of *The Alternative Press Annual*, is taken from 36 alternative magazines and newspapers, which are published by socialists, feminists, environmentalists, anarchists, radical people of color, politically active lesbians and gay men, and people working for equality and social justice. We have arranged the articles in five topical sections, with a postscript in tribute to pacifist and lesbian-rights advocate Barbara Deming who passed over in August. We have added a Directory with address and subscription information for each of the publications represented in the volume, plus an index.

I am once again indebted to many people for their assistance in compiling this volume, especially to the alternative press publishers, editors, and writers who make it so difficult to keep this book down to manageable size. Thanks also to Sandy Berman, head cataloguer at Hennepin County Library in Minnesota, Tim Ryan at SourceNet, James P. Danky, newspaper and periodicals librarian at the State Historical Society of Wisconsin, and Ellen Embardo, curator of the Alternative Press Collection at the University of Connecticut in Storrs, for recommending articles and reviewing the preliminary selections.

The following people also nominated articles for inclusion in this year's volume: Eileen Conan Broadbelt, Delphine Blachowicz of *Cross Country Currents*, Brad Edmondson and S. K. List of the *Ithaca Times*, Ronda Hauben, Rich Grzesiak of the *Philadelphia Gay News*, A. D. Winans of Second Coming, Inc., Polly and Mickey of *Broomstick*, Paula Kassell of *New Direc tions for Women*, Candace Watson, David Finkel of *Changes: Socialist Journal*, D. C. Erdmann of Merging Media, Paul Hoover of *Oink!*, Concetta C. Doucette, Richard Reynolds of *Mother Jones*, Marilyn Hacker of *13th Moon*, David A. Albert of New Society Publishers, Connie Fox, Bill Vitale of *The Mobilizer*, Ina Bransome of *Practice*, Jan Clausen of Long Haul Press, Kathleen Hughes of *Environmental Action*, Gary Keenan of *Science for the People*, Allison Meyers, Linda Unger of *Lucha/Struggle*, Farar Elliott of *Off Our Backs*, Susan Jamieson of *Breakthrough*, Doug Moss of *Agenda*, Steve Fankuchen of *Shmate*, Josh Gosciak of *Contact II*, Leonora H. Wienner of *New Age Journal*, Nathan Karp of *The People*, Jon Steinberg of *Health/PAC Bulletin*, and Ari Korpivaara of *Civil Liberties*.

The Contemporary Culture Collection at Temple University Library in Philadelphia served as the core collection of materials reviewed for this book, but I also drew heavily on the resources of the Alternative Press Collection at the University of Connecticut in Storrs and the library at SourceNet in Santa Barbara, California. The people at Temple University Press—David Bartlett, Michael Ames, Doris Braendel, Zachary Simpson, Mary Capouya, and Robert Taft—were responsible for converting a dog-eared stack of photocopies into the tight, crisp volume that you hold in your hands.

Reading for *The Alternative Press Annual*, 1985 has already begun. Previous volumes have benefited greatly from the nominations made by alternative press writers, editors, publishers, and readers. For the 1985 volume, again I am looking for news items, essays, poetry, songs, cartoons, photos, and drawings published in alternative magazines and newspapers. Materials should be well developed, should effectively address the vital social and political issues of the year or record the organizing and actions of people working for social change. The deadline for nominations of materials published in 1985 is November 15, 1985; materials received before October 1 will be in the first sort. Send a photocopy of the piece itself or the issue of the magazine or newspaper it appeared in, and make sure that the magazine or newspaper title, issue number, and date are in evidence.

If you are an alternative press editor or publisher and we are not already on your mailing list, please consider adding us to it. This will also ensure that your entry in the *Whole Again Resource Guide* is kept current. Address nominations to:

Patricia J. Case
SourceNet
P.O. Box 6767
Santa Barbara, CA 93160
ATTN: *The Alternative Press Annual*

Section 1

ORWELL WASN'T ALL WRONG

Newspeak and the Impoverishment of Language

by Lynne Clive

FROM *Fifth Estate* 18:4; whole no. 314 (Winter 1984): 6–8

In his appendix on language in the world of 1984, George Orwell explains that "Newspeak was the official language of Oceania and had been devised to meet the ideological needs of Ingsoc, or English Socialism." Newspeak was created for the ultimate purpose of thought control. By reducing the English language (Oldspeak) to a utilitarian skeleton, dispensing with all verb tense irregularities and syntactical complexity, and by scaling down word choice to a bare minimum, it destroyed the ambiguity of human communication and would eventually "diminish the range of human thought." Most people had not yet adopted Newspeak as their only means of communication, but it was intended that by the year 2050 Oldspeak would be made totally obsolete by the new Party language.

Perhaps 1984 analogies will become tiresome and overworked very early in the year. The year 1984 was 1948 for Orwell of course, and aspects of this "fictional" world are easily mirrored in any year of our modern myopic age. The uncanny truth of the analogies shouldn't surprise us. There are no off-the-wall coincidences here. We're on a treadmill and have been long before 1948; it's just that Orwell was astute enough, perceptive enough, to write it all down, and with such clear, sharp wit and honest irony that history seems to ring truer and truer each year. It *is* 1984 after all, and some things do just jolt you.

COMPUTER LANGUAGE SHOVED DOWN OUR THROATS

Newspeak isn't being openly imposed on us by our government, but the communications industry is shoving computers, computer systems, systems communications, and the vapid, facile language of computer technology down our consumptive throats. Computer companies are inundating schools with free computers in their mad rush to sell the world on this "new, practical, effective, efficient, invaluable mode of communication." Through school and television and video arcades, it is hoped that our vulnerable children will be easily won over to the cause of the computer revolution. By being exposed at every turn to the world of computer technology—in study, in play, in creative activity—they will become fluent in the language of systems communications, adept at responding with the right password and appropriate obeisance to computer command, and so set the stage for future generations.

Computerspeak and Newspeak are strikingly similar in certain respects. In both languages difficult spelling is changed and simplified. Many words are abbreviated, and new and efficient compound words are constructed. Traditional correct grammar and regular syntax are sacrificed for alleged clarity and simplicity in order to avoid the ambiguous or the possibility of shades of meaning. Abstractions of Oldspeak simply cannot be expressed in Newspeak. Orwell gives us an example: "The word *free* still existed in Newspeak, but it could only be used in such statements as 'This dog is free from lice' or 'This field is free from weeds.' It could not be used in its old sense of 'politically free' or 'intellectually free' since political and intellectual freedom no longer existed even as concepts, and were therefore of necessity nameless."

All other words that expressed antiquated concepts of freedom or equality were included in one Newspeak word: *crimethink*. Computers of course only accept responses constructed of their own limited vocabulary; all other responses are categorized as *syntax error*. The language of technology, like Newspeak, is of necessity standardized, streamlined, concrete and elementary. While in Newspeak you find such words as: Miniluv (Minister of Love), bellyfeel (blind acceptance), goodthink (orthodoxy), joycamp (forced labor camp), unperson, speedful, and uncold; in Computerspeak you have such words as: Basic and Fortran (two computer languages that are considered simple and straight forward), input, output, crash, feedback, interface, flip-flop, memopak, zeroflag, warm-boot, and linefeed. The powerful inner structure of a certain computer is called "Soul." One who works on computers is a "servoprotein." Computerspeak is simply destroying the former "archaic" meanings of abstract words such as: memory, truth, time, logic, think, freedom and friendship. It is mutilating some words and creating countless others from abbreviations. Words themselves, of course, are not spoken or written but "processed." What follows are two partial explanations of the processes of a new computer from a technology trade journal:

There are no tri-state gates, and no provisions for wired ORing of the outputs of two or more gates. Each has a 'O' delay; and there is no provision for adding the delays necessary to create flip-flops or adjust the circuit for dc convergence where feedback is used. Rather than arbitrary inputs, you must use signal sources for your inputs.

You must have a network listing, a pattern and have defined the order of your output node display in memory before involving simulator. If any portion is missing, your RUN will bomb-out requiring a RESET and PR 6.

LANGUAGE OF BIG BUSINESS AND ADVERTISING

We see in the already well established language of big business and advertising, the seeds of computerspeak. It is here that one observes the blatant, steady development of a world in which people are conceptualized as objects, as resources. I was recently talking about life with a young man who turned out to be a business administration student. Towards the end of our discussion, he told me that he had enjoyed "marketing" together. I replied, deeply insulted, that I wasn't sure what he was doing, but that I was merely discussing life with him. He insisted that we were both marketing, trying to convince the other of our point of view, selling ourselves. My concept of sharing ideas was much too archaic and only seemed to confuse him. In big business, particularly in management, there are such concepts as: network theory, queuing, quantitative analysis, programming, management style, motivation, demotivation, commercial awareness, performance appraisal, dysfunctional activity, hi-lo management. These are cold, fearsome words to my mind, but they have become all too familiar in a society that unquestioningly views commodities and consumption as its lifeblood.

My fear comes from the realization that these are not simply trade languages, isolated buzzwords, or the obscure jargon of specialized professions and activities. As big business and technology have exploited humankind, they have exploited its language in the process, just as Newspeak abused Oldspeak. And now, in turn, they invade our popular every-day speech. We find ourselves using such words as "input" and "feedback." We inadvertently trade our dictionary definitions of certain words like "soul" or "freedom" for the mutilated utilitarian definitions of a computer, and soon we will become oblivious to such flagrant travesty. We will be discussing life with a friend and find that we are marketing.

Yet it is the language of politicians which is so obviously characteristic of one of the most significant aspects of Newspeak. To one versed in Oldspeak, many Newspeak words mean the opposite of what they seem to be expressing. So, for example, "joycamp" was a forced labor camp, "goodsex" meant chastity, "miniluv" was the governmental agency responsible for law and order, and "doublethink" meant reality control. "Pax" or peace, meant war in actuality, and peace as we understand it simply did not exist as a concept in Newspeak. Clearly this must also be the meaning of the word for Ronald Reagan and Caspar Weinberger. There is an Environmental Protection

Agency—a term reflecting a warehouse concept of nature that falls deep into semantic absurdity—which sets guidelines for the dumping of toxic wastes. We have a Department of Defense—in actuality a Department of Offense—which initiates war and foments right-wing counter-revolution. We also have a Department of Welfare which distributes a miserable pittance to the poor to keep them poor.

Examples of political doublespeak abound. There are arms reductions talks and concepts of "build-down" while we continue to develop our nuclear and conventional arms capabilities by leaps and bounds. The three Party slogans of Ingsoc in 1984 don't seem all that absurd or illogical now that our ears are accustomed to the sincere teasetalk of promising politicians: (1) *War is Peace* (they *are* building up nuclear arsenals and feeding the entire war machine in order to ensure peace, right?) (2) *Freedom is slavery* (This is what we must explain to the people of Nicaragua, Guatemala and El Salvador.) (3) *Ignorance is Strength* (This would fit nicely as part of the slogan for America's finest: the Few, the Proud, the Marines.) This all begins to make sense once we let doublethink do its thing and listen seriously to our concerned Party leaders talk to us in the most refined dialect of Newspeak: *Duckspeak*, speech which, according to Orwell, issued from the larynx without involving the higher brain centers. Any one of these leaders could be described with the same Newspeak noun/adjective used to laud a party orator in Oceania: he was a *doubleplusgood duckspeaker*.

FRAGMENTED, COLD, UNEXPRESSIVE LANGUAGE

In this real world of 1984, we consciously and unconsciously respond to a myriad of very dangerous subtle and overt influences. It is an obvious fact that language profoundly reflects the environment, the culture, the lifestyle of the people who speak it. In an increasingly urbanized, suburbanized, streamlined environment where our wilderness is polluted, destroyed, smoothed over to make way for highrises, shopping malls, expressways, factories and nuclear power plants, it is small wonder that our senses are becoming dulled and our language impoverished. Our hearing is deafened by the roar of engines, our sense of smell deadened by burning poisons, and our frantic speech is fast becoming fragmented, cold and unexpressive.

My grandparents knew the names and the medicinal qualities of numerous wild herbs and grasses, the songs and names of a multitude of birds, the leaves and bark of countless trees, the phases of the moon. I know only categories and must search through books for lost details. Lewis Mumford speaks of the birth of language and man's environment: "If man had originally inhabited a world as blankly uniform as a 'high-rise' housing development, as featureless as a parking lot, as destitute as an automated factory, it is doubtful if he would have had a sufficiently varied sensory experience to retain images, mold language, or acquire ideas."

As we methodically lose our connection with the earth and its infinite diversity, our language becomes more and more refined, terse, standardized and insipid. As progress and technology transform our way of life and our physical surroundings, they eat away at our language, enfeeble our spirits, and perhaps without even the intention of controlling us, control us still by systematically destroying the creative options that sprout from a humane and naturally balanced world.

A MOUNTAIN OF MEDIOCRITY
And yet, you may counter, in spite of all these signs of the deterioration and degeneration of language, literature is flourishing, the written word lives as it has never lived before. There are more publications than ever before, more books, paperbacks, magazines, journals, newspapers and reviews. Perhaps this phenomenon represents a refusal on the part of individuals to accept the alienation created by a world of computerspeak and duckspeak. But the publishing business suffers the malaise of all big business; we are flooded with more published material than we could possibly consume and we are lost in a mountain of mediocrity. There are also more writers, poets, novelists, journalists, than ever before. At times it seems that everyone is talking or writing and that no one is listening or reading. The mountain keeps growing, of course, and one hardly knows where to begin reading or who truly has something to say that's worth listening to.

The Eastern European writer, Milan Kundera, writes about this phenomenon of literary over-abundance or "mass graphomania," as he calls it, in one of his stories. He explains it as a mass spirited effort to save oneself from the void. "The reason is that everyone has trouble accepting the fact he will disappear unheard of and unnoticed into an indifferent universe, and everyone wants to make himself into a universe of words before it's too late." (*The Book of Laughter and Forgetting*, 1980) It is a natural human need to be acknowledged, to be noticed, but this is only part of the older, more all-encompassing human instinct of reciprocity, which includes the active and the passive, the offering and the acceptance, the speaking and the listening. We are in danger of losing hold of the last threads of our humanity. "Once the writer in every individual comes to life (and that time is not far off)," Kundera tells us, "we are in for an age of universal deafness and lack of understanding." We need not accept Kundera's scenario as inevitable and inescapable, but we are forewarned. We must find a way to let our senses rest, refuse to speak the empty chatter of machines, seek out the immeasurable silence of the remaining wilderness, and step ever so carefully into this year.

Voting for President Is Like Changing Seats on the Titanic

FROM *It's About Times: Abalone Alliance Newspaper* (February/ March 1984): 2

Voting for President... is like changing seats on the Titanic

Photo by Rachel Johnson

Americans Are Far Less Free Today Than They Were a Year Ago
Supreme Court's 1983–84 Term

by Burt Neuborne and Charles Sims

FROM *Civil Liberties* 350 (Summer 1984): 12, 4–5

In the space of one genuinely appalling term of the Supreme Court, Americans lost their constitutional rights: (1) to travel abroad (*Regan* v. *Wald*); (2) to be free from preventive detention (*Schall* v. *Martin*); (3) to engage in low-cost political speech (*Taxpayer for Vincent* v. *City of Los Angeles*); (4) to be free from government supported religious observances (*Lynch* v. *Donnelly*); (5) to be free from unwarranted harassment by law enforcement officials (*INS* v. *Delgado, United States* v. *Leon*); (6) to privacy in their diaries, papers and personal effects (*United States* v. *Doe*); and (7) to competent counsel in criminal proceedings (*United States* v. *Cronic, Strickland* v. *Washington*).

In case after case during the 1983–84 term, a majority of the Supreme Court chose to resolve conflicts between the individual and the government in favor of the state. Although many will be tempted to characterize the Court's decisions as "conservative," it is far more accurate to describe them

Burt Neuborne is legal director and Charles Sims staff counsel of the ACLU.

as "statist." If the present trend continues—and we have no reason to believe that it will change in the near future—a fundamental alteration in the relationship of the individual and the state is likely to take place in American law.

Under our system—at least until very recently—a vigilant judiciary is our only formal guarantee of individual freedom. When, as has occurred this term, the Supreme Court functions, not as a vigorous guardian of the individual, but as a cheerleader for the government, individual constitutional rights cease to have independent meaning. Instead, they mean whatever the government wants them to mean.

A generation of Americans has come to maturity under a legal system in which the Supreme Court has provided sustained and effective protection for individual rights. Many Americans appear to have been lulled into believing that freedom is a natural state of political affairs and that our freedom is etched in constitutional stone. Reality is far less sanguine. Americans are not immune from political and social oppression. The waves of political hysteria which have periodically engulfed us—as well as our unfortunate history of racial, sexual and religious intolerance—bear painful witness to the need for effective institutional checks on the majority's power.

Unfortunately, the Supreme Court is now failing to provide that check. Individual freedom is the exception, not the rule. Liberty is an endangered species which is kept alive only by imposing effective institutional checks on the government's inevitable attempt to expand its power to control the individual. When the Supreme Court abdicates its role as protector of the individual, the fragile institutional structure which keeps us free is placed at risk. Moreover, when as has happened repeatedly during this term, the individuals whom the Court has elected to sacrifice to the government are the poorest and weakest in the society, the Court's greatest asset—its capacity for moral leadership—is mortally wounded.

FIRST AMENDMENT

Critics of the First Amendment are fond of charging that free speech is the exclusive province of the socially and economically comfortable. Defenders have been able to point to numerous Supreme Court cases in which poor people's rights to participate in public debate have been carefully protected. Unfortunately, the Court's First Amendment decisions this term make it very difficult to rebut the charge that the amount of First Amendment protection you have depends on the size of your wallet.

In two cases, the Court struck a major blow at poor people's speech. In *Los Angeles City Council* v. *Taxpayers for Vincent*, six members of the Court reversed the lower courts and voted to uphold a ban on placing election posters on public utility poles because the posters created "visual clutter." It is, of course, impossible for the poor to gain access to expensive forms of political speech. Placing campaign posters on utility poles is one of the only effective means by which the economically disadvantaged can participate in the electoral process. By countenancing the banning of campaign posters on public utility polls on grounds of aesthetics, the Court displayed a profound lack of concern for economically disadvantaged speakers.

Similarly, in *Clark v. Community for Creative Non-Violence*, seven members of the Court reversed a lower court decision permitting homeless persons to conduct a "sleep-in" in Lafayette Park across from the White House to dramatize the fact that they had nowhere else to sleep. Justice Marshall, writing in dissent, chastised the Court for failing to take seriously the attempt by the weakest among us to express themselves effectively.

In contrast, speakers with substantial economic resources fared much better. In *Capital Cities Cable, Inc. v. Crisp*, the Court ruled that Oklahoma could not require out-of-state cable broadcasters to delete liquor advertising from shows broadcast in Oklahoma, and in *FCC v. League of Women Voters of California*, the Court invalidated a ban on editorials by radio and television stations receiving funds from the Corporation for Public Broadcasting. In *Secretary of State of Maryland v. Munson*, the Court invalidated a ban on spending more than 25 percent of a charity's funds on fundraising.

While *Cable Cities*, *League of Women Voters* and *Munson* were all correctly decided and provide welcome support for First Amendment principles, the starkness of the comparison between rich and poor speakers is troubling.

In *Regan v. Time, Inc.*, the Court upheld a prohibition on reproducing a color picture of United States currency. The case demonstrates the danger of relying on the recent Supreme Court preoccupation with bans on content-based discrimination. In *Regan*, a provision of the statute permitted currency to be depicted in "newsworthy" settings. The Court found the distinction between newsworthy and non-newsworthy settings to be a forbidden content-based discrimination; but, instead of invalidating the statute, the Court simply eliminated the exception for "newsworthiness" and substituted an absolute ban.

Finally, in *Regan v. Wald*, the Court upheld the President's power to ban tourist travel to Cuba under the Trading With the Enemy Act. The Court's failure to affirm a careful and narrow opinion by the First Circuit which would have permitted travel was a major disappointment.

When one analyzes the term's First Amendment opinions, a disturbing trend emerges. Once the Court is persuaded that a restriction on speech is not based on its content, the remaining doctrinal restrictions appear to be dramatically relaxed. Instead of requiring a "compelling" interest in suppression, the Court requires merely a substantial interest—which is satisfied by interests as weak as avoiding visual clutter. Instead of requiring the government to proceed by the least drastic means, the Court merely requires that the regulation be "narrowly tailored." The power of the government to suppress speech—especially poor people's speech—in the guise of neutral regulation is now greater than it has been for a generation.

DISCRIMINATION

The Court decided three equality cases which posed no difficult questions. In *Hishon* v. *King & Spaulding*, the Court ruled that the ban on sex discrimination in Title VII was applicable to promotions from associate to partner in a law firm. In *Roberts* v. *United States Jaycees*, the Court upheld a Minnesota statute forbidding the Jaycees from denying membership to women. Finally, in *Palmore* v. *Sidoti*, the Court declined to permit interracial marriage to be used as a factor in child custody decisions. The Court also expansively construed a statute forbidding discrimination against the handicapped to apply to programs which use federal aid in nonemployment settings, *Consolidated Rail Corporation* v. *Darrone*, and construed the Educational Aid to the Handicapped Act as requiring services enabling handicapped children to attend school, *Irving* v. *Tatro*.

Despite favorable decisions in easy cases, however, the term was disastrous for the cause of equality. In *Grove City College* v. *Bell*, the Court gave an absurdly narrow reading to Title IX, holding that colleges receiving federal funds may engage in sex discrimination everywhere but the specific departments which actually receive the funds. Finally, in *Memphis Firefighters* v. *Stotts*, the Court rejected the decisions of virtually every lower court and ruled that consent decrees designed to remedy racial discrimination in employment were subject to "last hired-first fired" treatment when lay-offs were required. The result of the Court's refusal to require racially proportionate lay-offs even when necessary to protect a Title VII consent order threatens to result in the re-segregation of many police and fire departments. Moreover, the Court's loose use of language threatens literally hundreds of existing Title VII decrees.

CRIMINAL PROCEDURE

In no other field of constitutional law did the Court break so sharply from past precedent. Where the Court in recent years has made minor inroads on long-established rights, confining its decisions to the facts and declining to expand them, this year the Court seemed to lose its inhibitions against overruling doctrine that had been settled not only since the days of the Warren Court, but indeed since enactment of the Bill of Rights. In the area of Fourth Amendment searches and seizures, pre-trial detentions, and the Fifth Amendment right to remain silent, the Court restricted currently held rights and used language rife with possibilities for future incursions on long-established rights.

Preventive detention. In an extremely serious blow, Justice Rehnquist, writing for the majority in a 6–3 decision, upheld a New York statute authorizing pre-trial detention of accused juveniles whom a court had determined likely to commit future crimes before their return court date. *Schall* v. *Martin*. The Court held that as long as such detention provided for a hearing within a short period of time there was no violation of the Fourteenth Amendment's due process clause. In so ruling, the majority ignored the appalling conditions under which such juveniles are held; the minimal nature of the hearing at which they are remanded; uncontradicted evidence that judges were totally unable accurately to predict which juveniles might commit crimes if released on bail; and the fact that most of the juveniles held before trial as too dangerous to release on bail were rarely incarcerated even after conviction.

The Court's blithe rejection of expert testimony—and the views of professional groups like the American Psychiatric Association—that the prediction of future dangerousness is no more accurate than flipping coins in a courtroom makes it likely that the Court is ready to uphold preventive detention for adults as well.

Fourth Amendment. In the most damaging Fourth Amendment decision this term—indeed, the most damaging setback in seventy years—the Court severely weakened the exclusionary rule, by holding that evidence unconstitutionally seized may nevertheless be used in court, so long as it is a local magistrate, and not a policeman, who made the constitutional error. Since magistrates need not even be attorneys, and since many magistrates simply sign any warrant the police request, the remedy of suppression was indispensable; and now that deterrent is largely eroded. The Court's ruling in these cases goes far towards making the protections of the Fourth Amendment, to which the Court's opinions piously referred, mere symbolic pronouncements, whose violation will draw no sanctions whatsoever. *U.S.* v. *Leon*; *Massachusetts* v. *Shepherd*. Although these two cases apply only where the police have secured warrants, the Court has agreed to review a case next term which will give it the opportunity to further erode the rule in warrantless cases as well.

In another landmark decision whose pernicious effect will be felt for years to come, the Court held that Americans have no reasonable expectation of privacy in the land surrounding their homes. *Oliver* v. *U.S.* Stating that even fenced and guarded fields are not protected by the Fourth Amendment, the majority essentially held that even if the police commit trespass under state law their entry is not "unreasonable" under the Fourth Amendment. As a result, the police could apparently literally move onto an individual's land and surveil his activities from that vantage point full-time for weeks or months, and the Fourth Amendment would not be offended at all.

Fifth Amendment. Decisions eroding the right to remain silent were nearly as sweeping as this term's search and seizure holdings.

New York v. *Quarles* may well have begun the process of unravelling the protections long afforded by *Miranda*. In a split decision the Court held that police officers need no longer always issue *Miranda* warnings to those held in custody. Declaring that there were times when "public safety" required that police officers ask questions of accused persons first and inform them of their rights afterwards, the Court carved out an exception of notably uncertain scope to the clear and specific *Miranda* requirements.

Self-incrimination protections were further weakened when the Court upheld the government's power to require a test oath—an oath swearing that the individual has not violated a law—as a condition of governmental assistance for federal financial aid. Although test oaths were at the core of the evils against which the Fifth Amendment was originally adopted, the Court's holding effectively permits them of anyone seeking any kind of governmental assistance.

The Court's decision removes from the government the burden of proving at a criminal trial that individuals have violated the draft registration law, permitting it instead to simply refuse tuition assistance to any college students who refuse to swear that they have not violated the law. *Selective Service System* v. *Minnesota Public Interest Research Group.* In so doing, the Court has seriously weakened the protections against self-incrimination, and given Congress a blank check for further invasions of this vital constitutional right.

In another decision which both disregards long-established precedent and opens the way for further erosion, the Court held that business records voluntarily prepared by a sole proprietor were not protected as privileged under the Fifth Amendment merely because they were voluntarily prepared. *U.S.* v. *Doe.* By resting its decision on the voluntary preparation— the Court reasoned that where the record is "voluntarily" prepared in the first instance its production results not in "compelled testimony" forbidden by the Fifth Amendment but rather only in "compelled production" of "voluntary testimony" not protected by this narrow reading of the Fifth Amendment—the Court has opened the way to find that even personal diaries can be seized because the testimony inherent in such papers has not been "compelled" within the meaning of this new approach.

Sixth Amendment. The Supreme Court set extremely loose standards for the competency of defense counsel this term, holding that only in extreme cases could defendants make out claims of ineffective assistance of counsel. The court held in *Strickland* v. *Washington,* that the Sixth Amendment only required "reasonably effective assistance" of counsel and the defendant must overcome the strong presumption that counsel had been effective. Defendants will only be successful in their claims that their Sixth Amendment right to counsel has been denied when they have proven first that counsel's performance was deficient and secondly that the deficient performance "prejudiced the defense."

The Court further elaborated on these standards in *U.S.* v. *Cronic,* holding that only specific errors, and not the general circumstances surrounding defendant's representation, such as counsel's lack of experience as a criminal defense attorney and short period of preparation, were relevant in assessing whether the defendant had received adequate assistance of counsel.

CAPITAL PUNISHMENT
Accelerating its recent trend, the Court both repeatedly refused to stay executions ordered by state court judges, and vacated a number of stays which had been entered by federal appeals courts. As a result, more prisoners were executed this year than in any year since the 1960s.

Prisoners fared no better in cases decided by full opinion. The Court held this term in *Spaziano v. Florida* that a judge may impose a death sentence after a jury has already recommended life imprisonment.

And in a wide-ranging decision likely to affect hundreds of cases, and lead to an increase in the arbitrary impositions of death sentences, the Court held that the Eighth Amendment does not require state courts to conduct proportionality reviews in all death sentence cases. *Pulley v. Harris.* Paying little more than lip service to its repeated requirement that death sentences should not be imposed without adequate protection against arbitrariness, the Court held that the Constitution does not require appellate courts to compare death sentences with penalties imposed in similar cases. As a result, capital defendants convicted of similar crimes under similar circumstances will continue to receive widely disparate sentences.

CHURCH AND STATE
The Court seriously eroded the separation of church and state this term in its only major freedom of religion decision. The Court held that the city of Pawtucket's display of a nativity scene, municipally owned and maintained, did not violate the establishment clause. *Lynch v. Donnelly.* Ignoring the complaints of non-Christians and religious Christians alike, who objected to this secular use of deeply religious symbols, the Court held that Pawtucket's inclusion of the creche in its annual Christmas display was not religious but secular—depicting the historical origins of Christmas—and therefore that the city had not established Christianity.

ACCESS TO JUSTICE
In a landmark 5–4 decision, the Court dramatically restricted the opportunity to seek relief in federal courts in civil rights cases. Although plaintiffs with federal civil rights claims against state officials had long been permitted to include in their lawsuits that state officials were violating state law as well, the majority held in *Pennhurst State School & Hospital v. Halderman*, that the Eleventh Amendment prohibits federal courts from enjoining state officials who have not complied with state laws. As a result,

plaintiffs who have strong federal and state claims against state officials will have to sue in state courts, where political constraints tend to make their chances of winning less likely.

The Court sharply cut back access to federal courts in two other unfortunate decisions. First, it held that due process claims seeking relief for intentional deprivation of property rights by state officers must generally be brought in state court. *Palmer v. Hudson*. Second, the Court has eliminated the possibility of statutory attorneys fees awards to prevailing plaintiffs in civil rights cases challenging discrimination by public schools against handicapped students. The decision precludes effective enforcement of the very rights Congress has so carefully protected. Since, in most instances, it costs far more to bring a successful lawsuit seeking relief than to provide private schooling for the handicapped child, it is unlikely that many lawsuits will be brought to compel resistant school boards to comply with their obligations. *Smith v. Robinson*.

RIGHTS OF THE POOR
In a decision that split the Court along its basic conservative (Justices Burger, O'Connor, White, Powell, and Rehnquist) and moderate (Justices Brennan, Marshall, Blackmun and Stevens) lines, the majority struck down a district court's injunction requiring the Secretary of Health and Human Services to adjudicate disability claims according to judicially established deadlines. *Heckler v. Day*. Conceding that adjudicative delays prevented many from timely receipt of benefits, the Court nevertheless held that district courts could not force the secretary to comply with deadlines which Congress had not itself enacted.

The Court also cut back the ability of recipients of medicaid and medicare to challenge the secretary's regulations barring funding certain kinds of operations. The Court ruled that such rulings could be challenged only in a suit attacking the denial of reimbursement for an operation already performed—even though the secretary's very regulations had the effect of deterring doctors from performing the operations in the first place. As a result of this Catch-22, general regulations declaring various operations nonreimbursable are effectively insulated from any review. *United States v. Ringer*.

RIGHTS OF ALIENS
The Court severely weakened the rights of aliens in three decisions handed down this term. First, Justice Rehnquist held for a sharply divided Court that factory sweeps by Immigration and Naturalization officials did not constitute a "seizure" of the work place of the alien workers questioned by INS officers. *Immigration and Naturalization Service v. Delgado*. Despite firm evidence to the contrary, the Court ruled that the questioning itself was not

so intimidating as to make factory workers think that they were not free to leave.

A few weeks later, the Court went further, holding that the exclusionary rule does not apply at all in immigration proceedings. The Court's decision that illegally seized evidence—even evidence seized in intentional violation of the Fourth Amendment—can be used in immigration proceedings will effectively remove the Fourth Amendment's protections from Hispanic-American communities. *INS* v. *Lopez-Mendoza*.

Aliens who are political refugees fared no better. The Court unanimously ruled that deportation actions could be avoided *only* when a deportable alien showed a clear probability of persecution in his/her home country. *Immigration and Naturalization Service* v. *Stevic*.

CIVIL RIGHTS ACTIONS

For those civil rights cases not totally excluded from federal courts by the Court's access to justice decisions, this was a mixed term. The most serious blow was *Davis* v. *Sherer*, where the Court expanded its previous rulings that a plaintiff whose constitutional rights have been violated may not receive damages unless she shows that government officials violated clearly established law at the time of violation. The Court further ruled that officials are entitled to immunity even if they violated clearly established state regulations; notwithstanding constitutional and state law violations, officials will be liable for damages only if they violated "clearly established" constitutional rights.

In another setback, the Court held that a state could preclude a discharged school teacher from bringing suit under 42 U.S.C. 1983 and 1985 in federal court when the constitutional claims involved the same facts as the issues in the claims the teacher had previously litigated in state court. *Migra* v. *Warren School District*. Disregarding the strong federal interest in litigating federal constitutional claims before federal judges, the Court unanimously ruled that the state court judgment could be given the same preclusive effect in federal court as it would in state courts.

A Court That Never Says No

by Keenen Peck

FROM *The Progressive* 48:4 (April 1984): 18–21

Twice a month, and whenever an emergency arises, a judge holds court in the conference room on the top floor of the Justice Department building in Washington, D.C. The room, regularly "swept" to detect hidden microphones, is secured by a cipher-locked door. Seven district court judges preside on a rotating basis. Though hand-picked by Chief Justice Warren Burger, all are subjected to FBI background checks.

Eleven lawyers currently hold Government clearance to appear before the court. They have never lost a case. No one argues against them. One judge once overruled the lawyers, but merely because they had asked him to do so. That unique decision became the only published opinion ever to emanate from the conference room.

This is the Foreign Intelligence Surveillance Court. For the past five years, since May 1979, it has authorized "national security" wiretapping and bugging. Federal spy agencies must obtain approval from the special judges to conduct electronic surveillance within the United States. Applications to the court bear the signatures of the Attorney General and, depending on which agency makes the request, the Secretary of Defense, the Director of Central Intelligence, or the FBI Director.

At a time when more and more Americans are protesting U.S. nuclear and

---

Keenen Peck is an associate editor of the Progressive.

---

foreign policies, the tribunal poses a potential threat to dissidents at home. It authorizes wiretaps on persons believed to be "agents of foreign powers," and President Reagan has said more than once that he regards dissenters as tools of alien forces.

Every application brought before the extraordinary court has been approved—1,422 as of January 1983. In 1982, the last year for which figures are available, the Reagan Administration sought and received 473 surveillance orders, almost 50 per cent more than the Carter Administration obtained in 1980, the only full year it was required to seek court approval.

Why has the secretive court never rejected an application?

"The garbage drops out way before that," contends Mary Lawton, the Justice Department's counsel for intelligence policy, whose staff prepares the applications and represents the snoops. "The levels of review in the FBI and National Security Agency and here are so intense that the chances of a poor one getting in there are zilch."

"I am not necessarily persuaded," says Representative Robert Kastenmeier, the Wisconsin Democrat who chairs the House Judiciary Committee's subcommittee on courts, civil liberties, and the administration of justice. "It's an open question whether we're getting good, solid review of these applications."

Last summer Kastenmeier held the first public hearings on the court. Witnesses included Lawton, civil liberties advocates, and the former chief judge of the intelligence court, George Hart, Jr., who served from 1979 to 1983. Hart delivered his testimony in vague terms, but he inadvertently provided some insight into the court's perception of its duty:

"The judges of the court sit in Washington, D.C., to consider applications for orders authorizing the interception of foreign intelligence information by electronic surveillance, or other mechanical means," he told the subcommittee. "We seek to ensure that there is always a judge available to issue such an order."

The key words are "available to *issue* such an *order*"—which is quite different from ensuring the availability of a judge to *consider* an *application*. Hart, perhaps, equates impartial review with automatic approval.

Presumably, the court has the power to reject applications. Under the Foreign Intelligence Surveillance Act (FISA), which mandated the establishment of the court, the judges are charged with weighing the constitutional rights of Americans against the ostensible needs of the spy agencies.

Unfortunately, the court seems to attach greater import to the latter—at least from the scanty data that have seeped through the shroud of secrecy surrounding the body. In some instances, the judges have erred in favor of the intelligence community. But even where the letter of the law is upheld, constitutional rights stand in jeopardy. FISA's safeguards are paper thin, and its loopholes are gaping.

In a conference room on Constitution Avenue, of all places, the National Security State has been institutionalized.

FISA was enacted in 1978 after Congress and the media exposed a wide pattern of abuses by the Executive Branch. Senator Frank Church, who led the most intensive investigation into Watergate-era transgressions by the intelligence agencies, summed up the findings of his Select Intelligence Committee this way:

"Through the uncontrolled or illegal use of intrusive techniques—ranging from simple theft to sophisticated electronic surveillance—the Government has collected, and then used improperly, huge amounts of information about the private lives, political beliefs, and associations of numerous Americans."

FISA was supposed to put an end to such offenses.

The law was designed to "curb the practice by which the Executive Branch may conduct warrantless electronic surveillance on its own unilateral determination that national security justifies it," according to a 1978 Senate report on FISA. "Legitimate use" of wiretapping and bugging to obtain foreign intelligence information would thereafter be authorized by the Attorney General and a disinterested special court which, in turn, would be watched by Congress itself.

Six years earlier, the Supreme Court had held that warrantless *domestic* surveillance violated Fourth Amendment protections against unreasonable searches and seizures. But the high court explicitly reserved judgment "on the scope of the President's surveillance power with respect to the activities of foreign powers, within or without this country."

Congress stepped in to fill the breach. FISA allows court-approved electronic surveillance if there is "probable cause" to believe that the target is a "foreign power" or, more vaguely, an "agent of a foreign power."

A "U.S. person"—that is, a citizen, a permanent resident, or an organization that includes many American members—may not be considered an "agent of a foreign power" solely on the basis of activities protected by the First Amendment, the law states. However, the court can authorize snooping on Americans if the Attorney General certifies that they are engaged in clandestine activities on behalf of a foreign power that "may involve" a violation of criminal law.

According to a recent memo prepared by the Justice Department at the request of Representative Kastenmeier, "Even if the target is seeking unclassified or public information, this may be sufficient to obtain authorization of the surveillance if he is doing so at the direction of a foreign power."

The memo also notes, "During the past four years, the percentage of targets who are United States persons has increased, somewhat, due primarily to enhanced investigation of international terrorism."

When the Government overhears an American in the course of a foreign-related surveillance, it can retain the information if "necessary" to national defense or security—the same rationalization Richard Nixon invoked to spy on U.S. dissidents.

The intelligence court's standard for approving surveillance is weaker than the one used in criminal investigations. To obtain a warrant in a criminal case, the Government must show "probable cause" that an offense has been or will be committed; in an FISA case, the Justice Department must merely demonstrate that the target has foreign connections and that the premises to be bugged are used by that target.

Furthermore, the language of the Act limits the ability of the court to challenge Government claims. As Mary Lawton told the House subcommittee, "An FISA judge may look behind the certification only if the target is a U.S. person and then only on a 'clearly erroneous' standard." Put another way, if the papers are in order, the court has no choice but to approve the spy agencies' requests.

"The benefits of the structure are illusory," says John Mage, a New York lawyer who represents a Bulgarian diplomat charged with espionage on the basis of an FISA surveillance. While listening in on the Bulgarian, the Government overheard discussions among the diplomat, Mage, and another lawyer who, like Mage, is a "U.S. person." The Justice Department says it protected the rights of all parties by erecting a "Chinese wall" between prosecutors and FBI agents who monitored the microphones.

"Secrecy corrupts, and absolute secrecy corrupts absolutely," maintains Barry Scheck, professor at New York's Cardozo Law School and attorney in an FISA case involving supporters of the Irish Republican Army. "The statute permits political surveillance, and without a stretch, without a lot of malevolence, it permits abuse." Scheck believes the Government can "find a way into domestic political organizations" by targeting their foreign members.

"Until someone knocks on your door and says, 'Aha, you're a foreign agent,' you don't think it could apply to you," adds attorney David L. Lewis, who has also represented backers of the Irish Republican Army who were bugged under FISA. (In one case, the defendants were acquitted of conspiracy and various weapons charges; in the other, Scheck and Lewis are appealing convictions of gunrunning.) "Congress authorized the President to use the judiciary as a rubber stamp," Lewis says.

The tribunal has not confined itself to issuing surveillance warrants; between 1979 and 1981, the judges approved a series of physical break-ins—black-bag jobs—although FISA plainly grants no such authority to the court.

After the Reagan Administration took office, the Justice Department submitted an application "inviting" the court to renounce any power to sanction break-ins. The Executive Branch wanted to stake out exclusive authority over intelligence-related physical searches, and Judge Hart complied in the court's only published opinion.

Hart correctly delineated the court's jurisdiction in his 1981 ruling. But the fact that the judges had previously violated FISA provisions gives great cause for concern. How many other requests falling outside the parameters of the Act have been similarly approved?

Moreover, Hart's decision demonstrates that FISA does not stand in the way of Executive Branch abuses. Who can authorize black-bag jobs if not the intelligence court? The Attorney General and the President, answers Lawton.

A more disturbing loophole in FISA is that most people spied on with the blessing of the court never find out. Targets of FISA snooping are not notified—unless they are prosecuted. By contrast, targets of criminal surveillance must eventually be informed, even if the G-men hidden in the shadows heard not an inkling of villainy.

The American people have no sure way of knowing whether the FISA court is, in fact, endorsing unreasonable searches and seizures, allowing the indiscriminate dispatch of the "invisible policeman in the home," as Supreme Court Justice William O. Douglas termed electronic surveillance.

Even in those rare criminal cases where a tap or bug surfaces, the accused usually don't find out what prompted the eavesdropping in the first place. Under FISA, the Attorney General may ask the trial judge to review the surveillance application and the order in secret to protect national security.

Every judge who has been asked to conduct a secret review has examined the documents *in camera* and *ex parte* to determine the legality of the surveillance. Lawyers have argued to no avail that they need to see such information to prepare an adequate defense.

"While the alert eye of an advocate might be helpful in discerning defects in the [application] certificates, I see no reason to believe that an adversary proceeding is necessary for accuracy," opined the district court judge in the Irish Republican Army case now being appealed.

"We appreciate the difficulties of appellants' counsel in this case," the U.S. Court of Appeals in Washington, D.C., conceded to attorneys for two men incidentally overheard during an FISA surveillance. "They must argue that the determination of legality is so complex that an adversary hearing with full access to relevant materials is necessary. But without access to the relevant materials their claim of complexity can be given no concreteness. It is pure assertion."

Joseph Heller could not devise a sharper *Catch-22*, and Franz Kafka could not have conjured up a craftier prevarication.

To be sure, FISA provides for Congressional oversight as a check and balance against the intelligence tribunal. The Justice Department is required to file semi-annual reports on the court with the House and Senate Intelligence Committees. The committees, however, have neither the time nor resources to review the circumstances behind hundreds of surveillance orders. A staff assistant to the House committee says its members have examined a "handful" of applications; members of the Senate committee have publicly stated that their supervision is not ideal.

And because both intelligence committees operate largely in secret, the public can only speculate about what they learn. FISA requires minimal annual committee reports to Congress, but that provision expires this year. Kastenmeier has asked the House Intelligence Committee to continue reporting, and he predicts it will agree.

"Their oversight is off the record," says Kastenmeier. "Ours [the civil liberties subcommittee's] is on the record. We, as well as the intelligence committee in its own fashion, must review this court and its proceedings." Yet the Justice Department offered little information during Kastenmeier's hearings.

"We still do not know whether this court is working perfectly or whether it isn't working at all," Kastenmeier says. "One problem might be that we don't have a good mix of judges," he adds, noting that Warren Burger appointed "individuals not likely to rock the boat—senior judges, conservative judges." Kastenmeier acknowledges there are "open spots" in terms of what FISA regulates.

The biggest open spots relate to the National Security Agency. The NSA does not need court approval to monitor messages that leave or enter the United States. Nor must it have permission to monitor messages transmitted on lines used exclusively by foreign powers within the United States.

Author James Bamford highlighted another loophole in his recent book, *The Puzzle Palace*. According to Bamford, the NSA "has skillfully excluded from the coverage of the FISA statute as well as the surveillance court all interceptions received from the British GCHQ [Government Communications Headquarters] or any other non-NSA source. Thus it is possible for GCHQ to monitor the necessary domestic or foreign circuits of interest and pass them on to the NSA. . . ." Bamford points out the British did just this when the NSA snooped on American dissidents in the past.

Protection of our constitutional rights is an all-or-nothing proposition; once an erosive precedent is set, the entire foundation begins to slip.

That is usually the position of the nation's leading civil liberties lobby, but with respect to FISA, the American Civil Liberties Union placed itself in a curious position. After opposing FISA-type legislation for some four years, the ACLU stepped aside in 1978 and implicitly endorsed the final "compromise" bill, though it expressed dismay over the NSA exemptions and the absence of a procedure to notify all surveillance targets.

FISA was "the best we could get," argues Morton Halperin, director of the Center for National Security Studies and one of the ACLU lobbyists at the time. "FISA is working in the sense that it has defined the boundaries of national security wiretaps. In the absence of FISA, the Government was proclaiming the right to tap for whatever reason."

Halperin and ACLU attorney Mark Lynch urged Kastenmeier's subcommittee to compensate for the law's loopholes and ambiguities by ensuring strict Congressional oversight.

In light of today's admittedly weak oversight, however, are the rights of Americans being upheld by FISA? Is privacy better protected in 1984 than it was in 1978?

"A lot more could be done in the area, but it would be a mistake going back," warns Bruce Lehman, a Washington lawyer and former Congressional aide who helped draft FISA. "The thing that gave rise to the court was the assertion by the Justice Department that there was a residual power in the hands of the President and his appointees to engage in searches and seizures without regard to the Fourth Amendment." Lehman feels "safer and more comfortable" knowing that FISA exists.

"I feel considerably less secure," counters lawyer John Mage. Before FISA, he notes, the judiciary had reached no consensus on warrantless foreign-related snooping. But the second most influential court—the District of Columbia Court of Appeals—had imposed standards on the Executive Branch more stringent than those of FISA. "I see no advantage in Congressional approval of the legality" of national security wiretaps, Mage says.

The advisability of FISA could be debated *ad nauseam*. But some points are indisputable: First, no matter how hard Congress scrutinizes the intelligence court, the judges will continue affixing an imprimatur to the most reprehensible invasion of privacy—electronic surveillance, which the ACLU itself has called "the most intrusive and inherently unreasonable form of search and seizure."

Second, the current Administration displays the same kind of paranoia and loathing of dissent that marked the Nixon era. When the Nixonites tapped the phones of antiwar activists and suspected leakers (including Morton Halperin), they did so in the name of defense against foreign intrigue. Similarly, the Reagan Administration sees a KGB agent behind every nuclear freeze advocate and a Cuban inside every critic of its Central America policies. Reagan has freed the FBI to spy on domestic organizations, and he has heightened Government secrecy.

"You can't let your people know without letting the wrong people know," Reagan said last October in explanation of his tight lip about CIA activities directed against Nicaragua.

The subversion of constitutional rights often takes on a benevolent face. The attacks come not from evil people but from well-meaning bureaucrats, aided in this instance by well-meaning civil libertarians.

The basic freedoms of Americans will be in jeopardy as long as the citizenry fails to challenge the fundamental assumption of the National Security State—that any means can be used against the enemy presumed to lurk within our midst. The Foreign Intelligence Surveillance Court legitimates that assumption and assigns it a permanent place in the American landscape, even if that place is only a conference room in Washington, D.C.

Every Breath You Take

Forget About 1984, What's Big Brother Doing in 1985?

by Bill Weinberg and Joseph Zackelle

FROM *Michigan Voice: Michigan's Alternative Newspaper* 8 : 1 (February 1984): 1, 6–7

> Every move you make, every breath you take, I'll be watching you.
> —*The Police*

As we flipped our calendars to January this year, many of us were breathing a sigh of relief that the telescreens haven't arrived yet. Yet for some, that sense of relief is clouded by the possibility that we are being watched and manipulated in more subtle and insidious ways. Perhaps Big Brother needn't take the form of the mustachioed dictator of Orwell's nightmares. The corporate state is controlling us by means which we take for granted—even see as mere modern convenience.

Some of these means involve simple stealth. Some we openly cooperate with. Not only are Americans today scrutinized, counted, recorded and questioned by more government agencies, law enforcement officials and social scientists than ever before, but a quickly increasing percentage of our day-to-day activities leave distinct tracks in the memories of computer networks. The government has the equivalent of fifteen files on every household in America and computer records of our monetary transactions are no longer limited to airline flights and car rentals. Your daily grocery shopping, if not already subject to this phenomenon, will be soon.

YOU ARE WHAT YOU CONSUME

At the new super-market in your area, does the cashier skim over the universal product code of your purchases with a laser-scanner built into the check-out counter? Take a look at that receipt from your last trip to the new shopping mall. You will find all of your purchases itemized, right down to the brand name of each product.

The advent of universal product codes speeds up the check-out line and eliminates jobs—instead of having to hire somebody to change the price on products, the store can punch the change into the computer. It also enables computerized inventory systems to keep track of everything you buy. These records tell a great deal about contraception (and hence the frequency and orientation of your sexual activities) and even your tastes in literature (and hence a gleaning of your political beliefs). Books and magazines often have universal product codes today as well, and are itemized on your receipt (and their computer) right down to the title and author.

Computerized inventory systems are, by the way, often employed at libraries too. A brief overview of records can enable local authorities to instantly identify local radicals—and keep track of what they are reading. Files containing such records can easily be called up by anybody who is fairly competent with a computer keyboard and allegedly using the system for the routine and "legitimate" purpose of locating a library book.

The computerized inventory and universal product code systems were designed with an eye towards simplifying money transactions. Cash, checks and credit cards are falling out of favor because they are time consuming and/or easily stolen or forged. Bank cards—handy plastic strips with magnetized codes—are being heralded as the wave of the future.

Bank cards currently enable you to use those convenient automatic tellers so that you can withdraw cash after the bank has closed. You can even withdraw from the seat of your car. You can even smile for the camera: all automatic tellers are equipped with closed-circuit television which can video-tape every withdrawal, every transaction, twenty-four hours a day, at the bank's choice. Think about that the next time you walk by one.

Plastic will soon replace paper back at the shopping mall. Money will be directly deducted from your bank account as your bank card is inserted into the cash register and you enter your personal identification number (PIN code). Large chain stores will be the first to operate on this level, but as the practice filters down, plain old greenbacks will come closer to obsolescence—and it will become harder and harder to avoid dealing with banks, hide your income or work off the books.

It will also mean that your bank's computer will be linked with that of the shopping center's inventory system.

If these files are around, they will become available to the police or the IRS. The IRS already has access to your bank files. By knowing what, when and where you shop and make other money transactions, the authorities can know your life.

LAST FAIR DEAL IN THE COUNTRY

Freedom in America has been maintained by mobility—the ability to pull up the roots and start over somewhere else, leaving your past behind you. In this age of national police computers, that freedom is greatly limited; warrants now follow us all around the nation. With increasing use of computers in the economic sphere, that freedom threatens to wither entirely. The emerging system will allow authorities to trace the flow of people and dollars from sea to shining sea.

Recent programs have hastened this process. Already American cities and states are using computers to track and snare tax-evaders. New York City is using computers to check lists of business taxpayers against lists of property taxpayers, or check lists of one year's taxpayers against another year's. This method has exposed over 55,000 tax evaders, and netted the city nearly 100 million dollars of payments in the two and a half years since the program was initiated. The city has conceded that individuals and companies not paying any taxes at all have a better chance of getting away with it.

Meanwhile, the IRS has plans on the boards to build computer "lifestyle profiles" of all Americans to trace their incomes. Fortunately, they will (presumably) be starting with the richest. But provided there is no Congressional interference, they plan to eventually reach every citizen. The plan is to go all out on the little-known Section 7601(a) of the Internal Revenue Code, which permits IRS agents to "inquire after and concerning all persons" with a potentially taxable income. They hope to build these profiles by buying information from citizens and businesses via advertisements. Such advertisements have already been placed in appropriate journals in hopes that (for instance) your real estate agent will tell them how much you paid for your house. Eventually they may approach your supermarket to determine your average weekly food bill. Alternative lifestyles will come under greater scrutiny than those which conform to more mainstream spending patterns. Saving on your grocery money to buy a new stereo may get you some nice music and a tax audit. They are also actively seeking ways to discover barter transactions and garage sales so as to tax them as well.

If rich tax evaders are being made a scapegoat in the erosion of privacy, then so are migrant workers and other "illegal aliens." Legislation now pending before Congress would require all U.S. residents to carry a federally-issued "worker verification card," roughly modelled after those currently used in South Africa. The Simpson-Mazzoli Bill, as this twisted scheme is called, would institute sanctions against employers who hire undocumented workers. Purportedly designed to check the flow along the

Mexican border, it will allow the government to track us from birth to death via work permits plugged into a national computer network. Nobody would be able to work without a permit.

Even if this bill does not make it through Congress, Social Security cards are evidently evolving into a national worker identification system. They don't even have "not for identification" printed on them anymore. Already the new Social Security cards being issued are "tamper-resistant"—printed on banknote paper which is difficult to reproduce. Right now, nobody ever asks to see your Social Security card. But there must be some reason that Social Security is willing to spend three times as much to print the new tamper-proof cards.

More familiar, but hardly less chilling are the new draft cards being issued by the Selective Service System. Shortly after registering for the draft, young men now receive in the mail wallet-sized cards acknowledging such registration. Of course they aren't really draft cards, Selective Service hastens to reassure us, because men are not required to carry them. They were issued to facilitate the Solomon Amendment, which requires young men applying for financial aid and many federally-funded jobs to certify compliance with registration. As we go to press, the Supreme Court is yet to rule on the constitutionality of this measure, but until the decision comes down, the Solomon Amendment is in effect. Selective Service is also cross-checking state motor vehicle records and Social Security records with draft registration lists in an effort to snare non-registrants.

Perhaps most bizarre is the Treasury Department plan now under consideration to print money in a variety of colors, including pink and blue, to replace the familiar greenbacks now in circulation. The new colored money would have a metallic strip running vertically next to the face on the bill, allegedly to allow authorities to determine whether bills are being taken out of the country. Such, at least, are the allegations of Representative Ron Paul (R-Texas), who claims that the plan was disclosed to him at a November 3, 1983 meeting with the National Treasurer Katherine Ortega. The Treasury Department will concede only to considering changes to cope with counterfeiting. If they can follow the flow of such bills out of the country, they can follow them within the country as well. These "metallic strips" would enable them to trace money so that even those hold-outs who have resisted bank cards could be kept track of.

FOR WHOM BELL TOLLS—THE AT&T "BREAK-UP" AND YOU

The dismantling of the Ma Bell monopoly will have some paradoxical effects of consolidating power in the hands of the corporate and banking communities. The move makes possible many "advances" such as the establishment of lightning-fast exclusive communication networks for government agencies and other elite groups. These code-restricted systems link each call to a computer which in a matter of microseconds determines the

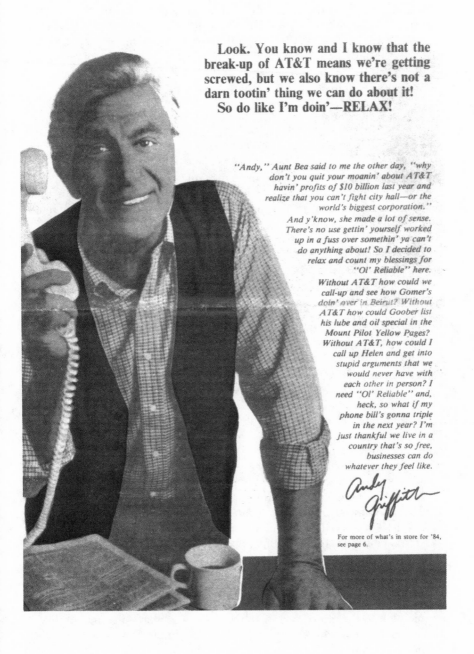

Look. You know and I know that the break-up of AT&T means we're getting screwed, but we also know there's not a darn tootin' thing we can do about it! So do like I'm doin'—RELAX!

"Andy," Aunt Bea said to me the other day, "why don't you quit your moanin' about AT&T havin' profits of $10 billion last year and realize that you can't fight city hall—or the world's biggest corporation."

And y'know, she made a lot of sense. There's no use gettin' yourself worked up in a fuss over somethin' ya can't do anything about! So I decided to relax and count my blessings for "Ol' Reliable" here.

Without AT&T how could we call-up and see how Gomer's doin' over in Beirut? Without AT&T how could Goober list his lube and oil special in the Mount Pilot Yellow Pages? Without AT&T, how could I call up Helen and get into stupid arguments that we would never have with each other in person? I need "Ol' Reliable" and, heck, so what if my phone bill's gonna triple in the next year? I'm just thankful we live in a country that's so free, businesses can do whatever they feel like.

Andy Griffith

For more of what's in store for '84, see page 6.

fastest and cheapest route available at that particular moment through any telephone lines controlled either by AT&T or contenders like ITT. These obscure systems, in addition to saving their users' time and money, have instant and impeccable tracing abilities. Computers keep track of every call made over such systems.

You can also start looking for computerized phones in airports and ritzy hotel lobbies. In response to widespread "phone piracy," both AT&T and MCI are producing separate phones for credit-card users—complete with slots for—you guessed it—magnetically-coded cards. AT&T's new credit card phones will even have video screens (at first to be used only for instructions).

While freeing the application of such innovations, the "break-up" actually does little to alter AT&T's position of supremacy. They lost functions which they were losing money on anyway, such as local service. They retain the lucrative functions. For instance, they still reap profits from Yellow Pages advertisements. Long distance rates will be dropping—and mutually beneficial arrangements are being worked out with corporations—the biggest long distance consumers.

Most significantly, phone companies will be able to utilize technology enabling instantaneous national money transactions. In the wink of an eye, infinite sums can be transferred from San Francisco to New York.

The opening up of satellite communications speeds things up on a global scale as well, and in effect creates a truly international currency market. It is now possible to track and monitor financial developments across the planet virtually at the moment they occur. Corporations can move currency or subsidiaries from one country to another in response to the slightest change in interest rates or political climate. Instead of having to keep their labor relations and marketing techniques responsive to local conditions, they merely move their functions to wherever meets their needs. Satellite communications, coupled with insensitivity to local conditions, eliminates the expense of flexibility. From corporate headquarters in Chicago or Dallas, executives can control speed and output of operations around the world.

Such instantaneous transactions mean that the supply of ready money is effectively increased. Revenue is moved more liberally, spent more freely and is therefore worth less, which makes for inflation.

At this point the shade of difference between a mere trend and a conspiracy becomes irrelevant. One way or another, we are becoming more visible and subject to manipulation. Information about our lives is recorded, centralized and accessible.

To defend this position of global domination, our leaders conscript and entice us into the armed forces, telling us that we have a responsibility as members of a free society. We must be prepared to go to war, always in the name of "freedom." "For every right that you cherish," Carter told us as he brought back draft registration, "you have a responsibility to fulfill."

We have closed circuit television and bullet-proof glass in our banks and post offices, ground-to-air missiles surrounding the White House, we are spied on, probed, and locked into an extensive computer network recording our every move.

The first thing we can do to resist the impending Big Brother system is keep aware of how it is being disguised and sold to us. Understanding how the system works is the key to evading it.

Limit your participation in the Recorded Economy—barter is the least traceable method. As slots for magnetized code-cards become more pervasive, hopefully so will the use of crazy glue and iron filings.

The U.S. Scramble for Olympic Gold

by Richard Hansen

FROM *The Guardian: Independent Radical Newsweekly* 36:43 (September 5, 1984): 9

LOS ANGELES—With the U.S. Olympic Team taking its national pride road-show to other cities, the Los Angeles Olympic Organizing Committee (LAOOC) here is reaping accolades of a different sort. U.S. business know-how and the free enterprise system took a bow when LAOOC President, Peter Ueberroth, announced that his original estimate of a $15 million surplus, or profit, from the 1984 Summer Games was "conservative."

The "success" was won with unprecedented commercialization of the Games. This commercialization prompted the mayor of Olympia to oppose the departure of the Olympic flame from that Greek city, and contributed to the Soviet Union's decision not to participate. The LAOOC conducted itself like a private corporation, closely guarding its registered trademarks, the "Star-in-Motion," "Sam the Eagle," and even the traditional five Olympic rings. Use of these symbols could be bought for some $500,000 or more, torchbearers across the U.S. paid $3,000 for their 1-kilometer thrill, and tickets for Olympic events sold at record prices. While city taxpayers theoretically did not have to pay a dime for the Games, neither do they now have any public improvements to show for their role as hosts. Instead, festive Olympic banners continue to wave—and fade—in the L.A. sun, donated, in part, to spare the Olympic committee the removal cost estimated at $10 apiece.

Reprinted by permission of *The Guardian*, which reprinted it from *Canalias, La Semana Cómica*, a Nicaraguan humor magazine.

It was, in the end, only the large corporations that benefitted from the Games, expending millions for the advertising exposure to be had by affiliating themselves with the LAOOC. Corporate sponsors spent a total of $140 million for that "official" privilege, with an additional $500 million reportedly spent on advertising campaigns linked to the Olympics.

It was a cleverly manipulated contest, exemplified by the $9 million fee paid by the Fuji film corporation for its official designation as exclusive film company of the 1984 Olympic Games. Kodak circumvented the sponsorship issue by paying $1 million for affiliation with the U.S. Olympic Team. In addition, Kodak contracted with ABC for $10 million in commercial spots in return for the promise that no other film advertisements would be aired. Similarly, Anheuser-Busch paid $11 million for its designation as official beer of both the Los Angeles and U.S. Olympic committees while Miller Brewing paid $3.1 million for the privilege of being named official sponsor of the U.S. Olympic Training Center.

Levi-Strauss pulled an advertising coup, paying the LAOOC $12 million as a corporate sponsor with much of the payment made in kind, so that with every U.S. medal winner, the Levi Logo came into direct camera view. The company supplied some 550,000 garments to 61,000 people, giving a 49-piece ensemble to each athlete and also outfitting Olympic committee employees and volunteers. But even this was not enough, as Levi-Strauss paid ABC an additional $18 million for commercials with the stipulation the Levis be the exclusive "outerwear leg-covering" advertiser. This $50 million Olympic marketing campaign culminates at a time when Levi-Strauss faces production cutbacks and layoffs.

Corporate willingness to swallow the high cost of affiliation, as well as the $500,000 ABC charged per television-advertising minute, underscores their faith in Olympic exposure. ABC, itself, paid an astounding $225 million for its exclusive media rights, anticipated some $100 million in production costs, and still expects a substantial profit.

TV AND RADIO CONTROLLED

In addition to its complete control over television coverage both here and abroad, ABC sought to control the radio media as well. This was to be accomplished by a "3-3-3 rule" negotiated with the LAOOC. Under that rule, other networks were to be limited to three minutes of live coverage only every three hours, and not to be presented more than three times each day. "Live coverage" was defined as any report aired within 100 yards of an indoor event and 500 yards from an outdoor event. Violations were to be dealt with by the removal of the offender's press credentials by the Olympic committee or lawsuit. This privilege cost the ABC radio network $500,000.

Protection of official sponsors' "rights" was the task of an investigative force set up by the LAOOC. Most often, the targets of these investigators were local community merchants attempting to make some money from the

Canalias: La Semana Cómica, Nicaragua

events taking place in their neighborhoods. As early as April, about 500 letters had already been sent to transgressors, 90% of whom the LAOOC admitted were innocent violators who did not understand that the ". . . Olympics aren't in the public domain." During the Games, U.S. District Court Judge Richard Gadbois—who had originally granted the Olympic committee sweeping powers to confiscate "illegal" material—was forced to admonish LAOOC detectives for their overzealous raids on unofficial souvenir vendors. These Los Angeles community merchants complained of the detectives' "Gestapo-like" tactics and abusive behavior.

Among some 100 such raids was the confiscation of a book entitled "24 Hours in the Life of Los Angeles, Olympic City '84" on the grounds that the usage of the word "Olympic" was unauthorized. The book is a collection of photographs, depicting a day's activities in Los Angeles.

Such heavy-handedness was only one aspect of the committee's effectiveness in controlling marketing of the Games at the sites themselves. As a result, the largely Black community that surrounds the main venue at the Los Angeles Coliseum was unable to profit from the Games. Merchants in the area purchased stocks of souvenirs, added to their normal inventories, and spruced up their storefronts in anticipation of Olympic crowds, only to find that shuttle buses bringing people to the Coliseum entered newly constructed fenced areas and discharged passengers so that they filed directly into the Coliseum, thus assuring only official concessionaires would get their business. Massive banners and posters were erected on the fences to shield visitors' views of local businesses and of substandard housing that dominates the area.

Six minority firms are suing LAOOC for $44 million in damages charging that it violated a number of verbal agreements, among them a pledge to allow the businesses to operate on the Olympic sites.

On the whole, Los Angeles small businesses gained little for their inconvenience during the Games. The events were attended by a largely local crowd, and businesses had little tourist trade on which to capitalize. Hotels reported numerous vacancies, and restaurants, theaters and amusement parks reported record low attendance. Only those few businesses involved in the production of official banners and pins reaped Olympic profits.

It was truly an Olympics for the high rollers, with some corporations willing to spend anything for the exposure to be had through Olympic affiliation. It was these corporations that provided the city with the majority of its out-of-town visitors as they flew their executives and aspiring employees to Los Angeles for hobnobbing sessions. The locals, apparently, went into hibernation, perhaps, watching the Games on television, as record sales in blank videotape seems to indicate. But despite home taping, ABC and the Olympic committee have planned yet a final capitalization of the Games. The "official 90-minute Olympic videocassette" is expected to hit the market by late September.

The Computer Revolution
Guess Who's Left Out?

by Patricia B. Campbell

FROM *Interracial Books for Children Bulletin* 15:3 (1984): 3–6

In a rush to bring computers into schools, educators are ignoring serious issues of equity—both in access and courseware content.

> When you get lonely you can talk to [the computer] and you can play a quiz game. It's a very smart machine.

> [With a computer] you could cheat in a test, get smart and know a lot of math. It could get you out of trouble.

The comments above were made by two fourth graders who had just joined the computer revolution. Like most students, they were excited about learning to use computers—and computer use in education is growing fast. It is

Patricia B. Campbell is the Director of Campbell-Kibler Associates, an educational research and evaluation firm located in New York City and Groton, Mass. Dr. Campbell is currently involved in software development as well as issues of computer equity.

estimated that in the past four years over 350,000 microcomputers have been introduced into the country's public schools.

While stories abound about students who will do just about anything to increase their access to computers, most youngsters working with school computers are wealthy, white and male. This is true outside of school as well. The ever-growing number of private computer camps, after-school and weekend programs serve middle-class white boys. Most minority parents just can't afford to send their children to participate in these programs.

Socio-economic status has a strong effect on who uses computers and how they are used. Race is a part of this pattern both because a greater proportion of minorities are apt to be poor and because of stereotypes about the "best ways" for minorities to use computers. Consider the following:

• Last year 67 percent of the wealthier public schools but only 41 percent of poorer public schools had microcomputers.

• More affluent suburbs teach programming and computer awareness, while less affluent urban and rural areas are more apt to use computers for computer-assisted instruction.

• One study of poorer elementary schools found that about 40 percent of predominantly white schools use computers for programming; for predominantly Black schools, the figure is closer to 10 percent.

• Programming has generally been seen as the purview of the gifted and talented and higher socio-economic status students, while drill and practice computer-assisted instruction is more frequently found with "disadvantaged" students.

• A California survey found the children of professionals more apt to use computers to program and for "creative approaches," while the children of non-professionals more often did reading and math drills and vocational work.

• A comparision of computer use in innercity Newark, New Jersey, schools and nearby suburban areas found that with few computers and still fewer sophisticated computers, even top Newark students quickly fall as much as two years behind their peers in better equipped suburban schools.

• Most software is written for English (or French) speakers. The lack of materials in other languages puts non-English speaking students at a serious disadvantage.

Given these and other similar findings, it is not surprising that one study concluded that current practices may reinforce existing socio-economic (and racial) inequities rather than foster educational equity.[1]

Explorations into why inequities in computer education exist are just beginning, but it is already clear that economic factors play a major role. Wealthier districts have more computers because they have more discretionary funds. Unlike previous educational innovations, this one is not being funded primarily by governments. Federal and state funds account for only about 30 percent of the funds allocated for computers; the other 70 per cent come from local tax levies, industry gifts and everything from PTA car washes to bake sales. As New Jersey Senator Frank Lautenberg points out, "Federal cutbacks in education aid are helping to widen the gap. The wealthier districts find a way to go ahead with computer purchases while the poorer districts cannot." In this time of the "New Federalism," who receives computer instruction is for the most part not who needs it, but who can afford it.

Of the government spending on computers, substantial amounts have been distributed under Chapter I (or its predecessor, Title I). Since these funds are used to provide remedial work for "disadvantaged" students, many districts feel that they can justify computer purchases only by limiting its use to basic skill "remediation" instruction. All this has implications for the relationship between computer use and the lack of empowerment for minority and poor students. As one district superintendent stated: "The students should control the machine, but what is happening is that the machine is controlling the students. School children are learning to be controlled by computers."[2] There are also serious implications for how well equipped poor children/minority children will be to find jobs as "computer literacy" becomes more important.

Computer equity is also affected by a factor that cuts across both economic and ethnic levels—gender. Although at least half of all students are girls, two out of every three students learning about computers are boys. When girls are involved, they tend to be clustered in the general introductory courses. "Hackers"—kids who spend most of their free time working with computers—are overwhelmingly male. When I interviewed 15 elementary and junior high teachers working with computers, 13 said that far more boys than girls come in for extra computer time before or after school. Boys are also more involved with computers out of school since, as noted, parents are more likely to enroll their sons in private computer camps and to buy them home computers. In private summer computer camps, boys outnumber girls by margins ranging from 3 to 8:1.[3] It is not surprising that the FBI crackdown on young people making unauthorized use of computer networks has caught only boys.

While only a little research has been done on why girls are being left out of the computer revolution (there is even less research on minorities), some distressing patterns are already visible.

The notion that computers are "math machines" appears to be a factor; computers have been viewed as "number-crunching monsters which historically were tamed by mathematical or engineering geniuses," i.e., by men.[4]

In a program designed to introduce computers to urban fourth and fifth graders, I asked students, "What can you do with computers?" The most frequent answer was "math." This answer—which is accurate but unnecessarily limited—may be due to the fact that computers were developed to work with large sets of numbers and that *calculators*, the precursors of computers, are almost totally number oriented. Even the word computer suggests a math connection.

Many more experienced people, who should know better, also consider computers as math related. This is the kind of thinking that leads middle schools and high schools to house computers in math departments, to encourage former or current math teachers to conduct computer courses and to require math prerequisites for computer courses when such knowledge is *not* needed.

As a result, computers are most often used in teaching math. In Massachusetts, for example, this is the most frequent instructional use of computers: 71 percent of the school districts responding to a State Department of Education survey reported such use. Stereotypic ideas about math, computer use and sex roles combine to give us the principal of a mid-western high school who last year explained that he limited computer use to boys because "they are going to be engineers."[5]

The perception that computers are "about math" has serious implications since math is so often seen, by students and adults alike, as a "male" domain, and "math anxiety" is more likely to affect girls than boys. Minority students are also affected by "math anxiety," so they, too, suffer from the math-computer connection.

Girls are also "turned off" computers by the ways that computers are introduced and used in the classroom. If boys introduce computers, or any new concepts, in the classroom, then students, both boys and girls, feel that the computers, or whatever, are for boys. Two stereotypes lead boys to be the ones who introduce computers to the class. First, the erroneous notion that preteen boys are stronger than girls means that teachers are more apt to choose boys to help carry the computer to the classroom. Second, the notion that boys are more mechanical leads many teachers to ask boys to help set up the computer and "introduce it to the class." I have seen this happen again and again: even when it is obvious that both girls and boys are interested in being involved, only boys are asked to help. When I ask teachers why they do this, the most common response is that they had been unaware of their behavior. (One teacher did say that she chose boys because they are stronger and seemed more interested. And when I demonstrated the computer in that class, some boys told the girls to sit down and get out of the way because "only boys know about computers.")

The computers-are-for-males syndrome is particularly common in the media. For example, almost 70 percent of the ads showing people and computers in recent issues of two popular computing magazines show only males; less than 3 percent showed only females.

As I write this, my second grade daughter has brought me her school district's newspaper. Its feature article is on computers; the accompanying picture, which is labeled "Computer whizzes sharpening their skills," shows five white boys (no girls) working with computers. This is not unusual. The cover of the New Jersey Education Association's policy statement on math and science shows a white boy at a computer—and inside pictures also show only boys on computers.

TV ads carry similar messages. It is a young white man who comes home from college a failure because his parents didn't buy him a computer, and it is a white baby boy whose parents feel that if he doesn't get a computer now it will be too late by the time he enters school. It is a pathetic boy, again white, about whom we read, "Because if he stumbles on sixth grade math, he may never catch up." Girls are rarely featured in these ads, and when they do appear it is in stereotypic ways such as the six-year-old girl in a frilly dress who gets a computer for her birthday. This "Buy-a-computer-or-your-child-[son]-will-grow-up-to-be-a-stupid failure" mentality harkens back to the worst of the door-to-door encyclopedia sales pitches.

Like the ads, most computer software seems to be male oriented, based on the assumption that only boys know about computers and only boys want to know about them. As one software/hardware developer commented, "Computer software is designed for boys, about boys, by boys."[6] Video games offer an array of "male" sports, battles, space wars and other macho forms of destruction. (An article about the macho, militaristic aspects of video games appears in Vol. 13, Nos. 6 & 7 of the *Bulletin*.)

Thanks to the factors noted above, boys are more likely than girls to come to school with prior computer experience. More significantly, girls do not "catch up" on computer experience in school. Teachers, themselves neophytes in the area, find it easier to limit computer use to those with experience. One elementary school teacher explained that she decided who would use the computer by "assigning two boys who already knew Apple." Her hope was that these students would then work with other students. Unfortunately, there is no better way to discourage elementary school girls than by putting boys in charge. In another instance, a software developer, field testing a program, observed a high school teacher introduce the field test with, "Which of you guys have computer experience?" Although prior knowledge wasn't necessary to what was being done, the five boys who said they had experience were those assigned to the computers.[7]

The small number of computers available for a large number of students may be the strongest influence limiting computer use. When the demand is greater than the supply, the more aggressive tend to usurp the limited supply, and thanks at least in part to our socialization, boys are more aggressive than girls. Girls who "give" their assigned computer time to boys frequently say they did it so that the boy "will stop bothering me." I have heard boys tell girls, when they are out of the teacher's hearing, that there isn't enough time for everyone to use the computer, so the girls had better not show up.

Educational Courseware

The accompanying article makes a convincing case that the current use of computers in education, far from promoting equity, actually reinforces unequal treatment of minorities and females. It remains to be asked: To what extent does computer courseware—the computer programs designed for classroom use—perpetuate racism, sexism and other forms of bias? Are the stereotypes, distortions and omissions that so plague school textbooks being repeated in computer courseware?

Some discount this possibility, on the grounds that software graphics are generally limited to stick figures and inanimate objects, and hence pretty much race- and sex-neutral. With technological advances, however, there is good reason to believe that computer programs will eventually become as proficient as the print media in projecting detailed images of all kinds. And there is already evidence of bias—in the terminology used, in the rewards given students for getting correct answers, in the "boy-oriented" materials being produced.

A brief look at the catalogs of computer courseware is not at all reassuring. Some courseware echoes the worst traits of the video arcade games. There is an emphasis on competition, macho sports and militaristic achievement. A single page of one educational catalog features "Math *Baseball*," "*Duelling* Digits" (one "*battles* the forces of ignorance"), "Math *Invaders*" and "Big Math *Attack*." Other offerings include "Tank Tactics" (in which students must structurally analyze words in order to "win a battle against the enemy's Super Tank"), "Alien Addition" (in which alien invaders can be stopped by firing a laser cannon with correct answers), "Demolition Division" (in which four tanks "must be destroyed by a correct answer") and "Battling Bugs" (self-explanatory). One game counters these exercises in militarism. It is "In Search of the Most Amazing Things," in which students "seek out, study and negotiate with the different cultures" of the (unfortunately named) "*Darksome Mire*."

Adding to this unappealing picture are such male-oriented programs as "Home Run Logic," which uses baseball terminology to "foster" systematic problem-solving, and "Bellringer," in which a "strongman" tries to ring a carnival bell. There are also the popular and prize-winning "Gertrude" programs—"Gertrude's Puzzles" and "Gertrude's Secrets"—featuring a bonnetted (obviously female) goose.

We should also be concerned about the selection of books used, for example, in language arts courseware designed for vocabulary and comprehension drills and games. There seems to be little concern for race, sex and class issues. One Apple Language Arts program, for instance, is built around children's books that have won Newbery Awards—awards that are not particularly sensitive to these issues.

Some educational organizations that review courseware do pose a question or two about equity in their evaluation forms, but these are generally superficial or assume that the evaluator is sensitive to race, sex, and other forms of bias. This is an assumption that is far from the mark. It is of utmost importance that, in addition to studies of courseware content, sensitivity programs be undertaken for courseware developers and that guidelines for evaluation be expanded in ways that are meaningful to race and sex equity and other content issues. Educators need to be reminded that stereotypic or biased software is no more acceptable in the classrom than any other biased instructional materials.

When I give computer demonstrations to groups of boys *and* girls, I regularly find myself surrounded by groups of *boys*, who literally fight to get through the crowd. Rarely is a girl willing to push through a group of boys. Occasionally some of the bigger boys will yell "let the little kids in," but the little kids given a path are always male.

This doesn't have to be the case. With a little effort, changes can be made. When I see boys clustering around my demonstrations, I ask girls to come over as well. Time spent watching a demonstration can also be regulated to ensure that everyone, female and male, gets a chance.

One summer program showed what could be done to increase equity in computer use. Designed to increase fifth and sixth graders' basic skills, the program attempted to counter the factors that discourage girls' access to the computer. The computers were not used in math classes, nor were they identified exclusively with math; the computers were used for writing and literacy, language arts, social studies, math, thinking skills and fine arts. Both female and male teachers and students introduced the computers. And there was no need to "fight" for a computer. Each student had access to one, and if a student chose to come in before or after school, a machine was available.

During the program, equal numbers of girls and boys began to work on computers outside of school hours. It must be noted that even this program did not fully escape the effects of stereotyping. In the afternoon, only girls worked with the female word processing teacher, while 85 percent of the students working with the male computer literacy teacher, doing "things like baseball math," were boys. Nonetheless, teachers reported that by the end of the program, any initial differences in boys' and girls' interest in and knowledge of computers had vanished.

Even small efforts to increase girls' computer use seem to have positive effects. In one urban junior high school the computers were part of the math department, all computer courses were taught by math teachers and all of the after-school "hackers" were male. Deciding to change this, one female computer teacher told the better female students how well they were doing and invited them to come in after school to work on the computers. Her encouragement was enough to change the sex ratio of the "hackers" from 100 percent male to 50 percent male, 50 percent female.

Here's another small effort that paid off. At one computer demonstration I gave, boys said that only boys could work on computers. I told them that the person teaching them about computers was a girl, even though a grown-up one, and that if girls didn't get an equal chance to use the computer then no one would. The teacher later reported that there was no more talk about who could use computers and who couldn't.

These anecdotes are in agreement with other findings. For instance, one study found that girls' participation increased if the computers were presented in the context of the arts rather than math.[8] If girls are given the extra encouragement needed to *begin* computer courses, their reluctance is lessened and sex differences in achievement disappear by the end of the course.[9] With appropriate encouragement, girls will use computers as much as boys—and perform as well or better. As teachers became more aware of girls' problems with access and regulate computer use, girls spend as much time as boys on the computer.

The computer is a newcomer to education, so stereotypes about computers are not as imbedded as they are in other areas. However, if we do nothing to counter current trends, then discrimination in computer access and use will become entrenched in our educational system, and both individuals and the country as a whole will lose. All students must be provided with equal access to the educational benefits of computers and to software that is free of racism, sexism and other forms of bias.

Notes

1. D. Watt, "Education for Citizenship in a Computer-Based Society" in *Computer Literacy*, ed., R. Seidel (New York: Academic Press, 1982).

2. C. Wilson, superintendent of School District 2, New York City, personal communication to Bradford Chambers, September, 1983.

3. P. B. Campbell, "Computers in Education: A Question of Access," paper to AREA, Montreal, April, 1983.

4. M. A. Marrapodi, *Girls and Boys: Equal Access* (New York: New York City Board of Education, 1983).

5. S. Kramer, Women's Action Alliance, personal communication, November, 1983.

6. R. Tinker, Technical Education Resources Center, personal communication, March, 1983.

7. A. Naiman, "Computers in Education: The Question of Equity," *SW Center for Human Relations Centerboard*, 1983, 41–45.

8. C. Berger, *Research on Women in Education Newsletter*, March, 1983, 2.

9. E. McCain, "Do Women Resist Computers?" *Popular Computing*, January, 1983, 66–78.

References

R. E. Anderson, "Computer Learning Inequities Are Found in Nation's Schools," *National Science Foundation News*, September 5, 1983.

H. J. Becker, "How Schools Use Microcomputers," *Classroom Computer Learning*, 1983, 4 (2), 40–44.

G. Burton, "Regardless of Sex," *Mathematics Teacher*, April, 1979, 261–270.

"Computers in the Schools," *Learning*, 1982, 11 (3), 30–31.

Computer Literacy Survey (Berkeley, CA: Computer Literacy, 1983).

E. Fennema, "Influences of Selected Cognitive, Affective and Educational Variables on Sex-Related Differences in Mathematics Learning and Studying" (Washington, DC: National Institute of Education, 1976).

E. Fennema and J. Sherman, "Sex-Related Differences in Mathematics Achievement and Related Factors: A Further Study," *Journal of Research in Mathematics Education*, 1978, 9, 189–203.

S. Greenberg, *Right from the Start* (Boston: Houghton Mifflin, 1978).

S. Kiesler, L. Sproull and J. Eccles, "Second Class Citizens?" *Psychology Today*, March, 1983, 41–48.

J. LeBaron, "Computer Use in Massachusetts Schools" (Wellesley, MA: The Commonwealth of Massachusetts Department of Education, 1983).

J. Lipkin, *Equity and Microcomputer Use in Public Education* (Washington, DC: National Institute of Education, 1983).

National Commission on Industrial Innovation, "California Computers in Schools Project" (Los Angeles: National Commission on Industrial Innovation, 1983).

K. Sheingold, "Issues Related to the Implementation of Computer Technology in Schools" (Washington, DC: National Institute of Education, 1981).

"Black on Black" Crime
The Myth and the Reality

by Bernard D. Headley

FROM *Crime and Social Justice* 20 (1984): 50–62

> Until we have the courage to free ourselves of many of the myths we know to be patently false, there will never be any serious alteration of the patterns of crime in this country.
>
> The Honorable John Conyers,
> United States House of Representatives

Few domestic or local issues in the United States (and to some extent Great Britain) in recent years have gripped the public's attention and become a platform for exploitative politicians more than the problem of "street crime." While the dominant white media never fail to underscore incidents of so-called "black on white" crime (i.e., "street crimes" committed by blacks against whites), attention is increasingly being drawn to the fact that "street crime" is essentially committed by low-income blacks against other low-income blacks (so-called "black on black" crime). The prevailing notion

Bernard D. Headley is currently teaching in the Department of Criminal Justice, Northeastern Illinois University, 5500 N. St. Louis Avenue, Chicago, Illinois 60625. He was formerly a Research Associate and Principal Investigator at Atlanta University's Criminal Justice Institute. The author wishes to thank Paul Takagi for his valuable suggestions in the preparations of this article.

being: the physical survival and well-being of the black community in America is threatened more by blacks killing or stealing from other blacks ("threats from within") than from external or systemic forces ("threats from without").

The notion is being articulated not only by the white capitalist media (who profit from stories about crime), but also increasingly by leading figures among the black petty bourgeoisie—politicians, academics, journalists, and law enforcement personnel—who, like their white counterparts, have a vested interest in promoting this belief. They benefit significantly from employment in an ever-expanding criminal justice industry.

The present discussion is an attempt to dispel the underlying myth that intra-race and intra-class directed "street crime" (i.e., "black on black" or "poor on poor" crime) represents the single most dangerous threat to the survival and well-being of black and poor Americans. Furthermore, I hope to show that the recurring presence of this myth tends to clutter a proper analysis of crime in black and working class communities and, more important, that the continued propagation of the notion of "black on black" crime (even among leading black intellectuals) indicates an unwitting internalization of one of white America's most cherished characterizations of black people, i.e., "Negroes are 'naturally' violent." At the same time it overlooks those crimes committed by white corporate America against black and working class Americans—crimes far more deadly and threatening to their survival than so-called "black on black" or "poor on poor" crimes.

Finally, I will argue that before discussions of "crime reduction" and "crime prevention" among black and working class Americans can take place, it is first necessary to view the phenomenon of "street crime" within the framework of a class analysis: the relation of dispossessed groups to the means of production.

ALARMING TRENDS

The myth that crimes committed by blacks against other blacks pose the single most dangerous threat to the black community is one that the black community itself (including the black press) has helped promulgate. And while there is no disputing the alarming trends in which blacks in the United States have criminally victimized each other, I will argue that when this phenomenon is placed in perspective with other forms of class victimization, our priorities will appear to be essentially misplaced. But first a look at some of the "frightening statistics," and at the way the phenomenon of "black on black" crime has been treated in one leading black publication.

So "horrifying" has been the phenomenon of "black on black" crime that *Ebony* magazine, only a few years ago, devoted an entire issue to its most grotesque aspects, citing at will the grim statistics. For example, the editorial pointed out that more blacks were killed by other blacks in the United States in 1977 than were killed in the entire nine-year duration of the Vietnam War. According to this editorial, "Most of the 5,734 blacks killed on the battlefields of Black America in one year (1977) could have survived Vietnam since Blacks who died there (5,711) averaged only 634 per year" (*Ebony*, 1979: 37). Based on these and other statistics, the editorial concluded that homicide is the leading cause of death among inner-city black males 15 to 44 years old, outnumbering deaths due to heart disease, cancer, sickle cell anemia, and other natural causes.

To reinforce the seriousness of the issue, the federal Law Enforcement Assistance Administration (LEAA) reported that for 1973, 87% of all robberies, rapes, and assaults involving black victims were committed by other blacks (LEAA, 1976; see also LEAA, 1975; Platt, 1978).

Again, there is no disputing the fact that the victims of "street crimes" are overwhelmingly poor people, particularly blacks and Chicanos, living in urban metropolitan areas. There is no arguing here that racial and national minorities, especially blacks, do have the highest rate of "street crime" victimization, and that in the few instances where perpetrators have been apprehended, they have indeed come from among the same superexploited sectors as their victims.

Undeniably, these are frightening trends that cannot be easily dismissed. Why poor blacks victimize other poor blacks is a question I shall return to, but we must bear in mind that viewing crime as a problem peculiar to a disadvantaged racial group becomes just one other way of blaming the victim. It diverts attention from the real causes of crime. Crime is not the result of blackness (which is what the notion of "black on black" crime implies), but rather a complex of social and economic conditions—a negative "situational matrix"—brought on by the capitalist mode of production, in which both the black victim and the black victimizer are inextricably locked in a deadly game of survival.

MORE DANGEROUS THREATS

Let us look objectively, however, at the prevailing notion that "street crimes" committed by blacks against other blacks constitute the most serious threat to the survival and unity of the black community. I suggest that if we examine black criminal victimization on a par with some less noticeable forms of victimization in the United States—which are no less criminal—directed against black and working class Americans, it should cause us to raise some questions about the "threat" of "black on black" or "poor on poor" crime.

Police victimization. One such form of external victimization, for example, is police brutality (what the police manuals blandly refer to as "deadly force"). Another recent *Ebony* magazine article cites that, nationwide, blacks constitute fully 45% of police homicides in the United States (see *Ebony*, 1981), a figure quite disproportionate to their representation in the total U.S. population of approximately 12%.

About 60% of all police homicides recorded between 1970 and 1972 in

New York City were black citizens (see *New York Times*, 1973). Clark (1974) reports that three quarters of all victims of police shootings between 1970 and 1973 were members of minority groups; about half were black and one quarter were of Hispanic ethnicity.

Takagi (1974), in his review of civilian deaths resulting from police use of force in California, reported that the incidence rate of such deaths increased by two and one-half times between 1962 and 1969, and that these rates have remained constantly nine times higher for blacks than for whites over the past 18 years. Robin (1973) investigated civilian deaths resulting from police force in Philadelphia that occurred between 1960 and 1970, and found that nearly 90% of those killed were black—whereas the local black community during this time accounted for only 22% of the population. At the same time, Robin reviewed statistics concerning police killings of civilians in seven other American cities (Akron, Chicago, Kansas City, Miami, Buffalo, Boston, and Milwaukee), and found black victims included among the dead more frequently than whites at ratios ranging from 6 to 1 in Akron, to 30 to 1 in Milwaukee.

Data cited by as conservative a figure as James Q. Wilson show that 5% of all blacks (over one million people) report themselves to have been unjustifiably beaten by the police (cited in Platt, 1978: 27). And Reiss, in an LEAA-financed study, found that the police used unnecessary force in fully 3% of all police-citizen encounters involving blacks, "representing hundreds of thousands of cases of brutality per year" (cited in Platt, 1978: 27).

In a most revealing article—"Violence in Detroit: A Bleaker View" (*The Progressive*, 1981)—it was pointed out that the police unit called STRESS (Stop the Robberies and Enjoy Safe Streets), which had come into existence in Detroit in 1971, in two short years had 22 killings to its credit. Similar to SWAT in Los Angeles and Atlanta, and BOSS in New York City, STRESS accounted for only 1% of the 5,500 Detroit police officers, but it soon had the highest per capita number of civilian killings by any urban police department in the country. According to the article, STRESS officers were responsible for 2.5% of Detroit's homicide rate in 1971.

Specific incidents of police homicide involving blacks as victims can be recalled ad infinitum. For example, there is the bizarre case that took place in rural Limestone County, Texas (80 miles south of Dallas), in June 1981. Three black teen-age males, who had no previous arrest records, were arrested by local white lawmen on trumped-up charges of marijuana possession. Under the most mysterious set of circumstances, they drowned while being transported across a lake in the custody of these officers. Apparently the youths had been handcuffed to each other while being taken across the water (a very extraordinary procedure for even the toughest police departments). The community believes it has solid evidence, showing a conspiracy on the part of the police officials to violate the victims' civil rights by killing them (see *Newsweek*, 1981).

In an unpublished list of incidents involving police violence against blacks, compiled by a reputable grassroots Montgomery, Alabama-based organization, the following cases—all taking place within the last two or three years—were documented:

• Birmingham, Alabama: A black woman sitting in a car was shot to death by police. Police answered a call regarding a robbery in progress. There was no connection with the woman. Police reinstated.
• Tuscaloosa, Alabama: Police turned a dog loose on a black child who was in the vicinity of a robbery.
• San Antonio, Texas: Policeman Veverka, who gave state's evidence against white police beating of (black) insurance executive (Arthur McDuffie) was acquitted by all white jury.
• Jackson, Mississippi: A disturbed pregnant black woman, Dorothy Brown, was shot down despite the attendance of a "slew of police."
• Deerfield, Florida: Black youth was in a crap game. Police broke up game, chased youth, had him on the ground, shot him in back of head. Ruled justifiable homicide by grand jury.
• Belle Glade, Florida: Jamaican man was part of a minor traffic accident. Taken to hospital by police and left hospital. [He] broke away from police and was shot and killed. Ruled justifiable homicide.
• Miami, Florida: (events leading to the McDuffie incident): . . . Dade County narcotics detective got wrong address and beat up black school teacher. No police indicted. . . . White highway patrolman molested 11 year-old girl. Got her in his car by saying she was suspected of stealing candy. Policeman received psychiatric treatment but was not removed from duty. . . . Moonlighting Hialeah police officer shot and killed black youth. He thought youth was armed. Actually, youth was urinating.
• New Orleans, Louisiana: Five police murders of blacks occurred after white policeman killed. Algiers area of city seems to be in state of seige. Mayor had to get rid of white police chief.
• Los Angeles, California: Reportedly two police who went to quell family disruption were subsequently arrested for rape of the eight-year-old daughter (Klan Watch, 1981).

Then, of course, there is the now ill-famed McDuffie incident. Arthur McDuffie, a black 33-year-old former marine and insurance salesman, was beaten to death by Miami-area policemen in December 1979. Several officers admitted that they had taken part in the savage beating, then smashed his motorcycle and falsified reports to make it look like an accident. McDuffie died of head wounds so severe that a Dade County medical examiner called them "the equivalent of falling four stories and landing between your eyes" (*Newsweek*, 1980). But after deliberating only two hours and 40 minutes, a six-man, all-white jury acquitted four white officers of all charges in connection with McDuffie's death. This startling verdict sparked three days of armed insurrection in Miami.

Finally, insult was added to injury when the white Los Angeles Police Chief (Daryl Gates) attempted to explain away the unusually high number of deaths of black suspects by police choke holds (12 since 1975) as being due to the fact that "some blacks may be more susceptible than normal people to injury when officers applied [the] choke" (*New York Times*, 1982).

From the above statistics and incidents, the case can be made that police violence directed against blacks in America represents a threat equally dangerous (if not more dangerous) to the physical survival and well-being of the black community to that of blacks killing other blacks.

Victimization at the workplace. To further dispel the myth of so-called "black on black" or "poor on poor" crime as the single most disturbing threat to black and working class communities, let us look at some additional external threats. Reiman (1979) relates that most of us, when we think of crime, do not imagine a corporate executive sitting at his desk calculating the cost of proper safety precautions and deciding not to invest in them. The odds are, according to Reiman, that what we see in our mind's eye is one person physically attacking another or robbing him/her with the use of threat or physical force. We visualize an attacker who is not wearing a suit and tie. In fact, at the thought of crime, most of us see a young, tough, "lower class" black male. But the case can be made that there are "non-criminal" actions ("crimes by any other name," as Reiman describes them) that take place every day and are far more dangerous to black and working class communities than the so-called "black on black" or "poor on poor" crimes.

Reiman (1979: 67–68) points out that work in America "may be dangerous to your health." In one year (1972), he writes, "A liberal estimate of the number of deaths caused by common crimes was 20,000." This is an alarming and considerable number, but it pales when compared to deaths on the job. Each year, according to Reiman's data, workplace injuries cause some 14,200 deaths—almost all of which are preventable by safety devices. In addition, he points out that some 100,000 people die annually of diseases that can be traced to coal tar, dust, asbestos, and other substances. All of these deaths are also preventable.

A recent *Washington Post* story relates the shocking information that federal agencies know the names of hundreds of thousands of people who have been exposed to cancer-causing chemicals on their jobs but, because of the "expense involved," have made no effort to tell them about the risk to their health. Nor has any effort been made to name or notify 21 million workers—one in every four—known to have been exposed to other hazardous materials; the government simply "waits for them to die" (*Washington Post*, 1981).

A most shocking case of corporate criminality against working class

Americans was recently revealed in the CBS Television newsweekly magazine, "60 Minutes." At the Tennessee Nuclear Specialties firm (TNS)—a
company which makes anti-tank penetrator shells for the United States Air
Force as part of a quarter-billion dollar contract—95 workers have been on
strike for well over one year because they became convinced that they were
being poisoned by exposure to radioactive uranium (see CBS Television
Network, 1981). Evidence was produced showing that on a "low week,"
workers are being exposed, on a daily basis, to an amount of radiation to the
entire body that is equivalent to five chest X-rays (100–200 milligrams).

One worker, Vincent Mango, complained of constantly being tired. "I
was weak. I lost a lot of weight," he said. Medical examinations showed that
he had a urinary uranium level in 1980 of 1,850–1,950 micrograms. According to medical experts looking into his case, the level of uranium found
in Mango's system, even by the company's criteria of 100 micrograms, was
over 18 times an "acceptable" level. One black worker, Albert Patton, who
had worked for TNS for six and a half years, contracted leukemia in the
summer of 1980. Medical doctors treating Patton reported that, "The type of
leukemia that he developed was in fact the type that is most commonly associated with radiation exposure."

In the case of TNS (as with a number of similar cases), the federal government (the supposed protector of all the people), by castrating regulatory
commissions and siding with giant capitalists, has made sure to protect the
interests of corporate and monopoly capitalism at the physical expense of
the American working class—even to the point of murdering them. These
are crimes that somehow never get counted in the FBI's "official" statistics.

A death resulting from a common or "street" crime may occur every 23
minutes (according to the FBI's 1980 statistics), but a death resulting from a
preventable industrial cause occurs every four minutes. I ask: Is permitting
hazards at the workplace a lesser crime than street violence?

Economic victimization. Other forms of criminal victimization of blacks
that somehow never get counted include shady business practices that are
often reported in ghetto areas—a form of property theft, if you will. Taub
(1970: 37–39) identifies some of these: bait-advertising of goods that are
"sold out" when the customer comes in to look at specials; telling the customer that an advertised special is not of good quality and that what he
really wants is some more expensive item; refusal to return deposits; mis-
representative sales contracts; used furniture sold as new; coercive pressures on buyers; attempts to collect nonexistent debts. All these practices,
so frequently complained of, have their roots in the powerlessness and the
lack of educational and financial resources of the urban poor.

Taub further notes:

> In today's consumer market, a specialized sales network has developed to deal
> with low-income blacks. The friendly smooth-talking dealer who makes the
> uneducated, poorly-dressed customer feel at home, gaining his confidence, of-

fering generous credit terms impossible to obtain elsewhere—and all this right in his own neighborhood—is much easier to deal with than a hostile downtown department store salesman (1970: 38).

Prices paid for needed items, however, reflect this "special service." A Federal Trade Commission report from not so long ago concludes:

> The low-income market is a very expensive place to buy durable goods. On television sets (most of which are the popular 19-inch black and white portables), the general market retailer price is about $130. In the low-income market a customer can pay up to about $250 for similar sets. Other comparisons include a dryer selling for $149.95 from a general market retailer and for $299.95 from a low-income market retailer; and a vacuum cleaner selling for $59.95 in the general market and $79.95 in the low-income market (cited in Taub, 1970: 38).

These are property crimes committed against poor and working class blacks in their own neighborhoods. They occur, as Caplovitz (1967) points out, with the full connivance of major banks and other lending institutions, which buy up dishonestly obtained contracts. According to Caplovitz, "The finance companies know what they are doing, as do the highly respected banks who lend to the finance companies." Ghetto blacks suffer to a far greater extent from these property crimes that never get counted than they do from housebreaking, purse snatching, and auto theft. Incidentally, not considered here are deaths and maltreatment due to improper medical care in emergency wards of hospitals, where most blacks go for nearly all medical treatment. There were some 20,000 of these deaths in 1974 (see Reiman, 1979: 72–74).

Taken together, therefore, the argument can be made that the violence that black and working class Americans suffer at the hands of the police and from industrial negligence constitute a far more serious threat to their physical survival than do violent "street crimes." Also, it can be argued that the daily rip-offs that blacks and other low-income groups experience at the hands of ghetto merchants represent an even greater economic and material threat than do "street" property crimes.

FACTS AND CAUSES

Generally in discussions of "black on black" crime there is the related myth that crimes committed by blacks against other blacks require a separate analysis from the larger social reality of crime in the United States. As observed earlier, the statistics on blacks harming and ripping off other blacks are alarming and indeed frightening. They cannot be dismissed or "explained away," and no attempt will be made to do so here, because "conventional" or "street crime" is neither an admirable nor an effective means of revolutionary action, and is in some respects reactionary—it pits the poor against the poor.

But as the black U.S. Congressman John Conyers (1979: 128) correctly observes, "the label 'black on black' crime gives the erroneous impression of a strange, aberrant, or exotic activity, when it is taken out of the context of the social and economic roots of crime." He continues, "The facts about Black crime have to be honestly examined and confronted. The meaning of these facts must not be misconstrued."

Let us try, therefore, to look objectively at the social and economic roots of "street crime" in the United States, because only as we look at these basic causes can we then address the incidence of crimes committed by blacks against other blacks.

First of all, given sufficient cause, there is nothing peculiar about one black criminally victimizing another black. Crime statistics from a number of U.S. jurisdictions have shown clearly that most criminal offenses, particularly of the "street" or urban variety, tend to take place within five or six city blocks of the offender's place of residence (see, e.g., Pyle, 1974), and that most homicides occur among relatives and acquaintances (see, e.g., Wolfgang, 1958). Because a significant proportion of the black population in the United States is systematically housed in overcrowded, segregated slum areas, it is therefore only logical that, given the known ecology of criminal behavior, the victims of "street crime" will more than likely be of the same race as the offender. In other words, the perpetrator of a "street crime" will generally victimize those closest at hand.

As Platt (1978) argues, there is no question that "street crime" is primarily an intra-class and intra-racial phenomenon, media stereotypes to the contrary. "White women are most likely to be raped by white men, young black men are most likely to be robbed by other young black men, and working class families are most likely to have their homes vandalized or ripped-off by strangers living only a few blocks away" (1978: 29).

What is at issue, therefore, is not the ecology of black or poor criminal victimization, but the social and economic forces that produce the victimizer. As has been argued extensively elsewhere (e.g., Platt, 1978; Gordon, 1976; Chambliss, 1976; Quinney, 1977; Krisberg, 1975), the real cause of crime in America lies *not* in the relation between victim and offender, but in the social relations engendered by the capitalist mode of production.

"Street crime," as Platt observes, "is not simply a *by-product* of the capitalist mode of production, a logistics problem to be solved by technocrats trained in 'system analysis.' Rather, it is . . . a phenomenon *endemic* to capitalism at its highest stage of development" (1978: 29. Emphasis his). In a capitalist society such as the United States, social and economic relations are basically competitive and generate substantial inequities in the allocation of material resources.

Capitalist societies are unable to guarantee economic security to most of their individual members; thus individuals must fend for themselves, finding the best available opportunities to provide for themselves and their families. Driven by fear of economic insecurity and by competitive desire to gain some of the goods unequally distributed in the society, many individuals will eventually become "criminals." Many forms of "street crimes" thus become logical, rational responses to the structure of institutions upon which capitalist societies are based. In fact, as Chambliss (1976: 6) so succinctly put it: "some criminal behavior is no more than the 'rightful' behavior of persons exploited by the extant economic relations."

IMPLICATIONS FOR SOCIAL POLICY

To dwell only on the myths relating to "black on black" crime (however important such an exercise is in and of itself) without devoting some space to the social policy implications that flow from the discussions presented here, and at least suggesting some short-term recommendations, is to run the risk of having this article dismissed as just another exercise in "radical polemics."

The social and policy implications surrounding the larger issue of blacks and crime in the United States (of which the phenomenon of "black on black" crime is simply one dimension) have been quite adequately addressed by Platt (1982). In that article (originally co-authored with Takagi and presented as a position piece for the National Association of Blacks in Criminal Justice) a number of what might be called "progressive short-term recommendations" were set forth—e.g., bringing equal justice to the bail system, abolishing mandatory sentencing, restoration of indeterminate sentencing, combating racism in criminal justice professionals, prosecution of corporate crimes and racist violence, and restoration of funding for community alternatives to imprisonment.

These are all realistic and practical objectives which, given the political will of the black and progressive leadership class, can be implemented in the short-run. However, if one were to deal specifically with the issues raised in the present discussion, a slightly modified and less comprehensive list of recommendations would emerge. The underlying theme of this article is to point out, if nothing else, the need for a new level of social awareness, a heightened consciousness in examining the problem of "black on black" crime. That is, it must be seen in perspective. At the same time, however, I have argued that "black on black" crime (particularly in poor and working class neighborhoods) must also be seen in all its ugly dimensions and that it should be thoroughly repudiated by all sectors of the black community. Consequently, I shall confine myself here to two basic sets of recommendations: one dealing with the myth, the other dealing with the reality of "black on black" crime.

A. Re-education of minority attitudes toward "black on black" crime. First of all, the black leadership class must actively challenge the two related myths: that "black on black" crime constitutes the most serious threat to the survival and well-being of the black community, and that this phenomenon requires a separate analysis from the larger social reality of crime in general. Black and progressive politicians, journalists, community and civic leaders, and intellectuals must be in the forefront in raising the level of the discussion of "black on black" crime, placing it in perspective with the larger and more serious crimes committed against black and poor Americans by the ruling sectors of the society. The effect of such a re-education would be an increased demand from the masses for a new level of social justice in the American society. This is not merely a call for "color blind" justice; as Platt argues: "So long as corporate and government crimes go unpunished, we cannot expect the selective punishment of working class crime to be an effective deterrent" (1982: 42).

B. Radical community involvement. Turning to the reality, the second recommendation calls for radical community organizing as a way of combating minority "street crime" victimization. Increasingly, local police have shown limited ability or willingness to combat predatory crime in black and working class neighorhoods. What is called for here is local leadership that recognizes and encourages neighborhood and community organizing for social defense; the type of communal and sometimes "primitive" forms of defense that rural black communities mobilized to resist the racist violence of hate groups like the Klan. Specifically, I am calling for nothing more than residents coming together and defining for themselves (free of official or academic intrusion) their own anti-crime measures and strategies for coping with crime and street criminals, then deciding how best to mobilize themselves for implementing these measures.

Under these circumstances, residents may (or may not) desire to use the local police as a resource agency—to make "official" arrests or aid resident groups in such activities as joint stake-outs. In other words, what is called for is a heightened sense of community vigilance without vigilantism. Only recently (and partly in response to a string of mysterious child killings) we witnessed the emergence of such neighborhood anti-crime groups here in the predominantly black working class neighborhoods of Atlanta, sprouting names like Atlanta Youth Against Crime, Atlanta Women Against Crime, and the Bat Patrol (the latter group, being the most aggressive in its anti-crime methods, did run into open conflict with the local police). There has emerged among these groups a collective sentiment that views the street criminal (black or white) as a parasite, a leech, a predator who should be resisted at all costs and by any means necessary.

Ultimately, however, as I have maintained throughout this discussion, the problem of street crime and street crime victimization can only be solved in the long term by a radical overhaul of the American political economy and the ideology that directs and guides the criminal justice system. An economy that generates gross levels of inequality and consequently relegates a substantial proportion of its population to permanent unemployment, joblessness, and demoralization—then uses its criminal justice system to control this surplus population—cannot hope to "free" itself of the menace of predatory crime.

References

Caplovitz, David
    1967   The Poor Pay More. New York: Free Press.
CBS Television Network—"60 Minutes"
    1981   "On Strike for Their Lives." Transcript Vol. 14, No. 9 (November 29).
Chambliss, William and Mankoff, Milton (eds.)
    1976   Whose Law? What Order? New York: John Wiley.
Clark, Kenneth
    1974   Quoted in New York Times (September 18).
Conyers, Congressman John
    1979   "Main Solution Is National Plan Correcting Economic Injustice." Ebony (August).
Ebony
    1981   "Police Deadly Force: A National Menace" (September).
    1979   "Black on Black Crime" (Special Edition—August).
Gordon, David M.
    1976   "Class and the Economics of Crime." In William Chambliss and Milton Mankoff (eds.), Whose Law? What Order? New York: John Wiley.
Klan Watch
    1981   Draft on Racial Violence. Montgomery, Alabama.
Krisberg, Barry
    1975   Crime and Privilege: Toward a New Criminology. Englewood Cliffs, N.J.: Prentice-Hall, Inc.
Law Enforcement Assistance Administration (LEAA)
    1976   Criminal Victimization in the United States: 1973. Washington, D.C.: U.S. Government Printing Office.
    1975   Criminal Victimization Surveys in the Nation's Five Largest Cities. Washington, D.C.: U.S. Government Printing Office.
New York Times
    1982   "Police Chief in Los Angeles Is Accused" (May 13).
Newsweek
    1981   "The McDuffie Case" (July 2).
    1980   "Death on Juneteenth" (July 20).
Platt, Tony
    1982   "Crime and Punishment in the United States: Immediate and Long-Term Reforms From a Marxist Perspective." Crime and Social Justice 18, pp. 38–45.
    1978   "'Street' Crime—A View From the Left." Crime and Social Justice 9 (Spring–Summer), pp. 26–34.
Progressive, The
    1981   "Violence in Detroit: A Bleaker View" (September).
Pyle, Gerald F.
    1974   The Spatial Dynamics of Crime. Chicago: University of Chicago Press.
Reiman, Jeffrey
    1979   The Rich Get Richer and the Poor Get Prison. New York: John Wiley & Sons.

Robin, Gerald
   1973   "Justifiable Homicide by Police Officers." Journal of Criminal Law, Criminology, and Police Science 54.

Takagi, Paul
   1974   "A Garrison State in a 'Democratic' Society." Crime and Social Justice 1 (Summer).

Taub, William
   1970   The Political Economy of the Black Ghetto. New York W. W. Norton & Co.

Washington Post
   1981   "Millions Not Told of Job Health Perils" (August 24).

Wolfgang, Marvin
   1958   Patterns in Criminal Homicide. Philadelphia: University of Pennsylvania Press.

Why the "War on Cancer" Isn't Working

by Peter Barry Chowka

FROM *Whole Life Times: Journal for Personal and Planetary Health* 33 (March 1984): 26–29

Although cancer is the second leading cause of death in the United States (after heart disease), public opinion polls continue to show that North Americans fear cancer more than any other health problem—probably because it presents the individual with more of a quandary than any other illness. Where does one turn when cancer strikes? The criticalness of the situation may make one hesitant to question the three therapies—surgery, radiation, and chemotherapy—favored by conventional medicine. Yet one hears increasingly about a myriad of so-called alternative, natural, sometimes illegal treatments—special diets, laetrile, stress reduction, and herbs, for example—and of practitioners who combine conventional and alternative approaches. (See Bernie Siegel, M.D.: A Yale Surgeon Cuts Through the Medical-Authority Myth, Whole Life Times, December 1983, and Does Mildred Nelson Have an Herbal Cure for Cancer?, Whole Life Times, January/February 1984.)

Peter Barry Chowka is contributing editor of Whole Life Times *and a journalist specializing in cancer and in the political dimensions of health care.*

In this issue, Whole Life Times *begins a series examining the cancer dilemma, first analyzing the failure of Western society to come to grips with the problem, particularly through our nation's current "war on cancer." Succeeding installments will review the most credible of the scores of alternative treatments that are available, and will look at the newest research and theories that are capturing the imaginations of both conventional and alternative practitioners.*

Please tell us how we can make this series more helpful to you; write to Peter Barry Chowka, Contributing Editor, Whole Life Times, *18 Shepard Street, Brighton, MA 02135.*

This past December a major anniversary passed almost without recognition: It was 12 years since the federal government and the private American Cancer Society (ACS) had declared all-out war against cancer. Back on December 23, 1971, there was fanfare in the historic East Room of the White House as President Nixon, joined by leaders of the country's medical establishment, faced the television cameras to offer "a Christmas present to the nation"—the unprecedented cancer crusade. "It will not fail because of lack of money," Nixon promised. "To the extent money is needed, it will be provided."

In fact, during the next decade the federal National Cancer Institute (NCI) alone spent $10 billion on conventional cancer research and treatment—more than was spent on cancer during the entire previous history of Western medicine. What the money bought, in the words of former Food and Drug Administration Commissioner Donald Kennedy, Ph.D., was a "medical Vietnam."[1]

The statistics speak for themselves: In 1983 cancer took the lives of just under half a million people in the United States—five times as many as were killed in the Vietnam and Korean wars combined. And except for a few rare forms of the disease, if you get cancer today your chance of surviving for five years after diagnosis is approximately one in three: roughly the same odds that faced a cancer patient in 1950.[2]

As the General Accounting Office (GAO), the investigative arm of Congress, reported in mid-1981, "We are demonstrably no closer to a cancer cure than we were 10 years ago."[3]

Yet despite this failing record, the cancer war's strategy of examining cancer on the microscopic, cellular level and developing methods of surgery, radiation, and chemotherapy drugs to attack the abnormalities seen there continues almost unchanged. In 1984 more money will be pumped into this effort than ever before—more than $1 billion in federal tax money alone.

A POLITICAL DISEASE

Almost unknown a century ago, cancer today has become an epidemic. One-third of us, according to the American Cancer Society (ACS), will get it; one-quarter will die from it. In many ways cancer is a tragic metaphor for modern times; a disease of excess—rare in primitive or agrarian cultures, prevalent in affluent, industrial societies. "We are not dealing with a scientific problem," explains Samuel S. Epstein, professor of occupational medicine at the University of Illinois. "We are dealing with a political issue."[4]

An analysis of epidemiological studies from around the world proves that 70 to 90 percent of human cancers are caused by factors in our environments, including diet and lifestyle,[5] Epstein asserts. A 1964 World Health Organization study confirmed that a large percentage of cancers are caused by "extrinsic factors," and concluded that the disease is largely preventable.[6]

Two decades later, while still not understanding the precise biochemical process which results in malignancy in the body's cells, scientists have developed a lengthy catalog of processes and products known to cause cancer, including synthetic food additives, diets high in fat and processed carbohydrates and low in fiber, ionizing radiation (including X-rays), industrial chemicals and wastes, air pollution, smoking, and chlorinated water. Virtually all of these causes represent profitable business interests—getting rid of them, thus preventing most human cancers before they begin, seems nearly impossible.

The medical establishment's overall strategy of treating the disease, especially cancer, after its occurrence, as opposed to preventing it, dovetailed well with the explosion of the carcinogenic culture following World War II. Everywhere, the environment at large (air, water, land), occupations, and individual lifestyles (food, exercise, stress) were undergoing rapid, profound changes from centuries-old traditional patterns to less natural ways, with a corresponding rise in rates of cancer and other degenerative diseases. Our economic system promoted these questionable changes, and in turn supported a medical system—which is now itself a $320-billion-a-year business—to treat the diseases that resulted. [See box: *A Bit of Medical History*]

CONFLICTS OF INTEREST

It became routine for executive officers of cancer-causing companies to sit on the decision-making boards of government research agencies, cancer charities, and cancer hospitals, resulting in the discouragement of prevention research. In one recent case President Ronald Reagan appointed Armand Hammer as chairman of the National Cancer Advisory Board (NCAB), government's top cancer panel, with responsibility for overall direction of the cancer war. Hammer is the chairman and president of Occidental Petroleum, which owns Hooker Chemical and Plastics Corporation—notorious

A Bit of Medical History

Economics and politics have played a large role in shaping conventional medicine's approach to cancer. This is no accident; it stems from a firmly entrenched trend in this country's medical history. Around 1900 a wide variety of medical approaches flourished here—among them homeopathy, nutrition, herbalism, midwifery, and the self-proclaimed "scientific" or "regular" doctoring of the physicians who had founded the American Medical Association (AMA) in 1848. Each healing approach had its own theories, practitioners, schools, and substantial respect from at least a segment of the public.

Then the nation's industrial leaders began using their considerable wealth and influence to establish AMA medicine as the only official form of health care. The young Rockefeller and Carnegie foundations led this campaign for what they called "medical reform." Alexander Flexner, a Carnegie Corporation employee, conducted a national survey of medical education for these foundations: His now-famous Flexner Report of 1910 strongly criticized "irregular" medical schools and recommended that scores of them (including most of the ones that admitted women or blacks) should close. Following the report's lead, philanthropists and public institutions withdrew support from these schools, and states began regulating them in ways that further assured their demise.

At the same time, local AMA chapters successfully influenced state legislatures around the country to severely restrict or outlaw the physicians' competition. Midwives, for instance, who attended 50 percent of U.S. births in 1910, were outlawed by the end of that year in all but remote rural areas. Meanwhile, industrialists poured millions of tax-deductible dollars into creating new AMA-style hospitals (1,652 between 1900 and 1910) and medical schools. It is difficult to estimate how much these contributions shaped the profession's approach to health, which from the earliest days focused on treating the symptoms of disease, rather than preventing it. The budding pharmaceutical industry, for instance, contributed massively to medical schools, ensuring that medical curricula would almost exclusively emphasize pharmacology—the sophisticated identification of symptoms and their suppression with drugs. One company alone—Eli Lilly—has contributed more than $250 million to medical education.

—Shelly Kellman and Peter Barry Chowka

For a more in-depth discussion and documentation of these events, see *Witches, Midwives, and Nurses: A History of Women Healers*, by Barbara Ehrenreich and Deirdre English, from The Feminist Press, Box 334, Old Westbury, NY 11568.

for its indiscriminate dumping of cancer-causing wastes into the environment, including at Love Canal in Niagara Falls, New York.

As Russell Mokhiber of Citizens Concerned About Corporate Cancer wrote to Hammer: "You cannot be expected to urge strict enforcement of the environmental laws, or otherwise encourage prevention of cancer—such a move would run against the short-term financial interests of your company." Hammer's appointment, Mokhiber suggested, represented "an insurmountable conflict of interest."

At the American Cancer Society, drug company consultants and others with a vested interest in promoting specific anti-cancer strategies regularly sit on governing boards. For example, Shields Warren, M.D. a lifetime member of the ACS board, is a director of the Mallinkrot Foundation, supported by the $250-million-a-year Mallinkrot drug company; Frank Dixon, M.D., of the ACS Council for Analysis and Projection is a consultant to the Eli Lilly drug firm.

This practice began in the late 1940s when a group of prominent industrialists (including Alfred Sloan, then president of General Motors) and motivational advertising experts (like Albert Lasker, head of the Lord and Thomas agency)[7] took control of the then-small ACS and built it up into the largest disease-oriented charity in the world. Today, with an annual budget approaching $200 million and thousands of local offices and paid employees, the ACS is arguably the most influential non-profit organization in the world.

Another leader of the modern ACS was Elmer Bobst. Bobst made millions of dollars for himself and billions for the drug companies he led (Hoffmann-LaRoche and Warner-Lambert); he is often referred to as the father of the pharmaceutical industry.

Not surprisingly, Bobst, active in the ACS for more than a quarter century, did his best to see that cancer research and treatment would focus exclusively on drugs. In his autobiography, Bobst brags that his ideas later "became the war on cancer."[8]

HALF AN ARMY

"The war on cancer was a boondoggle and a con job," Samuel Epstein states bluntly. "Initially Congress was conned by a group of the chemotherapy lobby in this country whose knowledge of cancer causation and cancer prevention was miniscule to say the least. The NCI has resisted any attempts to shift the emphasis from diagnosis and treatment to prevention."

"Everyone should know that the 'war on cancer' is largely a fraud, and that NCI and the ACS are derelict in their duties to the American people who support them," agrees two-time Nobel Prize winner Linus Pauling, Ph.D., whom *New Scientist* ranked among the 20 top scientific innovators of all time, in *The Cancer Syndrome* (Grove Press, New York; 1979).

On almost a dozen occasions during the past decade, Pauling has applied for small grants (around $200,000 each) to the NCI and the ACS to carry forward his promising work on cancer and vitamin C. With one exception, his requests have been denied.

In a recent interview at the northern California research institute that bears his name, Pauling described what he feels are the roots of the problem. "It's the system of peer review that appears to be responsible," he observed. "One thousand scientists and medical people are involved in this system, as members of committees that go over all applications for federal research money," he explained. The committees then rank the applications

---

An Expert Who Wears Too Many Hats

At the National Cancer Institute (NCI) the most glaring conflict-of-interest situation involved Dr. Phillippe Shubik. Shubik was a member of the National Cancer Advisory Board (NCAB), which sets NCI policy, from the board's inception in 1972 through early 1982; for years he was the only one of the 14-member group with expertise in environmental cancer. But at the same time that he served on the influential NCAB, Shubik was a paid consultant to 20-odd corporations and other groups, including at least eight drug companies and a number of firms (Coca-Cola, General Foods, Procter and Gamble, Royal Crown Cola) that produced and marketed suspected or known cancer-causing products and were thus affected by NCI decisions. Shubik also heads the Eppley Institute in Omaha, a cancer research and treatment facility that receives $4 million a year in NCI funds.

At one hearing before an NCI regulatory board, Shubik appeared and spoke in support of allowing NTA, a detergent additive manufactured by Procter and Gamble that preliminary tests had shown to be a carcinogen, to remain in use for three more years. When Shubik was asked whom he was representing, he replied, "Procter and Gamble." Umberto Saffiotti, Ph.D., who chaired the meeting, observed, "I never knew which hat he was wearing." Dr. Wilhelm Hueper, former chief of NCI's environmental cancer section, commented, "He's serving two masters."

Eventually, several congressional committees investigated Shubik but apparently he had violated no law. The influential *Cancer Letter* pondered why Shubik had been "singled out," since "nearly every scientific member of the [NCAB], the President's Cancer Panel, and the various advisory committees could be subject to such charges."

---

in order of worth. "But there's a conflict of interest," he noted. "The peer-review system people *themselves* apply for funds, and they recommend approval for the projects that others in this group—their friends—are involved in. They criticize novelty and originality and support the status quo in scientific research. If they started allocating funds for nutrition in relation to cancer, they might have to cut down on the funds for their own pet researchers."

INBRED RESEARCH

Each year, the federal National Cancer Institute (NCI) distributes more than $500 million in research grants and the private American Cancer Society (ACS) about one-tenth that amount. In addition, by defining the dominant trends in research, these institutions influence most others that disburse money for cancer—including drug companies, private hospitals, and cancer charities. Incredibly, the ACS admits in its 1976 *Annual Report* that $26 million—70 percent of its research budget—went that year to "individuals or institutions with which [ACS] board members from the medical and scientific community were affiliated."

In testimony before a subcommittee of the Committee on Government Operations of the U.S. House of Representatives in 1977, Irwin Bross, Ph.D., director of biostatistics at Roswell Park Memorial Institute in Buffalo, New York, the nation's oldest cancer research hospital, stated: "In any other part of government, it would be a corrupt practice for the persons giving out the money and the persons getting it to be the same people. It is a corrupt practice even when it is called 'peer review' or 'cancer research.'" Dr. Bross concluded: "This setup is not worth revamping and should simply be junked." [9]

THAT ELUSIVE CURE

If one pays attention only to the claims of the U.S. cancer establishment, one would believe that hope and a cure for cancer are just around the corner. In 1958, for example, Dr. John Heller, NCI director during the late 1950s, told *Life* magazine (May 5, 1958), "I'm glad to be alive these days. I've spent many years in cancer research. We are on the verge of breakthroughs." The title of *Life*'s 12-page cover story was, in fact, "Cancer—On Brink of Breakthroughs."

After so many years and billions of dollars have failed to produce such results, the establishment's continued optimism about the same therapeutic strategies provokes sharp criticism. Between 1969 and 1976 the occurrence of cancer rose as much as it had during the previous 35 years, asserts Epstein, a persistent, internationally recognized figure in the debate. "Our ability to treat and cure the major cancer killers has not materially advanced for decades," he contends. Nobel laureate Albert Szent-Gyorgi, M.D., Ph.D., goes even further: "For the last 100 years, cancer research has made practically no progress at all."

Even Vincent DeVita, M.D., director of the National Cancer Institute, admitted to the Associated Press (May 1, 1981) in a statement of unusual candor that "only about one-fifth of chemotherapy recipients are helped by the drugs."

Most tragically, this appears to be a situation in which the much-touted treatments may be worse than the disease. After spending several decades researching the byzantine world of cancer survival statistics, Hardin Jones, Ph.D., then a professor of medical physics and physiology at the University of California at Berkeley, declared in 1975: "My studies have proven conclusively that untreated breast cancer victims actually live up to four times longer than treated individuals." [10] Jones, a well-known dissenter from the mainstream approach to cancer, died in 1978; now his findings are being reexamined in medical circles in light of recent research about the long-term toxic effects of traditional cancer treatments.

Indeed, all of the 40 or so approved chemotherapy drugs, as well as radioactive substances, have long been known to be carcinogens themselves. As George W. Gray observed in 1941 in *The Advancing Front of Medicine* (McGraw-Hill, New York): "Frankly, all present methods of treating cancer are like so many firings of grapeshot at an unknown enemy in the dark. . . . Mutilation of a human body to extirpate a cancer is not a cure." Current

Interferon's Broken Promise

Interferon, a briefly heralded cancer fighter, provides a classic example of misdirection in the medical establishment's continuing attempt to cash in on drug-oriented treatments.

Interferon is a class of naturally occurring, non-toxic blood proteins that have an anti-virus effect in the human body by stimulating the body's own immune system. (Vitamin C helps to produce interferon in the body.) Interferon was first discovered in 1957 but curiously did not begin to interest the U.S. cancer establishment until two decades later when, via the new techniques of gene splicing, it could be mass-manufactured and sold as a drug.

In 1978, beleagured by mounting criticism, the cancer orthodoxy found itself in need of something promising. Virtually overnight the ACS seized on interferon, approving $6 million of its discretionary fund to purchase supplies of interferon from drug companies for human clinical trials—bypassing much of the lengthy protocol (five to 10 years of laboratory and animal studies) that normally precedes the human testing of any new drug.

Scores of pharmaceutical companies, encouraged by the ACS's high-power promotion and promise of funding, scrambled to get aboard the interferon bandwagon; they expected interferon to become the most profitable drug of all time. Approximately 20 new drug companies were actually formed simply on the basis of their promise to produce interferon. An investigation by ABC-TV's *20/20*, broadcast on October 22, 1981, revealed that, "The stock issues [these companies] floated on the strength of their interferon research multiplied overnight. . . . There were a lot of 'paper millionaires.'"

20/20 found that the companies had "lined up prominent scientists to act as so-called advisers, but in many cases those same scientists are also receiving federal tax money in the form of grants from the National Cancer Institute." For its part the American Cancer Society purchased a huge supply of interferon from a company called Life Sciences. But Life Sciences was in severe financial trouble until the ACS contract came in. Interestingly, two out of three members of Life Science's scientific advisory board were also on the ACS's interferon advisory committee, which approved the contract to Life Sciences; the scientists were also recipients of government research grants.

20/20 concluded that the "clubby" nature of cancer research and "overlap between the public and private sectors" posed a dilemma: "Is the public paying for the development in private industry, and what kind of return on investment is the taxpayer getting?"

Perhaps the more important question is what happens to promising cancer treatments that do *not* have the potential for generating massive profits? For years, other non-toxic treatments for cancer have been around—many of them, it turns out, more effective than interferon; none, however, seemed to be a moneymaker. Not a single one has made it to the stage of federally approved clinical trial.

Ironically, after all the hoopla, interferon has proven very disappointing, showing anti-cancer action in only 10 to 20 percent of cancer patients, and most of that temporary. Moreover, a study released on April 19, 1982, showed that interferon may *increase* the ability of cancer cells to spread into normal tissue. Dr. Shelby Berger, author of the study, noted (in the *New York Times*, April 20, 1982) that the findings "are certainly not a good indication for interferon."

evidence of this includes a study published in the *New England Journal of Medicine* (November 3, 1983) showing that a particular class of chemotherapeutic drugs (nitrosoureas, particularly semustine) used to treat gastrointestinal cancer increased the survivors' risk of developing leukemia five to 10 years later. In fact, the longer the patient survived the original cancer, the higher the risk of this fatal side effect.

The need for reliable data on such carcinogenic effects of individual drugs and combinations is heightened, Dr. Paul Calabresi points out, by the fact that chemotherapy drugs are increasingly being used to treat non-cancer disorders such as arthritis and multiple sclerosis.

THE RE-EMERGENCE OF NUTRITION

As the interferon boom was going bust in the spring of 1981 (see box, *Interferon's Broken Promise*), Ralph Moss, author of *The Cancer Syndrome* and a perceptive observer of the politics of cancer, predicted that the cancer establishment's next hype would involve retinoids: synthetic forms of vitamin A. In fact, medical orthodoxy rushed headlong not only into work with vitamin A but into the whole area of diet and nutrition. As with interferon, however, the establishment seemed determined to turn its nutritional insights into a new form of medication.

Nevertheless, the time was right for this advance. Throughout 1982 scores of independent scientific studies from around the world added weight to the evidence linking diet to degenerative disease, particularly cancer. In June 1982, to great national fanfare, the National Academy of Sciences (NAS) issued a lengthy report, *Diet, Nutrition, and Cancer*, which surveyed the recent literature and recommended a whole grain-, fruit-, and vegetable-centered diet as the best protection against cancer.

The question remains: Why has it taken half a century for this country's scientific and medical mainstream to even begin discussing the relationship between nutrition and cancer? And more tellingly, when will our cancer-fighting institutions put their money on this insight, allocating substantial funds to research on preventing and curing cancer through diet—not just with nutritional extracts and synthetic substitutes, but through broader dietary and lifestyle change? Hundreds of struggling scientists who have championed unpopular ideas, and millions of potential cancer victims, are waiting.

Notes and References

1. Donald Kennedy, Ph.D., "What Animal Research Says About Cancer," *Human Nature*, May 1978, p. 84.

2. Compare information in "Cancer—On the Brink of Breakthroughs," *Life*, May 5, 1958, and "One in Three New Cancer Patients Will Live Five Years," an Associated Press story published in the *Boston Herald*, December 15, 1980.

For statistics throughout this section, see also *Facts and Figures*, published annually by the American Cancer Society, 777 Third Avenue, New York, NY 10017; (212) 536-5400, and annual publications of the National Cancer Institute, Public Inquiry Section, Building 31, Room 10-A-18, Bethesda, MD 20205; (301) 496-5583.

3. "Inefficiency Stalling War on Cancer," *Los Angeles Times*, May 31, 1981.

4. Interview with Samuel S. Epstein. See his book, *The Politics of Cancer* (San Francisco: Sierra Club Books), 1978.

5. *Ibid.*, p. 23, and see reference no. 12, p. 514 of that book.

6. *Report of a WHO Expert Committee: Prevention of Cancer*, World Health Organization Technical Reporting Service, #276:1–53, 1964; cited in Epstein, *op. cit.*, p. 482.

7. Lasker, called "the Father of Modern Advertising" by Bobst (in Bobst's autobiography), made Kleenex a household word and created the postwar Lucky Strike cigarette campaign ("Reach for a Lucky instead of a sweet") that made smoking widely acceptable to women for the first time.

8. Elmer Bobst, *Bobst: Autobiography of a Pharmaceutical Pioneer* (New York: David McKay), 1973.

9. *The National Cancer Program, Part I: Overview of Program Administration*, hearings of the Subcommittee on Intergovernmental Relations of the Committeee on Government Operations, U.S. House of Representatives, June 14, 15, 16, and 23, p. 98.

10. *Cancer Control Journal* (Cancer Control Society, 2045 N. Berendo Street, Los Angeles, CA 90027), Vol. 3, No. 4, 1975. Also see Jones' study, "Demographic Considerations of the Cancer Problem," *Transactions of the New York Academy of Sciences*, February 1956.

The Medical Time Bomb of Immunization Against Disease

by Robert S. Mendelsohn, M.D.

FROM *East West Journal* 14:11 (November 1984): 46–52

*The greatest threat of childhood diseases lies in the dangerous and ineffec-
tual efforts made to prevent them.*

I know, as I write about the dangers of mass immunization, that it is a concept that you may find difficult to accept. Immunizations have been so art-
fully and aggressively marketed that most parents believe them to be the
"miracle" that has eliminated many once-feared diseases. Consequently, for
anyone to oppose them borders on the foolhardy. For a pediatrician to attack
what has become the "bread and butter" of pediatric practice is equivalent
to a priest's denying the infallibility of the pope.

Knowing that, I can only hope that you will keep an open mind while I
present my case. Much of what you have been led to believe about immunizations simply isn't true. I not only have grave misgivings about them; if I
were to follow my deep convictions in writing this chapter, I would urge
you to reject all inoculations for your child. I won't do that, because par-

Robert Mendelsohn, M.D. is the author of MalePractice *and* Confessions of a Medical Heretic *and editor of* The People's Doctor.

ents in about half the states have lost the right to make that choice. Doctors, not politicians, have successfully lobbied for laws that force parents to immunize their children as a prerequisite for admission to school.

Even in those states, though, you may be able to persuade your pediatrician to eliminate the pertussis (whooping cough) component from the DPT vaccine. This immunization, which appears to be the most threatening of them all, is the subject of so much controversy that many doctors are becoming nervous about giving it, fearing malpractice suits. They should be nervous, because in a recent Chicago case a child damaged by a pertussis inoculation received a $5.5 million settlement award. If your doctor is in that state of mind, exploit his fear, because your child's health is at stake.

Although I administered them myself during my early years of practice, I have become a steadfast opponent of mass inoculation because of the myriad hazards they present. The subject is so vast and complex that it deserves a book of its own. Consequently, I must be content here with summarizing my objections to the fanatic zeal with which pediatricians blindly shoot foreign proteins into the body of your child without knowing what eventual damage they may cause.

Here is the core of my concern:

1. *There is no convincing scientific evidence that mass inoculations can be credited with eliminating any childhood disease.* While it is true that some once common childhood diseases have diminished or disappeared since inoculations were introduced, no one really knows why, although improved living conditions may be the reason. If immunizations were responsible for the diminishing or disappearance of these diseases in the United States, one must ask why they disappeared simultaneously in Europe, where mass immunizations did not take place.

2. *It is commonly believed that the Salk vaccine was responsible for halting the polio epidemics that plagued American children in the 1940s and 1950s. If so, why did the epidemics also end in Europe, where polio vaccine was not so extensively used?* Of greater current relevance, why is the Sabin virus vaccine still being administered to children when Dr. Jonas Salk, who pioneered the first vaccine, points out that Sabin vaccine is now causing most of the polio cases that appear. Continuing to force this vaccine on children is irrational medical behavior that simply confirms my contention that doctors consistently repeat their mistakes. With the polio vaccine we are witnessing a rerun of the medical reluctance to abandon the smallpox vaccination, which remained as the only source of smallpox-related deaths for three decades after the disease had disappeared.

Think of it! *For thirty years kids died from smallpox vaccinations even though no longer threatened by the disease.*

3. *There are significant risks associated with every immunization and numerous contraindications that may make it dangerous for the shots to be*

given to your child. Yet doctors administer them routinely, usually without warning parents of the hazards and without determining whether the immunization is contraindicated for the child. No child should be immunized without making that determination, yet small armies of children are routinely lined up in clinics to receive a shot in the arm with no questions asked by their parents!

4. *While the myriad short-term hazards of most immunizations are known (but rarely explained), no one knows the longterm consequences of injecting foreign proteins into the body of your child.* Even more shocking is the fact that no one is making any structured effort to find out.

5. *There is growing suspicion that immunization against relatively harmless childhood diseases may be responsible for the dramatic increase in auto-immune diseases since mass inoculations were introduced.* These are fearful diseases such as cancer, leukemia, rheumatoid arthritis, multiple sclerosis, Lou Gehrig's disease, lupus erythematosus, and the Guillain-Barre syndrome. An autoimmune disease can be explained simply as one in which the body's defense mechanisms cannot distinguish between foreign invaders and ordinary body tissues, with the consequence that the body begins to destroy itself. Have we traded mumps and measles for cancer and leukemia?

I have emphasized these concerns because it is probable that your pediatrician will not advise you about them. At the 1982 Forum of the American Academy of Pediatrics (AAP), a resolution was proposed that would have helped insure that parents would be informed about the risks and benefits of immunizations. The resolution urged that the "AAP make available in clear, concise language information which a reasonable parent would want to know about the benefits and risks of routine immunizations, the risks of vaccine preventable diseases and the management of common adverse reactions to immunizations." Apparently the doctors assembled did not believe that "reasonable parents" were entitled to this kind of information because *they rejected the resolution!*

The bitter controversy over immunizations that is now raging within the medical profession has not escaped the attention of the media. Increasing numbers of parents are rejecting immunizations for their children and facing the legal consequences of doing so. Parents whose children have been permanently damaged by vaccines are no longer accepting this as fate but are filing malpractice suits against the manufacturers and the doctors who administered the vaccine. Some manufacturers have actually stopped making vaccines, and the lists of contraindications to their use are being expanded by the remaining manufacturers, year by year. Meanwhile, because routine immunizations that bring patients back for repeated office calls are the bread and butter of their specialty, pediatricians continue to defend them to the death.

The question parents should be asking is: Whose death?

As a parent, only you can decide whether to reject immunizations or risk accepting them for your child. Let me urge you, though—before your child is immunized—to arm yourself with the facts about the potential risks and benefits and demand that your pediatrician defend the immunizations that he recommends. If you decide that you don't want to have your child immunized, but your state laws say you must, write to me, and I may be able to offer suggestions on how you can regain your freedom of choice.

MUMPS

Mumps is a relatively innocuous viral disease, usually experienced in childhood, which causes swelling of one or both salivary glands (parotids), located just below and in front of the ears. Typical symptoms are a temperature of 100–104 degrees, appetite loss, headache, and back pain. The gland swelling usually begins to diminish after two or three days and is gone by the sixth or seventh day. However, one gland may become affected first, and the second as much as 10–12 days later. The infection of either side confers lifetime immunity.

Mumps does not require medical treatment. If your child contracts the disease, encourage him to stay in bed for two or three days, feed him a soft diet and a lot of fluids, and use ice packs to reduce the swelling. If his headache is severe, administer modest quantities of whiskey or acetaminophen. Give ten drops of whiskey to a small baby and up to one-half teaspoon to a larger one. The dose can be repeated in one hour and again in another hour, if needed.

Most children are immunized against mumps along with measles and rubella in the MMR shot that is administered at about fifteen months of age. Pediatricians defend this immunization with the argument that, although mumps is not a serious disease in children, if they do not gain immunity as children they may contract mumps as adults. In that event there is a possibility that adult males may contract orchitis, a condition in which the disease affects the testicles. In rare instances this can produce sterility.

If total sterility as a consequence of orchitis were a significant threat, and if the mumps immunizations assured adult males that they would not contract it, I would be among those doctors who urge immunization. I'm not, because their argument makes no sense. Orchitis rarely causes sterility, and when it does, because only one testicle is usually affected, the sperm production capacity of the unaffected testicle could repopulate the world! And that's not all. No one knows whether the mumps vaccination confers an immunity that lasts into the adult years. Consequently, there is an open question whether, when your child is immunized against mumps at fifteen months and escapes this disease in childhood, he may suffer more serious consequences when he contracts it as an adult.

You won't find pediatricians advertising them, but the side effects of the mumps vaccine can be severe. In some children it causes allergic reactions such as rash, itching, and bruising. It may also expose them to the effects of central nervous system involvement, including febrile seizures, unilateral nerve deafness, and encephalitis. These risks are minimal, true, but why should your child endure them at all to avoid an innocuous disease in childhood at the risk of contracting a more serious one as an adult?

MEASLES

Measles, also called rubeola or "English measles," is a contagious viral disease that can be contracted by touching an object used by an infected person. At the onset the victim feels tired, has a slight fever and pain in the head and back. His eyes redden and he may be sensitive to light. The fever rises until about the third or fourth day, when it reaches 103–104 degrees. Sometimes small white spots can be seen inside the mouth, and a rash of small pink spots appears below the hair line and behind the ears. This rash spreads downward to cover the body in about 36 hours. The pink spots may run together but fade away in about three or four days. Measles is contagious for seven or eight days, beginning three or four days before the rash appears. Consequently, if one of your children contracts the disease, the others probably will have been exposed to it before you know the first child is sick.

No treatment is required for measles other than bed rest, fluids to combat possible dehydration from fever, and calamine lotion or cornstarch baths to relieve the itching. If the child suffers from photophobia, the blinds in his bedroom should be lowered to darken the room. However, contrary to the popular myth, there is no danger of permanent blindness from this disease.

A vaccine to prevent measles is another element of the MMR inoculation given in early childhood. Doctors maintain that the inoculation is necessary to prevent measles encephalitis, which they say occurs about once in 1,000 cases. After decades of experience with measles, I question this statistic, and so do many other pediatricians. The incidence of 1/1,000 may be accurate for children who live in conditions of poverty and malnutrition, but in the middle- and upper-income brackets, if one excludes simple sleepiness from the measles itself, the incidence of true encephalitis is probably more like 1/10,000 or 1/100,000.

After frightening you with the unlikely possibility of measles encephalitis, your doctor can rarely be counted on to tell you of the dangers associated with the vaccine he uses to prevent it. The measles vaccine is associated with encephalopathy and with a series of other complications such as SSPE (subacute sclerosing panencephalitis), which causes hardening of the brain and is invariably fatal.

Other neurologic and sometimes fatal conditions associated with the measles vaccine include ataxia (inability to coordinate muscle movements), mental retardation, aseptic meningitis, seizure disorders, and hemiparesis (paralysis affecting one side of the body). Secondary complications associated with the vaccine may be even more frightening. They include encephalitis, juvenile-onset diabetes, Reye's syndrome, and multiple sclerosis.

I would consider the risks associated with measles vaccination unacceptable even if there were convincing evidence that the vaccine works. There isn't. While there has been a decline in the incidence of the disease, it began long before the vaccine was introduced. In 1958 there were about 800,000 cases of measles in the United States, but by 1962—the year *before* a vaccine appeared—the number of cases had dropped by 300,000. During the next four years, while children were being vaccinated with an ineffective and now abandoned "killed virus" vaccine, the number of cases dropped another 300,000. In 1900 there were 13.3 measles deaths per 100,000 population. By 1955, before the first measles shot, the death rate had declined 97.7 percent to only 0.03 deaths per 100,000.

Those numbers alone are dramatic evidence that measles was disappearing before the vaccine was introduced. If you fail to find them sufficiently convincing, consider this: in a 1978 survey of thirty states, more than half of the children who contracted measles had been adequately vaccinated. Moreover, according to the World Health Organization, the chances are about fifteen times greater that measles will be contracted by those vaccinated for them than by those who are not.

"Why," you may ask, "in the face of these facts, do doctors continue to give the shots?" The answer may lie in an episode that occurred in California fourteen years after the measles vaccine was introduced. Los Angeles suffered a severe measles epidemic during that year, and parents were urged to vaccinate all children six months of age and older—despite a Public Health Service warning that vaccinating children below the age of one year was useless and potentially harmful.

Although Los Angeles doctors responded by routinely shooting measles vaccine into every kid they could get their hands on, several local physicians familiar with the suspected problems of immunologic failure and "slow virus" dangers chose not to vaccinate their own infant children. Unlike their patients, who weren't told, they realized that "slow viruses" found in all live vaccines, and particularly in the measles vaccine, can hide in human tissue for years. They may emerge later in the form of encephalitis, multiple sclerosis, and as potential seeds for the development and growth of cancer.

One Los Angeles physician who refused to vaccinate his own seven-month-old baby said: "I'm worried about what happens when the vaccine virus may not only offer little protection against measles but may also stay around in the body, working in a way we don't know much about." His concern about the possibility of these consequences for his own child, however, did not cause him to stop vaccinating his infant patients. He rationalized this contradictory behavior with the comment that "As a parent, I have the

luxury of making a choice for my child. As a physician . . . legally and professionally I have to accept the recommendations of the profession, which is what we also had to do with the whole Swine flu business."

Perhaps it is time that lay parents and their children are granted the same luxury that doctors and their children enjoy.

RUBELLA

Commonly known as "German measles," rubella is a non-threatening disease in children that does not require medical treatment. The initial symptoms are fever and a slight cold, accompanied by a sore throat. You know it is something more when a rash appears on the face and scalp and spreads to the arms and body. The spots do not run together as they do with measles, and they usually fade away after two or three days. The victim should be encouraged to rest, and be given adequate fluids, but no other treatment is needed.

The threat posed by rubella is the possibility that it may cause damage to the fetus if a woman contracts the disease during the first trimester of her pregnancy. This fear is used to justify the immunization of all children, boys and girls, as part of the MMR inoculation. The merits of this vaccine are questionable for essentially the same reasons that apply to mumps inoculations. There is no need to protect children from this harmless disease, so the adverse reactions to the vaccine are unacceptable in terms of benefit to the child. They can include arthritis, arthralgia (painful joints), and polyneuritis, which produces pain, numbness, or tingling in the peripheral nerves. While these symptoms are usually temporary, they may last for several months and may not occur until as long as two months after the vaccination. Because of that time lapse, parents may not identify the cause when these symptoms reappear in their vaccinated child.

The greater danger of rubella vaccination is the possibility that it may deny expectant mothers the protection of natural immunity from the disease. By preventing rubella in childhood, immunization may actually increase the threat that women will contract rubella during their childbearing years. My concern on this score is shared by many doctors. In Connecticut a group of doctors, led by two eminent epidemiologists, have actually succeeded in getting rubella stricken from the list of legally required immunizations.

Study after study has demonstrated that many women immunized against rubella as children lack evidence of immunity in blood tests given during their adolescent years. Other tests have shown a high vaccine failure rate in children given rubella, measles, and mumps shots, either separately or in combined form. Finally, the crucial question yet to be answered is whether vaccine-induced immunity is as effective and long-lasting as immunity from the natural disease of rubella. A large proportion of children show no evidence of immunity in blood tests given only four or five years after rubella vaccination.

The significance of this is both obvious and frightening. Rubella is a non-threatening disease in childhood, and it confers natural immunity to those who contract it so they will not get it again as adults. Prior to the time that doctors began giving rubella vaccinations an estimated 85 percent of adults were naturally immune to the disease.

Today, because of immunization, the vast majority of women never acquire natural immunity. If their vaccine-induced immunity wears off, they may contract rubella while they are pregnant, with resulting damage to their unborn children.

Being a skeptical soul, I have always believed that the most reliable way to determine what people really believe is to observe what they do, not what they say. If the greatest threat of rubella is not to children, but to the fetus yet unborn, pregnant women should be protected against rubella by making certain that their obstetrician's won't give them the disease. Yet, in a California survey reported in the *Journal of the American Medical Association*, more than 90 percent of the obstetrician-gynecologists refused to be vaccinated. If doctors themselves are afraid of the vaccine, why on earth should the law require that you and other parents allow them to administer it to your kids?

WHOOPING COUGH

Whooping cough (pertussis) is an extremely contagious bacterial disease that is usually transmitted through the air by an infected person. The incubation period is seven to fourteen days. The initial symptoms are indistinguishable from those of a common cold: a runny nose, sneezing, listlessness and loss of appetite, some tearing in the eyes, and sometimes a mild fever.

As the disease progresses, the victim develops a severe cough at night. Later it appears during the day as well. Within a week to ten days after the first symptoms appear the cough will become paroxysmal. The child may cough a dozen times with each breath, and his face may darken to a bluish or purple hue. Each coughing bout ends with a whooping intake of breath, which accounts for the popular name for the disease. Vomiting is often an additional symptom of the disease.

Whooping cough can strike within any age group, but more than half of all victims are below two years of age. It can be serious and even life-threatening, particularly in infants. Infected persons can transmit the disease to others for about a month after the appearance of the initial symptoms, so it is important that they be isolated, especially from other children.

If your child contracts whooping cough, there is no specific treatment that your doctor can provide, nor is there any you can apply at home, other than to encourage your child to rest and to provide comfort and consolation.

Cough suppressants are sometimes used, but they rarely help very much and I don't recommend them. However, if an infant contracts the disease, you should consult a doctor because hospital care may be required. The primary threats to babies are exhaustion from coughing and pneumonia. Very young infants have even been known to suffer cracked ribs from the severe coughing bouts.

Immunization against pertussis is given along with vaccines for diphtheria and tetanus in the DPT inoculation. Although the vaccine has been used for decades, it is one of the most controversial of immunizations. Doubts persist about its effectiveness, and many doctors share my concern that the potentially damaging side effects of the vaccine may outweigh the alleged benefits.

Dr. Gordon T. Stewart, head of the Department of Community Medicine at the University of Glasgow, Scotland, is one of the most vigorous critics of the pertussis vaccine. He says he supported the inoculation before 1974 but then began to observe outbreaks of pertussis in children who had been vaccinated. "Now, in Glasgow," he says, "30 percent of our whooping cough cases are occurring in vaccinated patients. This leads me to believe that the vaccine is not all that protective."

As is the case with other infectious diseases, mortality had begun to decline before the vaccine became available. The vaccine was not introduced until about 1936, but mortality from the disease had already been declining steadily since 1900 or earlier. According to Stewart, "the decline in pertussis mortality was 80 percent before the vaccine was ever used." He shares my view that the key factor in controlling whooping cough is probably not the vaccine but improvement in the living conditions of potential victims.

The common side effects of the pertussis vaccine, acknowledged by *JAMA*, are fever, crying bouts, a shocklike state, and local skin effects such as swelling, redness, and pain. Less frequent but more serious side effects include convulsions and permanent brain damage resulting in mental retardation. The vaccine has also been linked to Sudden Infant Death Syndrome (SIDS). In 1978–79, during an expansion of the Tennessee childhood immunization program, eight cases of SIDS were reported immediately following routine DPT immunization.

Estimates of the number of those vaccinated with pertussis vaccine who are protected from the disease range from 50 percent to 80 percent. According to *JAMA*, reported cases of whooping cough in the United States total an average of 1,000–3,000 per year and deaths five to twenty per year.

DIPHTHERIA

Although it was one of the most feared of childhood diseases in Grandma's day, diphtheria has now almost disappeared. Only five cases were reported in the United States in 1980. Most doctors insist that the decline is due to immunization with the DPT vaccine, but there is ample evidence that the incidence of diphtheria was already diminishing before a vaccine became available.

Diphtheria is a highly contagious bacterial disease that is spread by the coughing and sneezing of infected persons or by handling items that they have touched. The incubation period for the disease is two to five days, and the first symptoms are a sore throat, headache, nausea, coughing, and a fever of 100–104 degrees. As the disease progresses, dirty-white patches can be observed on the tonsils and in the throat. They cause swelling in the throat and larynx that makes swallowing difficult and, in severe cases, may obstruct breathing to the point that the victim chokes to death. The disease requires medical attention and can be treated with antibiotics such as penicillin or erythromycin.

Today your child has about as much chance of contracting diphtheria as she does of being bitten by a cobra. Yet millions of children are immunized against it with repeated injections at two, four, six, and eighteen months and then given a booster shot when they enter school. This despite evidence over more than a dozen years from rare outbreaks of the disease that children who have been immunized fare no better than those who have not. During a 1969 outbreak of diphtheria in Chicago the city board of health reported that four of the sixteen victims had been fully immunized against the disease and five others had received one or more doses of the vaccine. Two of the latter showed evidence of full immunity. A report on another outbreak in which three people died revealed that one of the fatal cases and fourteen of twenty-three carriers had been fully immunized.

Episodes such as these shatter the argument that immunization can be credited with eliminating diphtheria or any of the other once common childhood diseases. If immunization deserved the credit, how do its defenders explain this? Only about half the states have legal requirements for immunization against infectious diseases, and the percentage of children immunized varies from state to state. As a consequence, tens of thousands— perhaps millions—of children in areas where medical services are limited and pediatricians almost nonexistent were never immunized against infectious diseases and therefore should be vulnerable to them. Yet the incidence of infectious diseases does not correlate in any respect with whether a state has legally mandated mass immunization or not.

In view of the rarity of the disease, the effective antibiotic treatment now available, the questionable effectiveness of the vaccine, the multimillion-dollar annual cost of administering it, and the ever-present potential for harmful, long-term effects from this or any other vaccine, I consider continued mass immunization against diphtheria indefensible. I grant that no significant harmful effects from the vaccine have been identified, but that doesn't mean they aren't there. In the half-century that the vaccine has been used no research has ever been undertaken to determine what the long-term effects of the vaccine may be!

CHICKEN POX

This is my favorite childhood disease, first because it is relatively innocuous and second because it is one of the few for which no pharmaceutical manufacturer has yet marketed a vaccine. That second reason may be short-lived, though, because as this is written there are reports that a chicken pox vaccine soon may appear.

Chicken pox is a communicable viral infection that is very common in children. The first signs of the disease are usually a slight fever, headache, backache, and loss of appetite.

After a day or two, small red spots appear, and within a few hours they enlarge and become blisters. Ultimately a scab forms that peels off, usually within a week or two. This process is accompanied by severe itching, and the child should be encouraged not to scratch the sores. Calamine lotion may be applied, or cornstarch baths given, to relieve the itching.

It is not necessary to seek medical treatment for chicken pox. The patient should be encouraged to rest and to drink a lot of fluids to prevent dehydration from the fever.

The incubation period for chicken pox is from two to three weeks, and the disease is contagious for about two weeks, beginning two days after the rash appears. The child should be isolated during this period to avoid spreading the disease to others.

TUBERCULOSIS

Parents should have the right to assume, and most do assume, that the tests their doctor gives their child will produce an accurate result. The tuberculin skin test is but one example of a medical test procedure in which that is definitely not the case. Even the American Academy of Pediatrics, which rarely has anything negative to say about procedures that its members routinely employ, has issued a policy statement that is critical of this test. According to that statement,

Several recent studies have cast doubt on the sensitivity of some screening tests for tuberculosis. Indeed a panel assembled by the Bureau of Biologics has recommended to manufacturers that each lot be tested in fifty known positive patients to assure that preparations that are marketed are potent enough to identify everyone with active tuberculosis. However, since many of these studies have not been conducted in a randomized, double-blind fashion and/or have included many simultaneously administered skin tests (thus the possibility of suppression of reactions), interpretation of the tests is difficult.

That statement concludes, "Screening tests for tuberculosis are not perfect, and physicians must be aware of the possibility that some false negative as well as positive reactions may be obtained."

In short, your child may have tuberculosis even though there is a negative reading on his tuberculin test. Or he may not have it but display a positive skin test that says he does. With many doctors, this can lead to some devastating consequences. Almost certainly, if this happens to your child, he will be exposed to needless hazardous radiation from one or more x-rays of his chest. The doctor may then place him on dangerous drugs such as isoniazid for months or years "to prevent the development of tuberculosis." Even the AMA has recognized that doctors have indiscriminately overprescribed isoniazid. That's shameful, because of the drug's long list of side effects on the nervous system, gastrointestinal system, blood, bone marrow, skin, and endocrine glands. Also not to be overlooked is the danger that your child may become a pariah in your neighborhood because of the lingering fear of this infectious disease.

I am convinced that the potential consequences of a positive tuberculin skin test are more dangerous than the threat of the disease. I believe parents should reject the test unless they have specific knowledge that their child has been in contact with someone who has the disease.

SUDDEN INFANT DEATH SYNDROME (SIDS)

The dreadful possibility that they may awaken some morning to find their baby dead in his crib is a fear that lurks in the minds of many parents. Medical science has yet to pinpoint the cause of SIDS, but the most popular explanation among researchers appears to be that the central nervous system is affected so that the involuntary act of breathing is suppressed.

That is a logical explanation, but it leaves unanswered the question: What caused the malfunction in the central nervous system? My suspicion, which is shared by others in my profession, is that the nearly 10,000 SIDS deaths that occur in the United States each year are related to one or more of the vaccines that are routinely given children. The pertussis vaccine is the most likely villain, but it could also be one or more of the others.

Dr. William Torch, of the University of Nevada School of Medicine at Reno, has issued a report suggesting that the DPT shot may be responsible for SIDS cases. He found that two-thirds of 103 children who died of SIDS had been immunized with DPT vaccine in the three weeks before their deaths, many dying within a day after getting the shot. He asserts that this was not mere coincidence, concluding that a "causal relationship is suggested" in at least some cases of DPT vaccine and crib death. Also on record are the Tennessee deaths, referred to earlier. In that case the manufacturers of the vaccine, following intervention by the U.S. surgeon general, recalled all unused doses of this batch of vaccine.

Expectant mothers who are concerned about SIDS should bear in mind the importance of breastfeeding to avoid this and other serious ailments.

There is evidence that breastfed babies are less susceptible to allergies, respiratory disease, gastroenteritis, hypocalcemia, obesity, multiple sclerosis, and SIDS. One study of the scientific literature about SIDS concluded that "Breast-feeding can be seen as a common block to the myriad pathways to SIDS."

POLIOMYELITIS

No one who lived through the 1940s and saw photos of children in iron lungs, saw a President of the United States confined to his wheelchair by this dread disease, and was forbidden to use public beaches for fear of catching polio can forget the fear that prevailed at that time. Polio is virtually nonexistent today, but much of that fear persists, and there is a popular belief that immunization can be credited with eliminating the disease. That's not surprising, considering the high-powered campaign that promoted the vaccine, but the fact is that no credible scientific evidence exists that the vaccine caused polio to disappear. As noted earlier, it also disappeared in other parts of the world where the vaccine was not so extensively used.

What is important to parents of this generation is the evidence that points to mass inoculation against polio as the cause of most remaining cases of the disease. In September 1977 Jonas Salk, the developer of the killed polio virus vaccine, testified along with other scientists to that effect. He said that most of the handful of polio cases which had occurred in the U.S. since the early 1970s probably were the by-product of the live polio vaccine that is in standard use in the United States.

Meanwhile, there is an ongoing debate among the immunologists regarding the relative risks of killed virus vs. live virus vaccine. Supporters of the killed virus vaccine maintain that it is the presence of live virus organisms in the other product that is responsible for the polio cases that occasionally appear. Supporters of the live virus type argue that the killed virus vaccine offers inadequate protections and actually increases the susceptibility of those vaccinated.

This offers me a rare opportunity to be comfortably neutral. I believe that both factions are right and that use of either of the vaccines will increase, not diminish, the possibility that your child will contract the disease.

In short, it appears that the most effective way to protect your child from polio is to make sure that he doesn't get the vaccine!

Section 2

IGNORANCE IS NOT STRENGTH

Pesticide Residues in Food: Your Daily Dose

by Lawrie Mott

FROM *NCAP News: A Publication of the Northwest Coalition for Alternatives to Pesticides* 4:2 (Summer 1984): 7–9

We all have to eat, but does our food contain more than a safe amount of pesticide residues? High levels of the pesticide EDB in muffin and cake mixes, cereals, and citrus, first brought to the public's attention by the news media rather than the regulatory agencies, suggest that the regulatory program designed to protect us from pesticide residues may be inherently flawed. Also, the extraordinary public concern over EDB demonstrated the need for information on a variety of basic questions concerning pesticide residues in food. As it now stands, consumers have no way of knowing whether their food contains pesticide residues. In 1983, the Natural Resources Defense Council (NDRC) commenced a study to investigate pesticide residues in food and the adequacy of government programs that seek to protect the public from these chemicals.

Lawrie Mott is project scientist for the Natural Resources Defense Council and is principal author of NRDC's recently published report, Pesticides in Food: What the Public Needs to Know. The report is available for $7.50 through NRDC, 25 Kearny Street, San Francisco, CA 94108; (514) 421-6561; or through NCAP. Ellen Kesten, illustrator for this article is a member of her county's task force on hazardous waste disposal.

REGULATION OF PESTICIDE RESIDUES IN FOOD

Pesticides are used extensively during the production of our food. During the last three decades, pesticide use has increased ten-fold, while crop losses to insects have doubled. By definition, most pesticides are highly toxic chemicals—toxic to insects, weeds, and other unwanted pests. Some are also harmful to humans and can cause cancer, birth defects, heritable genetic mutations, and nerve damage, among other debilitating or lethal effects.

Although all of us routinely face risk in our lives, many risks are largely a matter of individual choice. By contrast, consumers involuntarily risk exposure to pesticide residues in their food. We have no way to avoid ingesting these chemicals because we cannot determine what residues, if any, are present. Therefore, laws and regulatory programs are critical to protection of the public from involuntary exposure to this potential hazard.

The government should keep dietary exposure to pesticides to a minimum, for several reasons. First, very little information is available on the potential chronic health effects that might result from exposure to pesticides now widely in use. Furthermore, considerable uncertainty exists when linking pesticides to human health effects. Numerous Congressional and government reports have suggested that there are serious inadequacies in the existing government programs that regulate pesticides; several of these have also shown that public confidence in the government's protection of consumers from unsafe levels of pesticides in food is unwarranted.

In order for a pesticide to be licensed (registered) for use on a food crop, the manufacturer must submit health effects tests to the federal Environmental Protection Agency (EPA) to assess the risks of the chemical, including whether the chemical will cause cancer, birth defects, genetic mutation, or nerve damage. EPA uses these data to establish the maximum safe level, or tolerance, for pesticide residues in food. However, in many cases, EPA

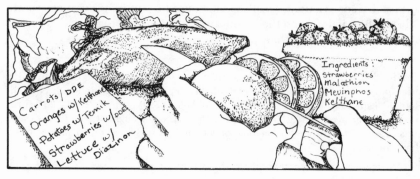

Ellen Kesten

Results of the NRDC Market Basket Survey

The NRDC market basket survey was conducted at four San Francisco supermarkets during August and September 1983. Samples were selected from the produce display shelves and delivered to an independent private Bay Area laboratory for pesticide residue analysis. An Advisory Board of scientists, physicians, and attorneys with expertise in relevant fields participated in the design of the NRDC study and interpretation of the results. The results of the survey are shown below.

PRODUCE SAMPLES WITH RESIDUES

Produce	Total Number Samples	Pesticide	Positive Results Residue (PPM)	Tolerance (PPM)	Detection Limit (PPM)
Broccoli	6	Dacthal	0.01	1	0.01
Carrots	8	Botran	1.1	10	0.01
		Trifluralin	0.01	1	0.01
		DDE	0.03	3.5	0.01
		Trifluralin	0.09	1	0.01
		Endrin	0.01	NT[a]	0.01
		Dieldrin	0.01	.01	0.01
		DDE	0.12	3.5	0.01
		DDT	0.03		
		Trifluralin	0.02	1	0.01
		DDE	0.05	3.5	0.01
		Trifluralin	0.15	1	0.01
Cucumbers	7	Dieldrin	0.01	0.1	0.01
Eggplant	6	Dimethoate	0.55	NT[a]	0.01
Grapes[b]	1	Dimethoate	0.07	1	0.01
Lettuce	8	DDE	0.03	7	0.01
		DDE	0.01	7	0.01
		Endosulfan	0.04	2	0.04
		Diazinon	0.02	0.7	0.01

Produce	Total Number Samples	Pesticide	Positive Results Residue (PPM)	Tolerance (PPM)	Detection Limit (PPM)
Oranges	8	DDE	0.01	3.5	0.01
		Kelthane	0.43	10	0.05
		Parathion	0.04	1	0.01
		Chlorpyrifos	0.01	1	0.01
		Ethion	0.19	2	0.01
		Methidathion	0.17	2	0.01
		Kelthane	0.17	10	0.05
		Methidathion	0.53	2	0.01
		Methidathion	0.05	2	0.01
		Chlorpyrifos	0.12	1	0.01
Potatoes	4	CIPC	0.17	50	0.01
		Aldicarb	0.05	1	0.05
		CIPC	0.01	50	0.01
		CIPC	0.12	50	0.01
Spinach	7	DDE	0.04	1	0.01
		DDT	0.02		0.02
		DDE	0.02	1	0.01
		DDT	0.02		0.02
		Dacthal	0.02	NT[a]	0.01
Strawberries	6	DDE	0.03	0.05	0.01
		Kelthane	3.01	5	0.05
		DDE	0.02	0.5	0.01
		Kelthane	1.07	5	0.05
		Malathion	0.01	1	0.01
		Mevinphos	0.28	1	0.01
		Kelthane	0.39	5	0.01
		Endosulfan	0.14	2	0.02
		DDE	0.01	0.5	0.01
		Kelthane	0.64	5	0.01
		Malathion	0.21	1	0.01
		Kelthane	0.07	5	0.01
		DDE	0.08	0.5	0.01
		Kelthane	3.7	5	0.01
		Mevimphos	0.02	1	0.01
Tomatoes	8	Botran	0.77	5	0.01
		Fenvalerate	0.02	10	0.02

[a] NT indicates no tolerances established for this pesticide on this particular commodity.

[b] This commodity was an alternate selection when the routinely-selected sample type was not available.

established tolerances *before* key health and safety tests were performed, and therefore cannot ensure that consumers are ingesting only safe amounts of pesticide residues.

The Federal Food and Drug Administration (FDA) is responsible for monitoring food in order to determine that EPA's tolerances or maximum safe residues limits are not exceeded. However, the analytical methods commonly used by FDA to test for pesticide residues are incapable of detecting two-thirds of the pesticides for use on food. In other words, the government cannot routinely tell at what level the majority of pesticide residues appear in our food.

In addition to monitoring food, FDA can remove from the market food with pesticide residues in excess of tolerances. Yet, FDA's enforcement action is greatly hampered by long delays between collection of food samples and completion of pesticide residue analysis. Consumers may be eating foods with high pesticide residue levels, simply because the laboratory results were not available until after the food had been sold.

Hold the Eggplant

The EPA estimates that you eat less than half a pound (7.5 oz.) of the following foods in a *year*. The amounts of pesticides they allow to remain on these foods are based on that estimate.

Almonds
Avocados
Blackberries
Boysenberries
Eggplant
Figs
Honeydew Melons
Leeks
Mushrooms

Summer Squash
  (e.g. zucchini)
Swiss Chard
Tangelos
Tangerines
Walnuts
Winter Squash
  (e.g. pumpkin)

These and over 60 other "low intake" foods are listed in R.D. Schmitt, EPA, "Update of Food Factor Tables," May 1, 1978.

NRDC'S STUDY

In 1983, NRDC initiated a study of pesticide residues in food in order to investigate the concerns raised by previously-released reports that federal and California pesticide residue programs did not sufficiently protect the public. One part of this investigation was a market basket survey for pesticide residues in fresh produce sold in San Francisco supermarkets. This survey was an attempt to gain a small representative sample of pesticide levels in ten different types of California-grown fruits and vegetables. The NRDC report also sought to independently determine whether the existing government programs detect all the toxic chemicals present. Because California supplies one-third to one-half the nation's fresh produce, the findings of this survey are relevant to other states.

The NRDC study resulted in three sets of major findings. First, 44% of the fresh fruit and vegetable samples contained residues of 19 different pesticides. This is *two to six* times as many residues as detected in California's monitoring of the same crop types. Many (42%) of the samples with detectable pesticide residues contained residues of more than one pesticide; several samples had four different pesticides present. Frequently, simultaneous exposure to more than one pesticide can increase the potential for other pesticides to cause adverse effects in humans. Yet, the government does not consider this effect when setting tolerances or "safe" residue levels.

Second, several of the pesticides detected are suspected or known carcinogens. EPA banned the use of some of these pesticides years ago because of their hazard to humans and the environment. Nonetheless residues of these chemicals continue to appear in our food. For example, DDT was the pesticide most commonly found in the NRDC survey, but the chemical was banned from use in the U.S. twelve years ago. This raises questions about the source of these residues. DDT has a half-life of 20 years in the soil, and the residues may therefore reflect continued contamination of produce by the chemical's presence in the soil. Another possible source is the use of the pesticide Kelthane, or dicofol. This chemical, which is virtually identical to DDT, contains DDT as a contaminant. The EPA permits use of the pesticide despite the fact that it contains a banned chemical. Several pesticides suspected of being carcinogens were discovered in the produce, and in each case the EPA is permitting their use on food in spite of their known or suspected dangers.

Third, although many of the pesticide levels found in produce were below the maximum allowable residue limits (tolerances) set by the EPA, these tolerances have been established at levels too high to protect consumers. The tolerances for several pesticides have been based on invalid scientific tests conducted by the Industrial Bio-Test Laboratories (NCAP NEWS, Winter 1981; *Amicus*, Spring 1983). For other chemicals, the government lacks certain critical health tests concerning whether the pesticide may cause cancer, birth defects, sterility, genetic mutations, or other ills. In other words, the EPA is permitting human exposure to pesticides in food even though it does not know what the outcome will be. EPA's tolerances for several of the pesticides discovered in this survey permit consumer exposure to exceed the maximum limit scientists believe to be safe for dietary intake. For three of these chemicals, consumer exposure may be at levels twice the maximum safe limits. Still other chemicals were found below EPA tolerances, but above the residue limits considered safe by the World Health Organization.

The flaws in EPA's tolerances are not unique to the pesticides detected in the NRDC study. The EPA tolerance-setting system allows pesticides to be present in food even though the chemicals are untested, have test data known to be false or fraudulent, or are carcinogens. In addition, EPA establishes tolerances based on certain assumptions of what comprises the average consumer's diet. Yet these figures may drastically underestimate dietary consumption. For example, EPA assumes we eat no more than *half a pound per year* of artichokes, avocados, blueberries, blackberries, cantaloupe or honeydew melon, eggplant, plums, tangerines, nectarines, or radishes. If consumers eat more than half a pound a year of these commodities, they are potentially exposed to more pesticide residues than EPA considers safe. EPA is now in the process of revising all food estimates used in setting tolerances.

NEED FOR REFORM

The results of the NRDC study demonstrate that existing government programs offer consumers a false promise of protection from potentially dangerous pesticides in food. However, there are a number of reforms that can be implemented immediately to prevent public exposure to unsafe levels of pesticides in food. The government should not permit the presence of any pesticide in food unless all required toxicology tests have been submitted to the government and the safety of the chemical has been proven. Residues of carcinogenic pesticides should not be allowed in food. Monitoring programs can be drastically improved by increasing the number of pesticides that can be detected in the food testing programs. Enforcement actions to prevent sale of food with illegal pesticide residues can be strengthened by requiring wholesale food distributors to record the destination of all crops from which samples were taken, to facilitate possible recalls.

In the long-term, the nation's farmers must move towards nonchemical methods of pest control. Techniques such as integrated pest management are already available to reduce the use of chemical pesticides. Biological agents, including the microorganism *Bacillus thuringiensis* and other natural parasites, can also be used to control pests. The government needs to support research to develop nonchemical pest control methods and to encourage the use of these techniques. In addition, the use of pesticides to rid produce of pests that result merely in cosmetic defects should be studied. Perhaps the use of chemical pesticides is only warranted when pests threaten the nutritional quality of food.

The results of the NRDC report and previous studies indicate serious problems in the way the government regulates pesticides in food. Many of these inadequacies can be addressed if federal laws are changed. Long overdue efforts are now underway in Congress to amend the nation's pesticide statute (the Federal Insecticide, Fungicide and Rodenticide Act) via H.R. 3818 introduced by Representative George Brown (D-CA) and the nation's food safety statute (the Federal Food, Drug and Cosmetic Act) via H.R. 5495 introduced by Representative Henry Waxman (D-CA). If enacted, these amendments would ensure that no pesticides are used on food crops before all the required health and safety tests have been submitted to EPA.

The strongest basis for optimism, however, is growing consumer awareness of the issue. This must be translated into pressure on the Administration and Congress to seek effective remedies that protect the public from unsafe pesticide residues in food. As public concern is translated into reform, consumers will have safe food.

U.S. Food Irradiators Wait for the Green Light

by S.K.

FROM *Not Man Apart* 14:9 (November 1984): 10

Although the Food and Drug Administration has yet to make an official ruling, the use of gamma rays to irradiate meat and produce appears to be headed for approval in the next few months. And despite the lack of information on the effects of irradiation byproducts on humans, the FDA seems confident that the consumption of irradiated food will not be harmful to American consumers. At the same time, food processors are jockeying for position in what could be a $50 million-a-year industry, if the FDA gives the green light.

"We believe that the uncertainties remaining are of no importance under our proposed regulation," Dr. Sanford Miller, director of the FDA's Center for Food Safety and Applied Nutrition, told a congressional subcommittee late in July. The proposed regulation, first published in the *Federal Register* on February 14, permits the treatment of fresh fruit and vegetables with up to one kilogray of radiation, and the sterilization of spices at up to three kilograys. At one kilogray, irradiation inhibits sprouting in potatoes and onions and kills some insects in fruit. At three kilograys, the irradiation will kill bacteria, mold, and yeast in spices. Although meat is not included in the proposed regulation, doses of 10 kilograys will completely sterilize a beefsteak, giving it a shelf-life of up to three years.

Most of the controversy around food irradiation concerns the lack of research done on the possible toxic and mutagenic effects of irradiated food when consumed by humans. (Radiation is not at issue here; the amount of energy used to irradiate food is not enough to induce radioactivity.) The chemistry of irradiation creates radiolytic products, which are also by-products of cooking, canning, and pasteurization. But irradiation produces unique radiolytic byproducts that are found only in irradiated foods. Although the FDA reported in 1980 that some irradiated foods may contain enough of these products "to warrant further study of their toxic effects," this study has never been commissioned.

Canadian food researcher Linda Pim noted that there have been studies cited in the *International Journal of Radiation Biology* suggesting that irradiated food can cause chronic reproductive and mutagenic effects in laboratory animals. Some animals that were fed irradiated wheat developed cells that contained more than the usual number of chromosomes. Despite these inferences, there has yet to be a study of the long-term effects of eating irradiated food.

Even the research data that do exist on irradiation have been called into question. The first approved use of irradiation in the U.S. was based on faulty data from animal feeding studies, FDA's Miller told the House Committee on Science and Technology. First granted in 1963, permission to irradiate canned bacon was rescinded in 1968 because of major errors in the way the experiments were designed and conducted. (Some of the later irradiation research was contracted to Industrial Bio-Test, a company whose management was recently convicted of falsifying lab-test results.) Despite the demonstrated problems with animal feeding studies, FDA researchers have continued to use them to back up the irradiation proposal.

And despite the continued delay on a final FDA decision, in September the Department of Energy awarded a $273,000 contract to a New Jersey firm to build a portable irradiator. Although the only legal items processors can irradiate now are spices (and only at low doses), this irradiator will be capable of sterilizing fruit and meat. Money to pay for the irradiator will come from DOE's Byproducts Utilization Program, which is supposed to promote the commercial use of the defense industry's nuclear waste. Although the most common fuel for irradiation is cobalt-60, DOE is hoping to persuade food processors to switch to cesium-137, a common nuclear byproduct.

Instead of nuclear warning symbols, most food processors are seeing dollar signs as they watch for regulatory barriers against irradiation to be dropped. The approval of higher irradiation doses for spices alone could mean $50 million worth of business a year, according to Martin Welt of Radiation Technology, another New Jersey firm. Although the company has only recently begun irradiating spices for domestic consumption, they have been irradiating strawberries and shrimp for export to countries where irradiated food is legal. According to *High Technology*, yet another New Jersey firm that uses irradiation to sterilize medical supplies, Isomedix, is gearing up for food irradiation.

The only problem these would-be food irradiators seem still to face is that of consumer acceptance. Many people view any nuclear technology as something to be wary of, and usually with good reason. This irritates irradiation proponents, and could throw a monkey wrench in their big-money plans. "In the U.S. a kind of 'technical neophobia' exists," the FDA's Miller told the congressional committee. "The public is inherently suspicious of new processes, particularly when the same technology is used for different purposes. . . . Industry ought to consider initiating some kind of public education program to demonstrate this is a safe and potentially valuable process."

Neophobia or no, consumer-advocate and public interest groups will lobby strongly for clear wording on irradiated food. Most commercial processors are hoping to be able to use euphemisms such as "processed with picowaves," or "treated with ionizing radiation." But this battle probably won't be as easily won by the processors. "We're going to insist on clear labeling," said Bob Scowcroft, who works on agricultural issues for FOE. "They're not going to be able to push this one through."

Fluoride: Miracle Cure or Public Menace?

by Russell Wild

FROM *Environmental Action* 16:2 (July/August 1984): 14–19

"A foreign substance is introduced into our precious bodily fluids, without any knowledge of the individual, certainly without any choice—that's the way your hard-core Commie works," theorized General Jack Ripper in the 1963 film, *Dr. Strangelove.* Ripper epitomized those excitable Americans of the then fading McCarthy Era who saw Communist infiltration in everything—especially in the new concept of fluoridation.

"Fluoride is the most monstrously conceived and dangerous Communist plot we have ever had to face," Ripper declared. The nation took a quizzical look at itself and roared with laughter.

But when the laughter died, something died with it—healthy skepticism. In post-*Dr. Strangelove* America, those who expressed concern over the U.S. Public Health Service's (USPHS) plan to add an odorless, colorless chemical to America's water supply were suspected of acute paranoia. Questioning fluoride's wondrous benefits or complete safety became comparable to questioning the existence of gravity.

Fluoride, or fluosilicic acid, the "fuming, corrosive liquid" (*Handbook of Chemistry and Physics*) used most often in the fluoridation process, is a byproduct of phosphate fertilizer production. It is provided to water authorities from a dozen or so corporations, including W. R. Grace & Company, Cominco American Inc., and Gardinier Inc. The liquid is measured and fed into water supplies in what the USPHS refers to as a "modern health miracle."

Fluoridation has been endorsed by most of the nation's major health organizations like the American Dental and American Medical Associations. And, as USPHS brochures will tell you, many civic groups, including the American Legion and the United States Junior Chamber of Commerce, have given their endorsements. It's almost an American institution. After all, the USPHS says fluoride can reduce 2 out of 3 cavities.

Roughly 60 percent of all Americans are drinking fluoridated water, and the USPHS is moving full-steam ahead to carry out its mission to bring the benefits of fluoridation to the other 40 percent as soon as possible.

In Dr. Strangelove, Gen. Ripper asks his aide, "Mandrake, have you ever seen a Commie drink a glass of water?"

But numerous reports and studies have emerged in recent years to warrant taking a closer look at this institution. A 1977 report by the National Research Council of Canada, citing over 500 studies, concluded that fluoride is an environmental hazard, inducing "metabolic and biochemical changes, the significance of which has not yet been fully assessed."

That same year our own National Academy of Sciences looked at fluoridation. Although it concluded that current concentrations in water supplies are "usually not great enough to be undesirable," the report also recommended further research. They suggested examining cancer death rates and congenital malformations in fluoridated and non-fluoridated areas, laboratory testing for carcinogenicity and chromosome damage and fluoride levels in the food chain.

Canada went further. In 1979 the Ministry of the Environment of Quebec issued a report citing dozens of independent studies, concluding that "Fluorides are highly toxic for humans and a narrow margin separates an 'acceptable level' from a toxic level." It recommended "an indefinite moratorium on water fluoridation." The Quebec government, even before the release of the report, suspended a bill that would have made fluoridation compulsory.

In light of these recent reports, it might well be asked why the USPHS remains undaunted in completing its mission. Or, to put it another way—was General Ripper really all that crazy?

Despite chuckles from friends, snickering from librarians, assurances from my own dentist and doctor that I would find only lunatics and fanatics, and warnings from public officials that I might never again be taken as a serious journalist, I set out to investigate fluoride.

Cited in the two Canadian reports and the Academy of Sciences report (although dismissed in the latter) are the studies of one Dr. John Yiamouyiannis. He is author of the recently self-published *Fluoride: The Aging Factor*. He is considered by many to be the leader of the anti-fluoridation movement. He is to some a prophet, to others, a modern-day General Ripper—maybe wackier.

"Kizilcaoren" is a village in Turkey where "even at the age of 30, the residents . . . experience walking difficulties and wrinkled facial skin. Upon falling their bones shatter like glass. Most of them will not reach the age of 50," *The Aging Factor* begins. Dr. Yiamouyiannis' diagnosis? The villagers ingest too much fluoride.

"Fluoride at levels as low as 1 part per million in the drinking water [Kizilcaoren's water has a natural fluoride content of 5.4 ppm] gives rise to an increase in the urine concentration of certain biological chemicals that signal the breakdown of collagen. . . . Disruption of this structural protein," Yiamouyiannis explains, "results in wrinkling . . . arthritis and stiffness of joints."

The symptoms observed in Kizilcaoren are generally not seen in the

United States. The abnormally high concentration of fluoride in the water there and the protein-deficient diet of the villagers make them highly susceptible to fluoride's toxicity. However, Yiamouyiannis maintains, in the United States, where fluoride is added to the drinking water at 1 part per million (a fifth that of Kizilcaoren), the deleterious effects of ingesting that fluoride, although not as visible, are indeed real.

Dr. Yiamouyiannis (hereon out Dr. Y) purports, on the basis of his own studies, that cities in the United States that fluoridate their water have significantly higher cancer mortality rates.

Not only is fluoride a dangerous poison, according to Dr. Y—it doesn't even fight tooth decay. Fluoridation, he claims, began as a "cruel hoax," in which industry officials persuaded the U.S. Public Health Service to pump an industrial waste product into America's water supply. The USPHS then formed "an unholy alliance with trade unions of medicine and dentistry [such as the AMA and ADA]."

Today, Dr. Y asserts, the USPHS and medical establishment, to "save their reputations . . . have intimidated, slandered, lied . . . even perverted the very principles of science itself in their attempt to cover up the damage they have done by promoting fluoridation."

Dr. Y has gained quite a following. His book is quoted regularly by members of the large anti-fluoridation movement. One USPHS official thinks that as much as 5 percent of all Americans may be devout anti-fluoridationists. Devout anti-fluoridationists are really the only kind. Belief in fluoridation as a medical hoax is accompanied always with a belief in fluoridation as a dental dud—and as a symptom of industrial greed.

On the other side, equally dogmatic, are fluoridation's staunch supporters. Asked about fluoridation, doctors transform into dental experts and dentists into medical experts, issuing blanket statements about the effectiveness and complete safety of fluoride. Highlighting the endorsements of their respective professional societies, they laugh heartily at any mention of controversy. Sometimes they get angry.

"I'm sorry if I've raised my voice, but I've seen too many kids suffering [from dental problems] not to get emotional," said Dr. Myron Allukian, D.D.S., Assistant Deputy Commissioner of Community Dental Health in Boston. He calls controversy over fluoridation ridiculous. "It's mostly this one guy running around the whole country saying all this stuff—a guy named Ya . . . Yam . . . Yamoo something."

Dr. Allukian advised me of the grave dangers involved in taking on this topic. "Naive journalists have been made fools of—they buy what these kooks tell them." Then, he added ominously, "talk to someone who'll give you the truth about fluoridation, so that won't happen to you." He suggested that such a man would be John Small, for the past 19 years the Public Health Service's "Information Specialist" on Fluorides and Health.

I found Small deeply ensconced in a cubicle in the USPHS's Bethesda,

Maryland complex, surrounded by an abundance of fluoride literature, much of his own authorship.

"Oh, John [Yiamouyiannis] is nothing more than a pain who has come up with a bogus, poorly researched book—pure junk," Small asserts. "There is no controversy about fluoride; as far as I'm concerned, it's a cut and dried case—fluoridated water does nothing but do a darn good job of fighting tooth decay.

"Listen," Small says chummily, "Yami sells his books, gives talks—he's making good money scaring people. Now, I don't do any evaluating—I'm just a switchboard. I hear something about fluoride that needs checking out—I get people—the best people in the world to look at it. We print what comes back."

But according to *The Aging Factor*, Small's job goes far beyond being "just a switchboard." According to Dr. Y, Small's job at the USPHS includes: "Covering up the harmful effects of fluoride" and working to "harass, intimidate, and destroy anyone whose publications, utterances, or activities work to the detriment of fluoridation." Small, alleges Dr. Y, "often calls upon other divisions of the Public Health Service to 'neutralize' studies showing adverse effects of fluoride."

Back to the switchboard analogy. Small offers the names and phone numbers to contact his "best people."

First I call William Bock, head of one of those "other divisions" of USPHS—Dental Disease Prevention at the U.S. Centers for Disease Control (CDC). The CDC has conducted its own studies regarding cancer death rates in fluoridated and non-fluoridated U.S. cities, with conclusions contrary to those of Dr. Y. "A crock," says Bock of Dr. Y's studies. "He misuses data, pulls things out of context, and misquotes. You know that quote on the back cover of his book, the one about Yiamouyiannis being conversant with the literature? That was my quote. What I said was 'Yiamouyiannis is conversant with the *antifluoridation* literature.' Just look at that book—you can tell it's garbage."

I looked at the book. Who's to say the "30-year-olds" who look like 70-year-olds in the photo aren't really 70? And his rendition of a fluoride-damaged spinal vertebrae looks suspiciously like a relief map of Cape Cod. Has he somehow managed to snow so many people? It was time to meet the famous Dr. Y.

Small informed me he'd be in town. Yet just a week before, I had spoken extensively with Dr. Y on the phone and he hadn't mentioned he was coming. "Probably didn't want you to see the company he keeps," said Small. He was giving a speech at a "Positive Living Expo" at the downtown Sheraton hotel. I got there at the tail end of a talk by a doctor on how milk contributes to sinus conditions. Dr. Y was then introduced as the world's foremost authority on fluoride. He took the platform.

"Fluoride has the most detrimental effect on humans of all toxic substances," he told an audience of 100. He went on to discuss chromosomal damage, damage to kidneys, premature aging, and cancer.

"But why," asked one listener testily, "is the government fluoridating, if what you say is true?"

Dr. Y described that "incestuous relationship" between government agencies and the industries they're supposed to regulate, and the extreme embarrassment that would surely be suffered by the Public Health authorities should the truth about fluoride come out.

At the end, as Small (seated in the second row with his wife) predicted, the books went on sale. At $10 apiece, Yiamouyiannis drummed up a dozen sales (two going to the Smalls).

I introduced myself to Dr. Y. He suggested we have dinner, and we did. Lifting his open palm, as if to stop traffic, he addressed the busboy carrying two glasses to our table: "No water for me, thank you." I was thirsty and hesitantly took a sip. Dr. Y watched me. "Do you drink beer?—Let me buy you a Heineken." (Holland has apparently not fluoridated since Dr. Y's cancer-mortality studies were presented to the Dutch Parliament in 1976.)

While reading my menu, I was instructed to beware of the dangers inherent (for reasons that were explained to me at length, but I forget) in margarine, ersatz sour cream, aluminum pots and pans, and especially, teflon. It was going to be a long evening.

We began discussing fluoride. I noticed that the man I was with, albeit a bit captious, and selling a story that was hard to swallow, was personable, seemed extremely intelligent, knowledgeable, confident in his claims, and— I may add—convincing.

Dr. Y encouraged me to speak to his experts. One of them is Dr. Dean Burk. Burk, if a kook, as his statements on fluoride have led some to allege, is certainly not your run-of-the-mill kook. He has had a long career in biochemistry, including 35 years at the National Institute of Cancer (USPHS). He has worked, he will tell you, along with many a Nobel Prize winner. Upon retirement from the Institute in 1974, he headed its Cytochemistry (tissues and cells) section. Since that retirement, Burk, driven by "good conscience," decided to reveal his former employer's promotion of fluoridation, for what it is—"mass murder."

Becoming aware of Dr. Y's work in 1975, Burk was impressed enough to join him in further calculating the cancer death rates for fluoridated and non-fluoridated cities. What these rates revealed to Burk were some 35,000 cancer deaths a year due to fluoridation.

"There's no question about it. We've checked and rechecked the data hundreds of times, and fluoride is a mass murderer," says Burk rather casually, disappearing behind a cloud of thick smoke from his protruding cigar. "I'm neither a missionary nor a martyr—I'm a scientist—and you won't find anyone with more credentials than me."

Many countries have decided not to fluoridate based on medical evidence,

Burk says. He describes the drive to promote fluoridation as an "Anglo-Saxon disease," because it is done only in English-speaking countries. His explanation for this is the same industry-government "hoax" envisioned by Dr. Y.

John Small claims this is nonsense. Western European countries "just never got around to it [fluoridating]," he says, "while some countries just don't give a damn about tooth decay." In Eastern Bloc countries, however, Small points out (and wouldn't Ripper be surprised) "they are heavily into fluoridation." He cites a Soviet document from 1974, which estimates 30 million Soviets drink fluoridated water.

Officials at neither the Western nor Eastern European embassies could confirm the status of fluoridation in their countries—except for the Belgian embassy. According to one Belgian embassy spokesperson, "It has been decided that the daily diet contains sufficient fluoride. Their [the Belgian public health authorities] feeling is that there is a definite tolerance level for fluoride—adding it to the water may break through that level and cause more harm than good."

Whether an "Anglo-Saxon disease," or a public health wonder, fluoridation was the brainchild of the U.S. Public Health Service. When it decided to begin fluoridation in 1945, it chose Grand Rapids, Mich. Considered an experiment, the USPHS set out to track dental decay in Grand Rapids (fluoridated to 1 ppm) for 15 years. It was also to monitor dental decay rates in neighboring unfluoridated Muskegon.

How, by that time, fluoridation had gained such scientific respect to be tried on the public, is open to interpretation. One of the USPHS examiners involved in the early fluoridation experiments, Dr. Frank McClure, writes in his *Water Fluoridation: The Search and the Victory*: "Events making fluoridation history unfolded slowly." In grand biblical style, he reminisces about his and his associates' years of research culminating in the announcement that fluoridation fights tooth decay and is completely safe.

But a quite different account of fluoridation history is given by antifluoridationists. In their account, McClure and his somewhat overzealous colleagues made their "astonishing" announcement about fluoridation without any sound basis. And there is talk of vested interests.

For instance, the Mellon Institute provided many of the studies of the '30s on which the USPHS based their decision to proceed with the Grand Rapids experiment. Coincidentally, the Institute was funded by the Alcoa Aluminum Company, which was eager to dispose of fluoride, a waste product of their aluminum production. And, the man who headed the USPHS in those days was Oscar Ewing—whose law firm represented Alcoa.

John Small claims that Alcoa has not sold fluoride since 1952. While that may be true, Alcoa apparently was selling fluoride to public health officials at the time of the Grand Rapids/Muskegon experiment—an experiment that would only be half completed.

2 out of 3 Cavities

The American Dental Association (ADA), not to mention *Consumer Reports*, approves only toothpastes with fluoride. That helps explain why 90 percent of all American toothpastes contain it. The other 10 percent can't carry the ADA seal of approval: "[This toothpaste] has been shown to be of significant value when used in a conscientiously applied program of oral hygiene and regular professional care."

Shown to be of significant value by whom? Even fluoride's greatest champion, Dr. Frank McClure of the USPHS, expressed doubt about the value of fluoride in toothpaste. He writes: "Endless displays of fluoride dentifrices . . . [on] radio and television have . . . [made] fluoride a universal household word. Hopefully, this publicity, false as it may be in some respects, will have favorable value in the promotion of water fluoridation."

Dr. Edgar Mitchell, who heads that division of the ADA which issues endorsements, said that the original ADA approval of fluoride toothpastes was "based on clinical tests done by Procter & Gamble Company in the late '50s." Asked if the makers of Crest with fluoride (which virtually cornered the market for 13 years) could be expected to be objective, Mitchell replied, "I see no reason why not." He explains that tests done since "do not always show positive effects," the reason being that "nowadays, cavities are so low as a result of fluoridation, it is hard to measure the effects of topical applications."

To Dr. Yiamouyiannis, fluoride toothpastes are a small part of what he envisions as the larger hoax of fluoridation. He warns that they can be extremely dangerous, especially for children, who are prone to swallow large amounts. "A family-sized tube," he alleges, "contains enough fluoride to kill a small child."

A spokesperson at Procter & Gamble could not say how much toothpaste children will swallow. She did, however, acknowledge that a family-sized tube "theoretically, at least, contains enough fluoride to kill a small child." But, she added, "that is virtually impossible—after the first 12 brushfuls or so the child would vomit."

Five years into the study, public officials of Muskegon, the unflouridated "control" city, were told of "marvelous success" in Grand Rapids. They decided they couldn't wait ten more years and fluoridated. Meanwhile, announcements were being made that the Grand Rapids/Muskegon experiment had revealed "2 out of 3 cavities" can be prevented simply by fluoridating the water supply. No one argued.

But what did the experiment really reveal? The examiners reported the number of decayed, missing, or filled (DMF) teeth in Grand Rapids children to have dropped by 65 percent. But several very important factors were never taken into consideration.

First, tooth decay was dropping even in pre-fluoridated Muskegon and probably in the country as a whole, due to increased awareness of proper dental hygiene, better nutrition in the postwar economy, etc. Second, the residents of Grand Rapids, aware they were being tested, may have been inclined to improve their dental hygiene habits. Third, the dental examiners could have been biased. As a study done by the Harvard School of Dental Medicine warned: "Interpretative and other examining errors in DMF studies may be large, easily exceeding a 100 percent difference in samples."

Anti-fluoridationists frequently question the effectiveness of fluoride in fighting tooth decay, an argument borne out in recent studies. A study done by Dutch scientists, as reported in Science News, showed fluoride of "dubious value" in reducing tooth decay. Similar findings were reported recently in studies done by the Forsyth Dental Center, comparing dental decay rates in fluoridated and non-fluoridated areas of the Boston suburbs.

Beyond fluoride's effectiveness, what about its safety? There is really no question that fluoride, long used as an insecticide and rodenticide, could be dangerous to humans. The important question is—how much?

Recent studies also show there is more fluoride in the food chain, primarily in processing food and beverages (a can of soup, made with fluoridated water, condensed, and then reconstituted with fluoridated water, will in effect, have been fluoridated twice before it reaches your table.)

A New Scientist article in May of 1983 compiled several reports from a number of scientific journals, including The Journal of the American Chemical Society, The British Medical Journal, The British Dental Journal, and Science. It concluded: "Individuals are receiving fluoride from a growing number of sources, and that too much fluoride can be harmful." In the opinion of the author, "a number of dentists [seem] to believe that if a little fluoride is good for you, then more must be better. This attitude is not only wrong, it is irresponsible."

According to the USPHS, an "optimum" level of fluoride depends somewhat on local conditions, but is roughly 1 part of fluoride per million parts of water. Or, assuming the average person consumes approximately one quart of water a day, the "optimum" should be about one milligram of fluoride a day.

But Quebec's Ministry of the Environment, in its 1979 report, stated: "There has been a substantial increase in fluorides in water, in food, and in the atmosphere. . . . The total quantity of fluorides ingested by normal adults (excluding those who drink abnormal quantities of liquids) [is] between 2 and 5 mg per day or more."

The 1977 National Research Council (NCR) report concurred: "Fluoride ingested daily in foods and beverages by adult humans living in fluoridated communities ranges from 3.5 to 5.5 mg." While the health effects of ingesting 5.5 mg. of fluoride are debatable, it is clear that the USPHS suggested level has been surpassed in Canada—where fluoridation is less prevalent than in the United States.

One way fluoride is being spread is through the air. The NRC estimates that 150,000 metric tons of fluoride were discharged over North America in

1972. "The emittance of fluoride from aluminum plants is so high," said one researcher from a Midwestern university, "that locals around every such plant in America have brought lawsuits for harm done to their livestock and the local vegetation . . . . The government standards are set by laboratories funded by the same industries that pollute. Naturally, the standards set are ridiculously lax."

At least one branch of the U.S. government has recognized airborne fluoride as a serious problem. In 1970, the U.S. Department of Agriculture claimed that "More worldwide damage to domestic animals is caused by fluoride than any other air pollutant." Mentioned were damage to lungs, liver, and kidneys, pulmonary damage, lameness, stiffness, and awkward gait. The NRC cited studies reporting samples of beef containing from 13.6 to 41.7 milligrams of fluoride per kilogram.

Recent studies indicate that children's diets alone, even in nonfluoridated areas, will yield in some cases over 1 mg. (the USPHS "optimum") of fluoride a day. When USPHS authorities came to Marin County, Calif., several years ago seeking to fluoridate the water, Dr. John Lee, a local pediatrician, was asked by the Marin Medical Society to study the issue before the organization would make an endorsement.

Even though Dr. Lee found an average daily intake of .9 to 1.5 milligrams of fluoride in diets—showing the county already was "optimally fluoridated" without adding it to water—the State Board of Health approved the move to fluoridate.

John Small, who is familiar with Lee's report, dismisses it, saying "the guy [Lee] isn't objective—he goes around and does talks on the evils of fluoridation." He also dismisses the Quebec report—"Pierre Morin [one of the 10 researchers who did the report] is an anti-fluoridationist from way back. Since these reports are, in his opinion, worthless, Small sees "no purpose in testing ambient levels of fluoride." Asked if it would hurt to test for ambient fluoride levels before fluoridating, he responded by reminding me that fluoridation has been going on for four decades without any apparent harm.

I mentioned that to John Lee. "That's their classic line," he responded. "That was also once the attitude about cigarette smoking—people died of cancer due to smoking long before tobacco was acknowledged as carcinogenic—but doctors didn't know what they were looking for."

Anti-fluoridationists see themselves facing a juggernaut. Norman Zimmerman, former senior toxicologist with the Michigan Toxic Substances Control Commission, went to the EPA last year to testify on the hazards of fluoridation. "The EPA officials gave us all [Pierre Morin from Quebec, Dr. Y, and several other opponents of fluoridation] but five minutes each to talk."

Zimmerman, however, is not the only one who feels it's hard to get a fair hearing. One head of a respected university research center (wishing to remain anonymous) recently sent the American Medical Association the re-

104 · Ignorance Is Not Strength

sults of his latest studies showing harmful effects of fluoride on the functioning of the kidneys. He received a curt note in response that said, "Let a dead issue remain buried. We don't want to give any additional fuel to the anti-fluoridationists." The study was returned.

One dentist from New York City no longer speaks out. When he voiced his concern over toxic effects of fluoride among associates, he was called before the ethics committee of the local dental association. He fears being viewed as a "quack" and being thrown out. "If you get kicked out, it means higher [malpractice] insurance. . . ."

John Lee doesn't care what anyone thinks—he is certain he's right. He criticizes the USPHS officials for presenting the members of California's Board of Health with data on fluoride intake as though it were current. "He later found the original study [one of McClure's] was from 1943. It was then I realized—there is more than scientific credibility on the side of fluoridation."

Evidence mounts to support anti-fluoridationists claims of fluoride's ill effects. A report done by Japanese scientists, appearing in the March 1984 *Cancer Research Journal* concluded that "a potential for carcinogenity of this chemical, which is widely used by humans, is suggested."

One upshot of the controversy caused by the Burk-Yiamouyiannis cancer study was the congressional subcommittee on intergovernmental relations calling on the USPHS in 1977 to do some laboratory tests of its own.

The tests are now being conducted by the USPHS's Institute of Environmental Health Sciences. Unfortunately, problems (apparently a deficiency in the diet of the laboratory rats leading to health problems), have delayed the results until 1988. "It breaks my heart," John Small says, "to see half-a-million [dollars] wasted and all those animals killed—but maybe it'll finally shut some people up."

But if before (or after) 1988, you have doubts, Dr. Yiamouyiannis suggests you stop using fluoridated products. By all means, he says, give up fluoridated water. You can buy bottled water," he says, "but the only sure way to remove fluoride from tap water is to use a distiller."

"Yiamouyiannis, as always, is full of it," counters Small. "You can use an activated bone charcoal or alumina filter, or reverse osmosis." The consensus among other sources is that both reverse osmosis and distillation are practical for home use. Distillation will do a more thorough job, but it is also more expensive.

For further information on fluoride, a few addresses are given below. But you've been forewarned—expect two very different stories.

There is in New York City a resource center where journalists with scientific questions may call to be put in contact with one of the many scientists the center has on file.

"Fluoride?" asked the receptionist. "Do you want to speak to a profluoridation scientist, or an anti-fluoridation scientist?"

"But I thought scientists are suppose to be neutral?" I asked.
"Not where fluoride is concerned."

For more information contact:
John Small, Public Health Service Building WWB, Room 506 Bethesda, Md 20205
American Dental Association, 211 East Chicago Ave. Chicago, Ill 60611
Dr. John Yiamouyiannis, Suite 202, BancOhio Plaza, Delaware, Oh 43105
Quebec Ministry of Environment, 2360 Chemin Ste-Foy, Ste-Foy, Quebec 61V 4H2, Canada

The State of the Nuclear Industry and the NRC
A Critical View

FROM Nucleus: A Report to the Union of Concerned
Scientists Sponsors 5:4 (Winter 1984): 3–5

*This was a presentation of the Union of Concerned Scientists to the Nu-
clear Regulatory Commission, Eric Van Loon, Executive Director; Ellyn
Weiss, General Counsel.*

Today marks an unusual occasion. This is the first time the Union of Concerned Scientists and the five NRC Commissioners have discussed nuclear
fundamentals.

There is little doubt that nuclear power is in trouble in America today.
The basic facts are familiar to us all: the cancellation of virtually every
plant ordered since 1974 and the unpromising outlook for reactor sales for
the rest of this decade. Since the TMI accident in 1979, 26 coal plants have
been ordered nationwide. These figures tell us that utilities continue to require new capacity, but they are declining to choose nuclear energy to meet
these needs.

The underlying reason for this direction, UCS believes, is that nuclear
power has lost the public's, as well as the investor's, confidence. There has
been a fundamental shift in public attitudes: a majority does not want more
nuclear power plants. American Nuclear Society's *Nuclear Report* of May
1983 found "the lowest level of support nuclear power has ever had, including immediately after Three Mile Island. . . ."

Why has the public become disenchanted with nuclear power? UCS sees four principal reasons:

- catastrophic accidents
- radioactive wastes
- industry ineptitude
- lack of trust in government

This fourth factor is especially important, and most directly within your purview: the public, in our view, believes that it is no longer being protected by its government—that there is no tough, effective cop on the nuclear beat. A consistent pattern of Commission actions broadcasts the message, intended or not, that safety is not this Commission's highest priority.

In order to restore a significant measure of confidence, the Commission must insist on safety first, institute measures to reinforce the "safety first" mandate within the NRC Staff, and act firmly toward an industry sorely in need of discipline.

With this prescription on the table, let me return to a diagnosis of the problem. In our view, the agency's shortcomings in its regulatory role have fallen into three categories: (1) the NRC has been unable or unwilling to resolve fundamental reactor safety problems; (2) the Commission has repeatedly tolerated a slow, reluctant or obscuring response to known safety hazards; and (3) the Commission and its staff have been hostile to those raising safety concerns.

I will present several examples of Commission action which illustrate the first two points, and UCS General Counsel Ellyn Weiss will follow with our views on the handling of public participation at the NRC.

The first example is the Bingham Amendment, introduced after the Three Mile Island accident, which casts doubt on how much the NRC knows about the level of safety at operating reactors. This amendment to the 1980 NRC Authorization Act, sponsored by Congressman Jonathan Bingham, directed the agency to identify which operating nuclear plants meet current safety requirements, and which generic, unresolved safety issues have technical solutions. A majority of the NRC Commissioners at that time objected to this task. The Commission majority conceded, in essence, that its staff was unable to determine which safety requirements had been applied in its licensing reviews. As you know, the Bingham Amendment was never implemented.

Sadly, delay and obfuscation have become a pattern. In recent months, we have seen two striking examples in the NRC's handling of the Indian Point emergency preparedness issue and the boiling water reactor (BWR) pipe cracking controversy.

A Commission majority selected the Indian Point nuclear plant, upwind from New York City—the nation's most densely populated area—to announce, in effect, that it would *not* stand behind its emergency planning regulations. And the Commission's quick reversal of an initial firm stance by the Staff on boiling water reactor pipe cracking undermined enforcement in this and future cases.

On July 14th, Harold Denton, not a frequent advocate of plant shut-downs, called for closing five BWRs for inspection. The next day, the Commission met with industry representatives and rescinded the order. A Staff member explained the recision to a reporter, "Industry gave them a good enough story that said [safety] . . . was outweighed by the costs of downtime to the utilities."

ENVIRONMENTAL QUALIFICATIONS: A CASE STUDY IN DELAY
A more extensive example of the NRC willingness to obstruct safety progress is the "environmental qualification" of electrical equipment needed to mitigate an accident.

Nuclear safety systems must be able to function during an accident. In a 1978 ruling, the Commission acknowledged that environmental qualification is *"fundamental* to NRC regulation of nuclear power reactors." Four years after this statement, more than 80 percent of the safety equipment still has not been shown to be capable of functioning in the harsh environment caused by an accident.

UCS first brought the environmental qualification issue before the Commission in November 1977 when we concluded that results from NRC-sponsored tests demonstrated the inadequacy of NRC's standards. Thereafter, the NRC asked nuclear operators to document the environmental qualification of equipment in operating plants. After two and a half years of utilities ignoring requests, the Commission set a compliance deadline two years hence.

A year later a group of utilities asked the Commission to postpone the "deadline" another year. The NRC Staff responded with a *two* year extension, and added exceptions that could allow unlimited delay. Meanwhile, a Staff evaluation report estimated that 15 to 40 percent of the equipment was "unqualified" and would need to be replaced.

When the June 30, 1982 deadline arrived, the Commission waived the "deadline" altogether, but provided no opportunity for public comment. A few months later, the Staff provided the Commission with a detailed equipment report. Altogether, 84.8 percent of the electrical equipment relied upon to protect the public in the event of an accident was not shown to be environmentally qualified, and only 6.6 percent of the equipment was fully qualified.

The most recent development is a Court of Appeals decision ruling that the NRC had violated the Atomic Energy Act, the Administrative Procedure Act, and its own rules when it suspended the deadline without providing public comment.

Since the Appeals Court ruling, NRC resistance has taken still another tack. More than four months after the Court ruling, still no opportunity for public comment has been provided. This is not surprising, however, since NRC attorneys told UCS after the Court ruling that even though UCS prevailed, NRC could exercise its discretion by doing nothing.

The handling of the environmental qualification problem is a glaring example of NRC's disregard for its statutory mandate.

THE CRGR: A SAFETY BOTTLENECK

The entire "backfitting" controversy, particularly the role of the Committee to Review Generic Requirements (CRGR), raises additional questions about the NRC's priorities and performance.

In general, backfitting is any change in a plant ordered by the NRC after the plant's construction permit is granted. In our view both the CRGR and the backfitting proposals to date aim toward establishing a system in which licenses can avoid backfitting.

Part of this irrationality derives from CRGR's use of cost-benefit analysis and probabilistic risk assessment (PRA) as analytic guidelines. Either one can be a tool that can be manipulated to produce a preselected result.

The legality of NRC's use of cost-benefit analysis is also questionable. NRC case law is remarkably consistent in affirming that costs are not a legitimate factor in safety decisions.

Nor can a process to assess safety improvements be rational if it is not accessible to all sides in the debate. CRGR is almost completely insulated from public scrutiny with limited access to relevant documents and only sketchy minutes of meetings.

We were utterly amazed at the Staff's triumphant boast: "There has been a substantial reduction in the number of new generic requirements since the inception of CRGR. Staff had projected 1900 new actions in FY-1982, whereas the actual number was less than 900." We had been unaware that CRGR's purpose was to clear the agency's regulatory docket.

THE HARTMAN ALLEGATIONS: UNANSWERED QUESTIONS

On November 7, 1983 indictments were handed down against the Metropolitan Edison Company for intentionally and systematically falsifying leak rate calculations at Three Mile Island Unit 2 for months before the March 1979 accident. Several questions about the NRC's handling of this matter go to the heart of NRC's credibility.

Considering that the NRC was informed in May 1979 of the facts underlying these indictments, how can it be that four and a half years later this agency has not taken any action?

How could the Staff continue to endorse the management competence and integrity of General Public Utilities (GPU) when it had evidence three years earlier that these charges were true?

If the Commission was secretly told that charges were substantiated while at the same time the Atomic Safety and Licensing Board (ASLB) which was adjudicating GPU's management competence on the record in public hearings, was led to believe that there were no serious questions about the utility's competence and integrity, that makes the adjudicatory process a charade.

It is possible that some—even at NRC—may not understand why the agency must care about the integrity of its licensees. You have no choice but to care. Like IRS auditors, your inspectors and technical staff are humanly capable of reviewing only a tiny fraction of the work done on these plants during construction and operation. South Texas, Zimmer, Midland and Diablo Canyon confirm that it is only too possible for a plant to be virtually completed with NRC approval, only to discover through a whistleblower, or otherwise, that your rules have been flouted.

RECOMMENDATIONS: A QUESTION OF MINDSET

From UCS's perspective, these and other examples illustrate an agency which has lost sight of its mandate.

Proposing a cure is difficult, since this is not a problem of rules or statutory authority. Our view, consistent with the Kemeny Commission findings, is that it is a problem of mindset. As a guiding principle, to reiterate Kemeny's view: "fundamental changes" are "necessary" in NRC's attitude. It must change from complacency to a view "that says nuclear power is by its very nature potentially dangerous and, therefore, one must continually question whether safeguards already in place are sufficient to prevent major accidents."

You as Commissioners may well feel and believe that changes have been major and that tough-minded vigilance is now the NRC norm. Whatever your intentions, however, your actions speak louder—and convey an opposite pattern.

The standards of integrity and carefulness you demand of the Staff are as important as the standards you set for yourselves.

In addition to the cases already discussed, we could cite many examples of Staff actions that undermine NRC's integrity as a regulatory agency. The Staff giving an early draft of the TMI Lessons Learned report to GPU and later deleting statements critical of the utility; a similar early "review" of the quality assurance study on Diablo Canyon by the licensee, with the Staff accepting many of its proposed changes, are examples of, to put it in the vernacular, Staff "coziness" with the industry it is supposed to keep at arm's length.

Needless to say, Staff members involved in these activities should not be rewarded with promotions, citations or bonuses.

You will need to maintain an attitude of questioning skepticism as you proceed to the issues on your regulatory agenda. We will turn to a few of those issues now.

SOURCE TERM

It is now quite clear that each accident sequence at each reactor will have its own unique "source term" that defines the quantity and chemical form of radioactive materials released to the environment as a result of a reactor accident.

Industry spokesmen claim the TMI accident "proved" that the release of radioactivity from a severe reactor accident had been drastically overestimated. No such fact was proven at TMI.

It is premature to be discussing the magnitude of possible source term reductions and their implications for emergency planning and other regulatory concerns. The Commission should evaluate its present source term research program, and reorient and expand it. Only then will it be possible to determine the degree to which reactor accident risks have been overestimated, and the steps that need to be taken in the light of the new information.

SAFETY GOALS

The Commission is midway through a two-year "evaluation period" in its consideration of quantitative Safety Goals.

Without reliable probabilistic risk assessment (PRA) results, quantitative Safety Goals have no meaning because it is impossible to assess compliance. The results can be manipulated by a judicious choice of assumptions, data base, and models.

We therefore urge the Commission to embark on an alternative program whereby qualitative evaluation methods are used to analyze many more reactors.

A comprehensive qualitative program will contribute more significantly to the protection of public health and safety than the present, PRA-based, quantitative Safety Goals program. UCS General Counsel Ellyn Weiss now will address the public participation part of our statement.

PUBLIC PARTICIPATION: ILLUSION AND REALITY

I want to begin by thanking you for this invitation. Because I am a frequent adversary, I have never been able to talk to you outside of that context, so I appreciate this opportunity.

To those of us who have represented intervenors in NRC proceedings, this agency presents a puzzling paradox. Although its overriding obligation, under the law, is to protect public health and safety, the public is made to feel an unwelcome interloper in NRC's proceedings.

I have heard the opinion expressed numerous times, often by experienced attorneys involved in their first NRC case, that they have never seen a system so weighted against the presentation of the other side's point of view. And that is under the current rules. New proposals to "reform" the licensing process generally move toward closing the system even more.

Let me be more specific. The licensing process actually begins when an applicant for a construction permit submits information to the staff for what is called a "completeness" review. The completeness review does not deal with issues of substance. The substantive Staff review and the documents that embody it are at that point months from publication. Even the applicants' basic licensing documents are in preliminary form: it is typical for a dozen or more amendments to be issued in the months before and during the actual hearings.

However, the licensing "clock" starts when public notice is given, even though NRC's substantive review has just begun. This has some extremely unfortunate effects.

First, intervenors' attempts to gather the information necessary to stipulate contentions and go to hearing are treated as "delay." Ironically, intervenors must formulate their contentions before the Staff's own review is completed.

In addition, the Licensing Boards, which are under orders from the Commission to move proceedings quickly, often view intervenors as impediments to achieving that goal.

The Staff's advocacy of the applicant's position places it, from the very beginning, in an adversary position towards any intervenors. No matter how technically credible intervenors may be nor what issue they raise, the Staff makes virtually no attempt to meet to consider whether their technical concerns have merit and if any corrective action may be necessary.

Instead, the immediate response is to find justification for opposing the intervenors' position on all substantive and procedural issues, and that stance continues during the entire licensing process.

Throughout the process, it is the goal of the applicant and, generally, also the Staff, to keep potentially troublesome information off the record. Rules are interpreted in the narrowest possible way to exclude relevant evidence and disregard serious safety issues.

In the recent past, the Commission has begun to actively interject itself into ongoing proceedings to narrow the issues being considered or to remove them altogether from the hearings, and therefore, from the purview of *on-the-record* public participation. This has happened several times in the TMI Restart case, Indian Point, Zimmer, and other cases.

We do not dispute the Commission's right, indeed duty, to maintain control over its proceedings. But in these cases the Commission has intervened to *remove* issues from the hearings. I am aware of no instance where the Commission has intervened in the other direction.

CATAWBA DECISION AND THE DOUBLE STANDARD FOR INTERVENOR CHALLENGES

I would like to mention two other developments that add reinforcement to the public's view that the Commission is hostile to the public's right to present arguments on the record.

The Commission reviewed an Appeal Board decision (the Catawba decision), holding that it was unfair and contrary to the Atomic Energy Act for the Licensing Boards to require intervenors to meet the special standards for late-filed contentions when they could not have filed the contentions earlier; specifically in this case because of the unavailability of the emergency plan that was the subject of the contention. It was impossible for intervenors in that case to know, not having access to a plan, whether it was acceptable, and if not, in what specific ways it might be objectionable.

The Commission reversed the Appeal Board in a remarkable decision that frankly left many people in disbelief.

The second development is the doctrine devised by the NRC that, in my opinion, epitomizes a siege mentality that reflexively resists public participation: the limitations on intervenor sufficiency challenges.

It is the Commission's position that when it amends a license to add some new requirement, the utility may claim a hearing to challenge the *need* for that requirement, but the public is precluded from challenging its *sufficiency* to cure the safety problem in question. This is true even when it was the public that first brought the safety problem to NRC's attention.

I regret that this practice has recently been upheld by a panel of the D.C. Circuit Court of Appeals in *Bellotti v. NRC*. Although that case is still ongoing, this regressive policy should be changed regardless of whether it is held to be legal or not.

UCS's views on current proposals to "reform" the licensing process, and our suggestions for meaningful change, are certainly well known to you since they have been presented in congressional hearings as well as on the record of your administrative proposals.

But the Commissioners may not fully appreciate the atmosphere of mistrust that has, unfortunately, shaped the debate on licensing changes.

Intervenors' worst fears about the direction of licensing "reform" are confirmed by the first set of NRC's proposals which were a laundry list of the industry's complaints about public participation. These proposals went solely in the direction of cutting off or restricting participation and made not a single move toward correcting the imbalances in the process or encouraging the presentation of alternative views.

I commend you for establishing the Ad Hoc Committee to review these proposals. However, the well had been already poisoned. Members of the public perceived that the purpose of licensing reform was to exclude them rather than to address the inequities and inefficiencies in the process.

The members of the public and the representatives of state and local governments who participate in your cases are entitled to a fair and accessible forum. They do not receive that now. What they too often get is a system which provides them with the technical formalities of due process—the grudging minimum required under the law—but makes it clear from the outset that they are seen as troublesome obstacles.

NRC pays twice for this. The first price is the NRC's loss of credibility. This applies not only to individuals who are unalterably opposed to nuclear power and as to whom you might conclude credibility is impossible, but also to Congress, state and local governments, and other citizen groups with pro-safety and pro-consumer agendas whom you cannot afford to have as automatic adversaries to your initiatives. The second price is loss of diversity in views on technical and policy issues.

UCS does not seek a system that is more adversarial or more legalistic. On the contrary, we seek the minimum requisites of a fair hearing: an opportunity to present a case and to critically question the other side.

Regardless of how UCS feels about the wisdom of future nuclear expansion, there are over 80 plants licensed now with more on the way. That reality dictates one mission that we must share, to see that the plants are constructed and operated safely. Effective public participation and an agency which accords the public respect and fairness, both in words and practice, are necessary to achieve that goal.

Turkey of the Month
Not to Worry

FROM *Northern Sun News* 7:3 (April 1984): 2

Turkey of the Month
Not to Worry

A Department of Energy spokesman at Hanford, Washington, explaining why no announcement was made after the smokestack at a plutonium plant was found to be leaking radioactive material into the atmosphere: "The thing is this—we have incidents happening over here all the time."
—The Progressive

Reprinted by permission of *Northern Sun News*.

Are Natural Disasters Natural?

by Jon Tinker

FROM *Socialist Review* 14:6, whole no. 78 (November/December 1984): 7–25

Taken from a speech given to the World Affairs Council of Northern California in San Francisco on April 5, 1984, based on a forthcoming Earthscan paperback published jointly with the Swedish Red Cross. Copies may be purchased for $5.50 from Earthscan Washington Bureau,1717 Massachusetts Avenue NW, Washington, DC 20036.

In the year of our Lord seventeen hundred fifty-five, the city of Lisbon, capital of Portugal, then one of the greatest colonial and imperial powers, was rocked by an earthquake and then swept by fire.

Mr. Richter had not yet invented his scale, so no one measured it accurately. But geologists now reckon it was the most powerful quake in history—and the most powerful there ever could be.

Lisbon was wiped out as effectively as if it had been atom-bombed. Sixty thousand people perished—and Christendom was rocked to its psychological foundations. Sixty years earlier, when Port Royal, Jamaica, then the Caribbean capital of piracy and vice, had disappeared beneath the sea in another earthquake, the right-thinking of the day had unanimously applauded the event as a well-planned act of divine judgment.

It is always comforting when God can be seen so clearly to endorse the views of the respectable. But when Lisbon was obliterated, only the most pious found it easy to convince themselves of God's benevolence and omnipotence at one and the same time. Had He not offered to spare Sodom and Gomorrah if only one virtuous man could be found? And could all—or even most?—of the sixty thousand who perished, in one of Christendom's most Christian cities, really have deserved death?

The faith of Europe was shattered. In France, the great libertarian philosopher Voltaire helped shake it a bit more with his finest book, *Candide*, in which he mocked the efforts of his Catholic character Dr. Pangloss to justify the destruction of Lisbon in terms of an all-powerful yet still loving God, who was supposed to direct the affairs of the planet so that "everything was for the best in the best of all possible worlds."

There were other effects, too. If God had that much power at his command, it clearly paid to be careful. The king of France vowed to give up his mistress—no doubt he changed his mind later, but it's the thought that counts.

I want to discuss whether these natural disasters—floods, droughts, famines, hurricanes, tsunamis, as well as earthquakes—are acts of God or acts of man.

What causes these disasters? And what causes the suffering they trigger off? Do we react intelligently to them—both afterwards and before? What is the role of environmental degradation and mismanagement in causing disasters—and in magnifying their human impacts? When disasters happen in the third world, and droughts and famines seem to be on the increase in Latin America, Asia, and Africa, do we react properly? Is disaster relief part of the solution—or part of the problem?

What is a disaster? We might say it's an unusual event which does a lot of damage, especially if it kills or injures a lot of people. But how many is a lot?

A team at the University of Colorado suggested a disaster should be defined in terms of $1 million of damage or 100 people killed or injured. Even the apparently concise definitions based on dollars and lives can be misleading. For instance, a tornado which destroys only a few homes may do over $1 million in damages in a wealthy United States suburb, and thus be a "disaster." But a widespread typhoon might destroy hundreds of third-world huts without causing $1 million in damages, and thus not be a "disaster."

Our perception of what we mean by a "disaster" is *largely social and political*. All the natural disasters and civil strife killed over 142,000 people a year throughout the 1970s, according to the Swedish Red Cross report *Prevention Better Than Cure*, published in June 1984. Yet each year some 15 million children die of malnutrition-related causes. The deaths of these children, which are nowhere defined as a "disaster," are predictable; governments and their agents in the fields of health and welfare know which children are at risk. United Nations organizations have recently devised relatively inexpensive ways of saving about half these children. As yet there is little indication that governments and agencies will put up the money. It could be that this non-stop disaster is politically acceptable. Despite the problem of definitions, a few generalizations are possible.

There has been a sharp increase in disasters from the 1960s to the 1970s and an even bigger jump from the 1970s to the first few years of the 1980s (see Figure 1). Fifty-four per year in the 1960s, and eighty-one per year in the 1980s. Half as many again. Why? The number of people affected by disasters has jumped from 28 million per year in the 1960s to 48 million per year in the 1970s (see Table 1).

And *casualties* are rising even faster—far more quickly than is explained by population growth. Twenty thousand per year were killed in the 1960s, and 143,000 per year in the 1970s. Why? Why a sixfold increase in casualties, when the numbers of disasters and people affected only rose by about fifty per cent? (See Table 2.) We seem to be becoming both more prone to disasters—there are more of them—and much more *vulnerable*—they kill more people. Why? Are the "triggers"—wind, waves, rainfall, continental movements—becoming more unruly? Neither the climate (associated with drought, flood, and cyclones) nor geological processes (associated with earthquakes, volcanic eruptions, and tsunamis) appear to be changing significantly. If nature is not changing, why are natural disasters becoming more frequent, more deadly and more destructive?

The answers seem to lie in an analysis of just who suffers in disasters. The Lisbon earthquake of 1755 killed rich and poor alike. Modern disasters don't. They kill, overwhelmingly, poor people in poor countries (see Figure 2).

Tokyo, Japan, and Managua, Nicaragua, are both *prone* to earthquakes. But Tokyo can afford strictly enforced building codes, while the poor of Managua live in top-heavy adobe shacks on steep hillsides. They are much more *vulnerable* than the Japanese. In the 1960s and 1970s, Japan suffered forty-three disasters, killing twenty-seven hundred people. In the same twenty years, Peru had thirty-one disasters—thirty-one compared to forty-three—but they killed ninety-one thousand people. Ninety-one thousand against twenty-seven hundred. Put another way, the average Japanese disaster killed sixty-three people. The average Peruvian disaster killed over twenty-nine hundred people.

Peru is not as prone to disaster as Japan, but it is fifty times more vulnerable. The reason is, basically, poverty.

Let's look at one type of disaster: floods. According to United States government statistics, five million people per year were affected by floods worldwide in the 1960s, and over fifteen million per year in the 1970s. Nearly a three-fold increase. We'll come back to why there are more floods, but let's look first at whom those floods hit.

In the industrial countries of the North, physical barriers and other flood-

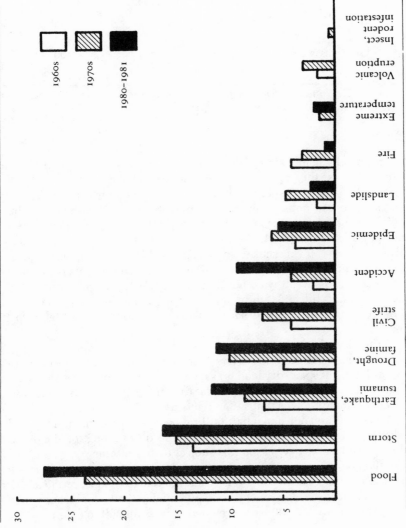

FIGURE 1: AVERAGE RECORDED ANNUAL DISASTER EVENTS IN THE WORLD, 1960–1981

☐ 1960s

▨ 1970s

■ 1980–1981

Flood
Storm
Earthquake, tsunami
Drought, famine
Civil strife
Accident
Epidemic
Landslide
Fire
Extreme temperature
Volcanic eruption
Insect, rodent infestation

SOURCE: *Prevention Better than Cure*, Swedish Red Cross, 1984, based on League of Red Cross and USOFDA statistics.

TABLE 1: NUMBER OF PEOPLE AFFECTED PER YEAR BY DISASTERS

Type of event	1960s	1970s
Drought	18,500,000	24,400,000
Flood	5,200,000	15,400,000
Civil strife/conflict	1,100,000	4,000,000
Tropical cyclone	2,500,000	2,800,000
Earthquake	200,000	1,200,000
Other disasters	200,000	500,000
	27,700,000	48,300,000

SOURCE: *Prevention Better than Cure,* Swedish Red Cross, 1984, based on League of Red Cross and USOFDA statistics.

control mechanisms, along with well-enforced zoning laws and building codes, decrease the population's vulnerability to floods.

Yet in the major cities of the third world, between thirty and seventy-five percent of urban populations live completely outside the law. They build their own houses; they squat on privately owned or government land; or they pay a fee to occupy illegally subdivided land, which nevertheless usually gives a measure of security. In most major third-world cities, the proportion of the urban population living in such illegal settlements is increasing.

Obviously, the wealthy do not want dangerous land: land prone to flooding by rainfall, tides, or storm surges, or hills and ravines prone to landslides during rainstorms or earthquakes. So this land is available to the poor.

In the city of Guayaquil, Ecuador, six hundred thousand out of a total population of over one million live in squatter communities built over tidal swampland. For some, dry land is as much as a forty-minute walk away, over rickety timber catwalks. Small wonder that in the 1983 floods in Guayaquil it was the shanty-towns that suffered most.

In Mexico City, one and a half million people live on the drained bed of Lake Texcoco. When it rains, their land becomes a bog, or floods completely. And in the dry season it is subject to dust storms.

In Bangladesh, perhaps fifteen million people—always the poorest—live less than ten feet above sea level. When the Ganges floods, or the sea rises after a hurricane, many must die. In 1970, when both things happened at once, 150,000 to 200,000 were drowned. It was difficult to count.

THE DYNAMICS OF DISASTER
Let's take a closer look at those Ganges floods. Floods are caused by rain, you will say. A heavy monsoon, you get floods. Well, no. Floods in the In-

TABLE 2 : NUMBER OF PEOPLE KILLED PER YEAR IN DISASTERS

Type of event	1960s	1970s
Drought	1,010	23,110
Flood	2,370	4,680
Civil strife/conflict	300	28,840
Tropical cyclone	10,750	34,360
Earthquake	5,250	38,970
Other disasters	2,890	12,960
	22,570	142,820

SOURCE: *Prevention Better than Cure,* Swedish Red Cross, 1984, based on League of Red Cross and USOFDA statistics.

dian subcontinent are triggered by the monsoons, but they are caused by deforestation and soil erosion. They are acts of man, not acts of God.

The Himalayas, the greatest mountain range in the world, feeds three massive rivers. The Indus flows south from Kashmir to India and Pakistan. The Brahmaputra, flowing east through Tibet, runs down to India and Bangladesh. And the Ganges flows south, east, and then south again through India to join the Brahmaputra in Bangladesh.

Once, the forested slopes of the Himalayas, and the thickly vegetated soil the trees protected, soaked up the annual monsoons like a giant sponge, releasing the waters throughout the year. The rivers rose and fell seasonally, in relative moderation.

Not any more. Last year, a report came out called the *State of India's Environment 1982*, edited by Anil Agarwal. In the middle Himalayas, it reported, the forested area has dropped from one-third to barely six or eight percent. "From Kashmir in the west to Assam in the east," Agarwal wrote, "the story is the same. Below 2000 meters there are literally no forests left."

Instead of flowing more or less predictably year round, those three great rivers flood uncontrollably in the weeks and months after the monsoons, and run relatively dry later on. In 1978, two thousand Indians drowned and sixty-six thousand villages were inundated. And remember that in India one village can contain up to several thousand people. The cost was over two billion dollars.

Without trees, the sponge effect is diminishing. The soil is washed off the hillsides and into the rivers, eroding irreplaceable farmland and plunging the peoples of Nepal and the other mountain regions into deeper poverty. The silt fills the stream beds, causing rivers to overflow their banks into the villages alongside. Hydroelectric and irrigation dams silt up. Much of the topsoil of the Himalayas ends up in the Bay of Bengal.

FIGURE 2: DISASTER MORTALITY PER EVENT, 1960-1981

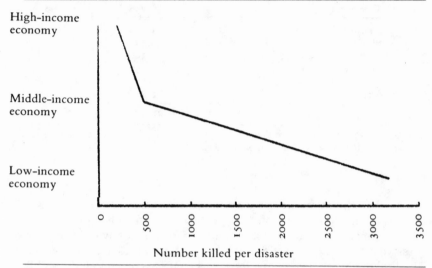

SOURCE: *Prevention Better than Cure*, Swedish Red Cross, 1984, based on League of Red Cross and USOFDA statistics.

This process has, to some extent, been going on for thousands of years. But the inexorable pressures of rising population, and increasing demands for timber (accelerated by modern logging methods), the needs for fuelwood, and for more land to cultivate, have combined to speed up deforestation and erosion to an alarming extent.

The pace of change is frightening. In a mere five years, from 1973 to 1978, the average dry season river flows of the Ganges basin dropped by eighteen percent. More and more, the monsoons wash straight off the Himalayas, flooding the valleys and plains below.

The pattern is the same in China, where floods are nothing new. An 1871 flood on the Yangtze pushed the water a staggering 275 feet above normal in the Yangtze Gorges. And the Yellow River is thought to have drowned two million people in 1887. Erosion in the Yellow River's catchment area has meant it carries a heavy silt burden down to the plains, where it now stands twenty-five feet above the surrounding land. When it breaks banks, the results are devastating.

After the 1981 Yangtze floods in Sichuan province, a Chinese journalist wrote a report for Earthscan on China's own analysis of the causes. Deforestation in the Yangtze catchment started early in the last century, when trees were cut for imperial palaces. The process accelerated during China's

disastrous "Great Leap Forward" toward rapid decentralized industrializa-
tion, which included a campaign to establish backyard iron furnaces that
needed wood for fuel. In the 1960s more forests were felled for the "grain
first" campaign.

In Latin America, especially in the Andes, deforestation and soil erosion
cause mud slides as well as floods. In 1977, the Colombian government discovered that seventy-five percent of its land surface was affected by erosion—and when you allow for the fact that part of Colombia is in the Amazon rainforest, you can see that the rest of the country is almost wholly
eroded. Again, it is the urban poor who suffer most from floods, in the
barrios or slums which sprawl on low-lying land, ravines and steep slopes
around all the big cities.

If it isn't too much rain, it's too little. Drought, and its companion famine,
are stalking many parts of the world today. Northeast Brazil, an area larger
than Texas, is now in its sixth year of drought. There are a few very rich
sugarcane planters, and an awful lot of very poor, largely landless peasants.
Last year, ninety percent of the harvest was lost in some areas, and the
people were reduced to eating cacti and lizards.

Brazil has drought relief, of course. There are work schemes, in which
the government pays the peasants to construct dams on some of the big
plantations, helping to keep the water away from the peasants' own land.
The workers are paid. It is just enough to buy two rolls of bread per day for a
family of five. They must often walk for two or three hours to reach the work
sites, and after being assembled in cattle corrals for roll call they may lose a
day's wages if they are a few minutes late.

Like other disasters in the third world, the Brazilian drought hits hardest
at the poor. The *New York Times* reported last spring that twenty-five million out of thirty million in northeast Brazil were affected, with fifteen million suffering hunger and thirst. In Pernambuco state alone there are reports
of forty-five thousand deaths as a result of the drought in the past five years.

But it is not only in the third world that this happens, or, at least, has
happened. Drought hit the High Plains here in the United States in the
1890s, and there were widespread reports of deaths from malnutrition and
starvation. There were similar reports in 1910 from the Dakotas and east
Montana. In each case, there was little relief effort, or even admission of the
problem, because the state governments were trying to promote their regions as prime farmland to new settlers.

Those of us brought up on John Steinbeck remember the results from the
Grapes of Wrath. Thousands of farmers were ruined and evicted, and they
and their families streamed west into California. Steinbeck's Okies didn't always like what they found there, but there was at least somewhere else to
go. Today, as drought and famine stalk Africa from Senegal in the west to
Ethiopia in the east, the people have nowhere to go. There are no fertile
empty lands left to colonize. There are no Californias in the third world.

In Ethiopia a terrible famine is brewing once again. The mountain regions, where most of the people live, are barren and eroded. Every now and again, you see a small Coptic church perched on a hilltop. Traditionally, no one touches the trees in the churchyard, so you can see what the land was once like. Sometimes, the soil is several feet higher inside the churchyard wall, with bare rock outside. When drought comes, what little soil remains is too exhausted to crop, and the people starve.

Several years ago, Ari Toubo Eibrahim, the minister of agriculture in Niger, said that his ministry had done away with "scientific" definitions of drought which depended on measuring quantities of rainfall. It now uses another definition: "Not as much water as the people need." This may be somewhat imprecise, but in fact it represents a new way of looking at drought which could be helpful to agricultural and soil scientists. Drought is when people haven't got enough water to survive: enough to drink, to water their animals, to grow food for themselves and fodder for their animals. To a farmer, drought is not necessarily about rainfall. In fact, one Nigerian city on the southern border of the Sahel region receives more rainfall per year than does London.

AGRICULTURE AND ENVIRONMENT

We hear a lot about the Green Revolution. New seeds, pesticides, and fertilizers have in some areas boosted food production miraculously, notably in the wheat fields of the Punjab in India and the rice paddies of Indonesia and southeast Asia.

But the Green Revolution has not reached most of sub-Saharan Africa. There, food production is going down. Not just food production per person, but food production per acre. Thirty years of so-called development, thirty years of foreign aid, has left African agriculture far worse off than when we started.

At any one time, there are about forty thousand foreign experts in Africa. They cost around one hundred thousand dollars per year each, when you allow for salaries and travel costs and moving expenses and home leave and school fees. That's four *billion* dollars' worth of so-called experts per year. I don't know how many work in agriculture, but it's certainly quite a lot. The net result of their efforts, year after year, has been to institutionalize famine in many parts of sub-Saharan Africa.

The agriculture they have introduced, focusing heavily on cash crops for export, instead of food crops for people to eat, works well enough in good years, when the rains come and prices in the world commodity markets are high. But in a slump, as we have now, and in a drought, as we have now, the result is disaster.

The United Nations' Food and Agriculture Organization in Rome is a pretty conservative organization. It has been criticized in the past—and

rightly so—for not ringing the alarm bells, because to do so would embar-
rass third-world governments, calling attention to their own mismanagement. A few months ago, FAO said that more than 150 million people in
twenty-four countries, in west, east, and southern Africa, were, and I quote,
"on the brink of starvation."

How has this happened? Let me describe it in the Sahel, the arid region
just south of the Sahara, which stretches from Mauretania in the west
through Mali, Niger, Chad, and east to the Sudan.

First, the more fertile, better-watered lands to the south have shifted over
to cash crops for export: cotton and peanuts. The cash crops are needed to
earn the foreign currency to import oil. Peasant agriculture has pushed
northward into drier lands which really should not be cultivated at all. Traditionally, these lands were left fallow after a few years of cultivating the
staple crops of millet and sorghum, to allow the soil to recover and the
humus content to build up under the natural grasses. Now under the pressure of rising populations, they are cropped again and again, until yields
per acre fall steadily away to the vanishing point. Eventually, there is a
drought, and the dessicated soil turns to dust. The desert takes over.

As the soil fails, the peasant farmers push further north, into the sub-
desert pastures, which were the rangelands of the nomadic peoples, grazing
with cattle and camels, sheep and goats. The rangeland is squeezed through
expanding farming, and the herd sizes increase because of rising population, more waterholes bored by the aid agencies, vaccination which reduces
herd mortality. The result is overgrazing. Again, this works in good years.
But when the drought comes, and come it will, there is not enough pasture
for the flocks and they die. The nomads are pauperized, drift south to the
towns, starve.

The great Sahelian drought of 1968–1973 killed somewhere between one
hundred thousand and two hundred fifty thousand people and reduced a
million or more to destitution and food handouts. But the drought was
nothing very unusual. What was new was the vulnerability of the people
and their agriculture. Drought *triggers* the crisis, but does not *cause* it. The
Sahel has always been drought-prone. Now it is more and more drought-
vulnerable.

Measurements of the flow of the Niger river, and old maps of the size of
Lake Chad, give us a yardstick for rainfall in the Sahel. The 1907–1908
drought, and the 1913–1917 drought, were just as bad as in 1970. What is
new, however, is the increased vulnerability, which hits hardest at marginal
peoples in marginal lands.

So what can be done about it? The Sahelian governments, through their
Permanent Interstate Committee for Drought Control in the Region (CILSS),
and the main aid-giving governments, through the Club du Sahel, have
agreed that food self-sufficiency must be the overwhelming target of devel-

opment assistance. In fact, they agreed upon it some years ago, after the 1968–1973 disaster. The United States Agency for International Development has gone further, and set as its main priority the improvement of grain production, especially through rainfed agriculture.

But neither the donors nor the recipients carry this out in practice. From 1975 to 1980, the Sahel had some $7.5 billion in foreign aid. Only twenty-four percent of this went into agriculture and forestry. And most of this was not spent in the rural areas, but in support facilities in the towns. Even the money spent in the rural areas tended to go towards roads and dams, because they are more fun for presidents and ambassadors to open, and they use foreign construction companies and consulting engineers, which is politically better back home. Overall, of the $7.5 billion, only eight percent went to rainfed cropping, and of that nearly all went not toward growing food for local people to eat but toward cash crops of cotton and peanuts for export. So much for food self-sufficiency as the great priority.

Drought and famine, like floods, are increasing. They are not caused by too little or too much rainfall, but by environmental mismanagement. They are acts of man, not acts of God, and they hit hardest at the poor.

There are other natural disasters: earthquakes and tidal waves and volcanoes and hurricanes. These are surely unpredictable, aren't they? These are surely acts of God?

Yes, the event itself is an unpredictable "act of God." No one knows when there is going to be an earthquake. But the disaster is not so much the event itself, as the damage it does to people, and that can be magnified and intensified by environmental mismanagement. Again, earthquakes seem almost to seek out the poor. The 1976 Guatemala quake killed twenty-two thousand, injured seventy-five thousand, and left a million of the nation's six million homeless. Fourteen towns were totally destroyed; in another seventeen towns fewer than one-third of the buildings were left standing.

Who suffered most? In the rural areas it was, of course, the poor, because in the rural areas nearly everyone *is* poor. In Guatemala City, almost all the twelve hundred dead and ninety thousand homeless were in the slum areas, built in ravines and gorges which are highly susceptible to landslides when earthquakes occur.

When a hurricane hits the Caribbean islands, the damage to villages along the coasts is far greater if the protective coral reefs have been blasted up for building materials, or poisoned by pollution; if the coastal mangrove forests have been cut down or used for landfill; if the people have been forced by poverty and high land prices and landlessness in the countryside to live in vulnerable squatter settlements on low-lying coastal land.

I hope I've said enough to make four points.

First, natural disasters are not really natural. Some are caused by man, like floods and famines.

Second, the human impact of all is magnified by environmental mismanagement.

Third, vulnerability to disasters is far higher in the third world, and is largely a matter of poverty.

Fourth, for these reasons, disasters and the deaths they cause are increasing rapidly.

DISASTER RELIEF: THE ROLE OF PREVENTION

I want to discuss briefly how we react to disasters, and to talk about disaster relief, I am going to suggest that far too often, maybe in the majority of cases, disaster relief is part of the problem rather than part of the solution.

One of the myths about disasters is that after an earthquake or a flood, or during a famine, people sit around in numbed helplessness waiting for helicopters to fly in with blankets and food. The truth is almost exactly the opposite: it is the delivery of food and blankets which causes this dependence and inactivity.

Strangely, the organizations that have the most experience with natural disasters—the governmental and nongovernmental aid and relief agencies—tend to treat them as "unnatural" events, excusing "unnatural acts" on the part of these agencies.

On a normal day-to-day basis, a third-world community—whether a nation, city, or shantytown—is an extremely complex network of deals, debts, kinships and relationships. During a disaster these relationships do not vanish; they aid the recovery and rebuilding process. Relief agencies tend to barge into a society as aliens, and interfere with the food, clothing, housing, and business activities of that society without in any way being answerable to the people with whom they are interfering. The only other times in which one society does this to another on such a scale is during warfare.

Ian Davis, a director of the Evangelical Alliance Relief Fund and an expert in housing after disasters, attacked the "helplessness myth" again recently. He said of agencies that intervene in foreign disasters, "The activity into which they intrude is the local ad hoc process that takes place after every disaster. This is the way a given third-world society buries its dead, cares for its wounded, clears the debris and eventually rebuilds its homes."

After the 1976 Guatemalan earthquake, the Red Cross delivered three thousand tents to the town of San Martín. Some $850,000 had been collected, and Red Cross brochures later included photos of the neat rows of tents. In fact, the Guatemalan army had to march people into the camps at gunpoint. They left soon afterwards. They wanted to be near their possessions and their livestock. After two weeks, only seven of the three thousand San Martín tents were occupied.

Vast quantities of food and aid were sent in. The quake had not affected crops, and coincided with a bumper harvest. The *New York Times* commented that so much food was sent in that "we knocked the bottom out of the grain market for nine to twelve months," doing far more harm to the farmers than the earthquake had.

So much food aid went into Bangladesh after the 1971 civil war that market prices fell, farmers planted less, food production fell . . . and the relief agencies sent in more food. In 1975 the World Food Program asked donor countries to stop food shipments: the more food aid, the more starvation, they said. That same year, the Bangladesh field director of U.S. Save the Children resigned because of the effect food aid was having.

It may appear churlish to question the worth of international relief efforts. The problems connected with military aid, long-term food aid, and even much development aid make disaster relief—getting food, medicine, and shelter to populations suddenly bereft of these things—seem like benign and selfless charity.

But disaster relief is a mess of incorrect assumptions and mixed political and economic motives. It is becoming more and more doubtful whether relief is the best way to help the afflicted people.

Disaster relief needs to be completely rethought. The medical profession is concerned with preventive medicine as well as with curing the sick. Relief agencies need to shift towards preventing disasters. Disaster prevention isn't easy. And it won't replace relief work. But it should complement relief efforts. How should we work toward this?

First, we can identify the disaster-prone areas of the world, and the disaster-prone regions within countries. Second, we can identify those people who are most vulnerable, which means overwhelmingly the poor. Third, we can try to reduce their vulnerability.

Take floods in India. It is possible to identify those villages that are most prone to flooding. The better off in these villages have concrete platforms for their huts, and their houses do not wash away. The poor have huts with wooden posts that are just stuck into the ground, and they *do* wash away. A program to help the poor in those flood-prone villages to build concrete bases to their homes would be better than stockpiling blankets against the next flood.

Moreover, scientists, politicians, decision-makers, and the general public have been very slow to make the basic distinction between the *trigger* and the *disaster*. Most of the money and scientific effort devoted to natural disasters has been spent on studying climatological and geological triggers— over which man has very little control—rather than on studying the wide range of human actions—over which man does have some control—which bring more disasters upon humans yearly.

Researchers have tended to study only the physical events, and these events are technically very complex. "In practice, then, natural hazards have been carefully roped off from the rest of man-environment relations," writes Canadian geographer Kenneth Hewitt. "There is no place for any sort of 'grass roots' input; no way for any but the 'experts' to break into the technical monologue." Yet floods and droughts are grass-roots phenomena that disrupt the lives of millions of people each year, the majority of these victims relying on the grass roots of subsistence agriculture. Because researchers have concentrated on the physical aspects of disasters, rather than the social and political aspects, governments have been lured into putting their trust in grand physical prevention and mitigation measures: dams, early warning systems, satellite studies. These have had little effect in the third world.

There are a growing number of disaster experts, dubbed "radicals" by many of their technology-oriented colleagues, who see the efforts of the relief establishment as resulting in *making more people more vulnerable* to disasters. The radicals say that it is the people living on the margins in both city and countryside who are both most prone and most vulnerable to disasters. They see the numbers of these "marginalized" people growing, both because of increasing populations and because of a world economic order that steadily increases the gap between the North and the South. The radicals see the relief agencies as the agents not of the victims but of wealthy Northern governments. The agencies' prime concern is to return disaster victims to the "status quo." Yet it is precisely that status quo that makes them prone and vulnerable. In maintaining the status quo, the radicals argue, the agencies ensure that disasters will continue to increase in the third world. And disaster mitigation work relying on high technology merely *reinforces the conditions of underdevelopment.* "Since it is the institutional and structural order which is at fault, disaster research and relief should formulate models and strategies which challenge this order," writes geographer Eric Waddell. "These should be based on the preservation and reinforcement of indigenous responses and involve a minimum of internal intervention (national or international)."

The disaster processes involved in drought and famine "can only be met by a development process, aimed at prevention of causes," argues Swedish Red Cross secretary-general Anders Wijkman. "Disaster assistance has to go hand in hand with development assistance and would be futile on a short-term basis. It has to be a development process that improves the conditions of both the natural environment and many millions of poor people—a mass movement, literally at grass-roots level."

The more thoughtful relief agencies, and the more thoughtful staff who work for the relief agencies, want to move, and are moving, in this direction.

ENVIRONMENTAL DEGRADATION AND WAR
I want to say one final word about the worst disaster of all, one that is indisputably human-made and not an act of God: war. I believe there is one cause

of war that is increasing, and is almost wholly neglected. Environmental degradation: the deforestation and erosion which I was talking about as the cause of floods and famines.

When Columbus first saw the Caribbean island of Hispaniola, he described it as "filled with trees of a thousand kinds, so tall they seem to touch the sky." Today, Haiti covers the western third of Hispaniola, and Columbus would not recognize it. The trees no longer touch the sky. In some districts, fifty per cent of the soil is eroded down to bare rock. Nearly every big rainstorm washes mud down into the streets of the capital city, Port au Prince. Siltation has halved the effectiveness of the Peligre Dam, which represents half of Haiti's hydroelectric potential.

The same is true in most of the Caribbean islands and Central America. Jamaica issued postage stamps toward the end of the colonial period which described it as "The Land of Wood and Water." Not any more. As in Haiti, the woods have mainly gone, and the streams now alternate between floods and drought.

As populations grow and the environment deteriorates, so poverty deepens and desperate people search for a way out. For Jamaica, one result was emigration, first to Britain, and then to the United States. Today, one Jamaican in five lives in the United States.

Jamaica's was an ordered and peaceful emigration. From Haiti, hundreds of thousands, perhaps as many as a million, fled illegally to other islands and here to the United States. Some were probably political refugees, escaping the vicious dictatorship of Baby Doc Duvalier. But most of the boat people were *environmental* refugees, leaving an island whose ecological base has been so damaged that it can no longer support its growing population—even in the poverty and misery for which Haiti is famous.

Haiti has produced environmental refugees. The Central American mainland has produced environmental revolutions, and now, ominously, environmental wars.

What are you to do if you are poor and landless; if there are no jobs in the cities and no soil in the countryside; if all the best land is given over to cotton or bananas, and owned by a few rich families or multinational corporations; if all the poor land is already occupied and reoccupied by other peasants nearly as poor as you are; if every year there are more and more of the poor and landless; if any attempt at peaceful political change is ruthlessly suppressed? In these circumstances, is it surprising that many turn to revolution, armed uprising, guerrilla movements?

Present United States involvement in Central America started in El Salvador, where the United States is assisting the government in civil war against peasant-based guerrillas, turning into an international military crisis something that is fundamentally an environmental problem. A 1982 report on El Salvador writes of "almost complete deforestation, massive soil erosion and loss of soil fertility, siltation threatening massive soil erosion and loss of soil fertility, siltation threatening hydropower developments, large-scale extinction of flora and fauna, diminishing groundwater resources, deteriorating water quality and widespread health-threatening environmental pollution. . . . The majority of Salvadorans are hungry, illiterate, infested with parasites, malnourished, poorly housed, underemployed and have little opportunity for self-improvement."

The report concludes that "the fundamental causes of the present conflict are as much environmental as political, stemming from problems of resource distribution in an overcrowded land."

Who would write such a report? A left-wing journalist? An ecological group? A pro-Castro propagandist? The Sandinistas? It was none of these. It was a report commissioned by the United States Agency for International Development.

The "fundamental causes of the present conflict are as much environmental as political, stemming from problems of resource distribution in an overcrowded land." Much of the Indian subcontinent, most of sub-Saharan Africa, the Caribbean, Central America, and the Andes are all on the verge of ecological collapse, moving rapidly into a deepening downward environmental spiral.

Regional ecological collapse is not just an environmental disaster. It is also a direct threat to the self-interest and security of all of us in the rich, industrialized nations. We all live on the same small planet. As we continue to damage it, to reduce its capacity to support our species, we destroy our own future. Poverty and environmental degradation cause disasters. They are not acts of God.

Soil erosion and landlessness, poverty and hopelessness, lead via social and economic unrest to political action, to guerrilla movements, to revolution, and now, increasingly, to superpower confrontations. Let us not believe, we in the rich world, that we can for long isolate ourselves from soil erosion in El Salvador, from floods and hunger in India, from famine in Ethiopia and the Sahel.

WAR IS NOT PEACE

Eight Mistaken Theses

by Tomas Borge

FROM *Lucha/Struggle* 8:1 (February 1984): 14–22

Toward the close of 1983, both Tomas Borge, of Nicaragua's Sandinista National Liberation Front (FSLN) and Roberto D'Aubuisson, of the Nationalist Republican Alliance (ARENA) of El Salvador, were denied visas to enter the United States. Just prior to this incident, Ernesto Cardenal, Nicaraguan Minister of Culture, was detained by the Immigration and Naturalization Service for three hours upon his entry into the U.S., and was interrogated about his political affiliations and objectives in visiting the United States.

The equation of these Central American figures was obviously meant to demonstrate the U.S.'s stance against "terrorism," regardless of its ideological character, and to show itself as the guardian of the mythical political center.

Tomas Borge is a founding member of the FSLN, and quite obviously a leading figure in Nicaragua Libre. By branding him a "terrorist" of the caliber of Roberto D'Aubuisson—long recognized as a motivating force behind death squad activity in El Salvador—is to brand the Sandinistas as a brutal, irrational and unpopular force. From this Reagan administration premise that thus characterizes the FSLN flow a whole series of myths and baseless stereotypes.

In the speech below, offered upon Borge's refused entry to the United States, the Interior Minister outlines the actual character of the Nicaraguan Revolution and addresses the falsehoods about it expounded and diffused by the Reagan administration.

Before the visa to visit the United States was denied us, we had the intention of traveling to educational centers which had invited us. We had also hoped to meet with Congresspersons and journalists representing broad sectors of the North American media. Everything seems to indicate that Mr. Reagan's administration feels that North American citizens have no right to listen to the voices of Nicaraguans.

We wish to speak to you from a country that is at war. We are not only in a war against underdevelopment, a war which we wished to wage. But we are also at war against military forces organized by the North American administration.

U.S. governing circles openly discuss the amounts to be assigned to covert operations against Nicaragua. For us, these operations mean air raids, sabotage of productive centers, massive migration and economic losses. These operations also signify death.

What does not seem to be much discussed is the right of one country to attack another. What is not discussed is the right of a powerful country like the United States to decide the destiny of a country that is nearly 80 times smaller in size and in population.

There is much discussion about the internal situation in Nicaragua. The Sandinista Revolution is called into question. But there is little discussion about the presumed right to intervene in Nicaragua.

This war, in which the United States is directly involved, today costs the North American taxpayers millions of dollars. Tomorrow this war may cost the North American people thousands of lives, as it is costing us Nicaraguans at present.

United States public opinion is daily presented with a series of affirmations about Nicaragua that are plainly and simply false, or else are half-truths. On the basis of these affirmations an attempt is made to justify to the North American people an increasing involvement in a war against Nicaragua.

We would like to briefly analyze some of the principal theses that the Reagan administration presents concerning Nicaragua. Each of these theses is managed so as to create a sentiment of support by North American public opinion for the actions the administration has taken to destroy the Sandinista Popular Revolution.

Let us see what these theses are:

FIRST THESIS: CENTRAL AMERICA IS THE ARENA FOR AN EAST-WEST STRUGGLE

It is true that Latin America, in its entirety, is poor and backward. Central America is poor and backward even with respect to the rest of Latin America. The per capita income of Latin Americans is 1,554 dollars per year; that of Central Americans is 472 dollars. That of North Americans is approximately 10,000 dollars. Some 6.7 percent of Latin Americans live in Central America, but they produce only 2 percent of the gross national product of Latin America.

Life expectancy in Central America is about 50 years, according to the fraudulent official data that Central American governments have historically provided. Central Americans live an average of 23 years less than persons born in the United States. There are places in Central America where infant mortality reaches the figure of 200 per 1,000 births. In the United States, infant mortality is only 13 per 1,000 births.

Five percent of the population—the richest sector—appropriated, until the revolutionary victory, 43 percent of everything our country produced. These figures are not much different from other existing realities in Central America. When I say that there are zones in El Salvador where there is one medical doctor for every 4,000 inhabitants, I am citing a figure that is more or less the same for the rest of Central America. I am sure that you are not unaware of the fact that in developed countries the proportion is one medical doctor for each 520 inhabitants.

Central America has been victimized by dictatorships, each of which might have provided a verse for the Apocalypse. The last dictatorship suffered by Nicaragua lasted nearly half a century. It has been conservatively calculated that the National Guard, Somoza's army, assassinated more than 300,000 Nicaraguans. Since 1954, more than 100,000 persons have been assassinated in Guatemala. And the Salvadorans, since 1979, have paid the same quota that we did in the final stage of our struggle against Somoza: nearly 50,000 human lives.

Hunger, dear friends, is not a conflict between East and West; hunger is a conflict between the dictatorial regimes and our peoples, who are hungry as well for justice. "General Hunger" is the commander-in-chief of Central American peoples.

This sophism concerning the East-West conflict is, therefore, a deliberate lie to justify aggressions against our peoples.

The problem must be posed in other terms. Ours is a struggle of national affirmation and it is a struggle that has the objective of ending under-development, social injustice and oppression.

Would it not be more logical if, rather than making and unmaking dictators, rather than arming and training oppressive armies, rather than supporting selfish oligarchies, rather than perpetuating underdevelopment by means of a profoundly unjust international economic order, the United States were to support profound social change, stop opposing peoples, stop arming oppressors? Would it not be more logical if the United States were to orient its gigantic technological proficiency toward the overcoming of hunger and misery, not only in Central America, but amongst two-thirds of humanity?

SECOND THESIS: NICARAGUA THREATENS THE NATIONAL SECURITY OF THE U.S.

We did not know we were so great and powerful.

Nicaragua is 80 times smaller than the United States, and it has almost 90 times fewer inhabitants. The total cost of manufacturing the United States' B-1 strategic bombers alone is 62 times greater than the annual budget of the Republic of Nicaragua.

How can we be a threat to the national security of the United States? Militarily it is absurd to attempt any comparison, besides which, our doctrine, as well as our armament, has a strictly defensive character.

It has even been stated, overstepping all logic, that we might threaten the Panama Canal, as if we had either the desire or the military capability to do so. Some sustain that this danger derives from the fact that we "export" the revolution—as if revolutions were cotton or coffee.

Faced with the evident weakness of all these arguments, at a certain moment it was said that nuclear missiles pointed at the United States would be installed in Nicaragua. Nobody has asked us to install missiles in Nicaragua, nor have we requested missiles of anyone.

THIRD THESIS: A CIVIL WAR IS UNDER WAY IN NICARAGUA

An attempt has also been made to create the impression that a spontaneous conflict has developed in Nicaragua, in which a part of the population is fighting against revolutionary power.

It is enough to have a minimum of common sense, enough to visit Nicaragua, to realize the extraordinary degree of popular support that our revolution enjoys.

What then, is the origin of the war? It has become axiomatic that the military forces that attack Nicaragua come from Honduran and Costa Rican territory and that the intellectual and material author of this invasion is the government of the United States. To affirm the contrary is to reduce the obvious to a scandalous lie. Of course, the lie bears fruit, and this was the philosophy of the German Third Reich which upheld the maxim: "Lie and lie again; something will remain."

On the other hand, it is an historic law that revolution necessarily produces counter-revolution. When the United States won its independence, there were also some 100,000 opponents who went to Canada. In Nicaragua, this counter-revolution, though weak, is inevitable. The strength acquired by this counter-revolution originates with a political decision by a government which, while maintaining diplomatic relations with Nicaragua, has determined to make war on Nicaragua.

The United States government, acting through the Central Intelligence Agency, reassembled members of Somoza's former National Guard who were dispersed throughout Guatemala, Honduras, El Salvador and the United States, forming them into what was ultimately called the Nicaraguan Democratic Front. These former members of Somoza's army were concentrated by the United States in Honduran territory. These counter-revolutionary forces commenced harrassing our military installations. At the same time, by means of radio and through direct agents who based their appeal on the separatist tendencies of some leaders of the Miskito population, they were able to draw a sector among them into counter-revolutionary activity.

These forces act from bases located in Honduran territory; their activities on our soil count on the rearguard and logistical support of the Honduran army and the financing, planning and intelligence information supplied by the CIA.

None of this is rhetorical. The so-called Nicaraguan Democratic Front acts from Honduras and has three command echelons: the lowest, composed of former officers of Somoza's National Guard, who are in turn commanders of the principal "task forces"; an intermediate command level made up of Honduran army officers, one former officer of the Somoza army and the CIA station chief in Tegucigalpa; and the high command, made up exclusively of North Americans, officers of the CIA and the Southern Command of the North American army located in Panama. This latter defines the strategy of the armed aggression against Nicaragua.

Is this a war between Nicaraguans? Or is it an external aggression? Can there be a civil war when one of the bands is organized, directed, armed and financed from abroad?

Civil war in Nicaragua? A civil war is what exists in El Salvador. The affirmation that there is a civil war in Nicaragua is an effort to legitimize political cynicism; it is an attempt to create the image that there exists in Nicaragua a situation analogous to that in El Salvador; it is a useless attempt to propose a possible solution at the Central American level from a position of force and blackmail.

FOURTH THESIS: NICARAGUA TODAY IS A SATELLITE OF THE CUBANS AND SOVIETS

It is still fresh in the memory of Nicaraguans that the highest authority in our country during the time of Somoza, was the ambassador of the United States. We are struggling, fundamentally, to be masters of our decisions. This is an elementary principle of national pride.

This affirmation that Nicaragua is dominated by the Cubans and the Soviets seems to be based on an ignorance of the pride and the forces of national feeling of the Nicaraguans. In honor to truth and with full knowledge of the facts, I can affirm that neither the Soviet ambassador nor the Cuban ambassador, nor Fidel Castro—with whom we have frequently conversed—nor the Soviet leader, Yuri Andropov—with whom we have also spoken—has ever told us what we must do. To think the contrary would be to accept that we have no criteria of our own, that we have no respect for the blood of our martyrs, that we are simply puppets. All the North American friends with whom we have spoken are witnesses to our national pride.

Who among you can believe that we lack the audacity and valor to make our own decisions? Were we sufficiently dishonorable to surrender ourselves, there can be no doubt whatsoever that it would be much easier and much more comfortable to surrender ourselves to the government of the United States.

Our international policy is non-aligned and Third World. This cannot only be measured through occasional votes in the United Nations, but in all the variety of relations we maintain with European, Asian, African and, naturally, with American nations.

Only 8.8 percent of our foreign commerce in 1982 was with socialist countries. We trade twice as much with Western Europe or with the United States as with all the Socialist countries combined.

Where is the Soviet and Cuban dominion? In the political sphere we are extremely jealous of our independence. In the economic sphere we have relations four times greater with non-socialist countries than with the socialists.

We have received respectful treatment from Cuba and the Soviet Union, without any sort of condition. This is the same treatment we would like to have from the United States, a relationship of mutual respect and cooperation.

FIFTH THESIS: THERE IS A TOTALITARIAN DICTATORSHIP IN NICARAGUA

Constructing a new state is like erecting a new structure on the ruins of a building that has been struck by a cataclysm. In Nicaragua, we have to change everything down to our very mental concepts, inasmuch as it was a country ruled by indifference, corruption and selfishness. Although it seems difficult to believe, in Nicaragua under the Somoza dictatorship, honesty was looked on askance.

With its feet firmly planted in this reality, with all its contradictions and incongruities, the Sandinista National Liberation Front designed a policy of alliances to confront the Somoza tyranny: a policy that had its continuity in a pluralistic and participatory conception following the revolutionary victory.

The concrete expression of this pluralism and participation is the Council of State. In the Council of State are represented seven political parties, seven labor organizations, five private enterprise organizations, diverse religious sectors, universities, youth and women's organizations, etc.

In this same context, we have committed ourselves to holding elections, opening the electoral process in 1984 to arrive at its culmination in 1985. In this way we are accomplishing what was promised in 1980, a few months after the Triumph. On 21 February, the exact date of the elections, which are scheduled for the first months of 1985, will be announced.

During these years we have carried out a series of reforms whose only objective has been to advance on the road to democracy, teaching 40% of our population to read, creating a totally new judicial system to replace the dictatorship's corrupt system, stimulating a people that was oppressed for a half century to organize itself and to participate in the decisions that effect its destiny. All of this has been accomplished in five years. Have the North Americans forgotten that in their country the first elections were held in 1789, thirteen years after the Declaration of Independence?

How easy it would be for us, goaded by the calumnies of each morning and each afternoon, harassed from all angles, to toss overboard the postulates and principles enunciated by our National Revolutionary Directorate. Nevertheless, we have demonstrated irrefutably that we continue to be a non-aligned nation with a pluralistic dedication.

In our country a Law of Political Parties has been approved that assures the right of all these parties to seek power.

The levels of popular participation have no precedents in our history. More labor unions have been created during these four years of Revolution than in all preceding Nicaraguan history. The entire people is organized: agricultural workers, owners of small and medium-sized businesses, women, youth, city dwellers, businessmen, professionals, students: all these have a voice in a country that was always starved for words. The decisions of our revolutionary Directorate are as closely linked to the sentiments of our people as blood is to arteries. This too is democracy.

The accusation of totalitarianism has sought arguments in a supposed suppression of freedom of the press. In Nicaragua there are nine newspapers: three dailies and six weeklies. Of the three daily newspapers, one is the official organ of the FSLN; the other two, NUEVO DIARIO and LA PRENSA, are private. There are 46 radio stations, of which 25—or 55%— are privately owned. Through these and through LA PRENSA the declarations and analyses of parties opposing the FSLN are transmitted every day. What is being censored? That which every State censors when confronted with a war situation, as was the case of the North American State during World War II.

How can we avoid censoring news items that promote speculation with basic products with the purpose of distracting our people from defense tasks? How can we avoid censoring news that attempts to confuse the population with the end of obstructing military service in a situation which requires the defense of the homeland?

Defense of the homeland is also a democratic act.

SIXTH THESIS: NICARAGUA VIOLATES HUMAN RIGHTS AND PRACTICES REPRESSION AGAINST THE MISKITOS

It is necessary to commence by saying that the North American administration has contentedly proclaimed that there is a notable improvement in the observance of human rights in Guatemala, El Salvador, Chile and Paraguay, and that in Nicaragua the respect for human rights has deteriorated and continues to deteriorate. The comparison is odious, because they speak of the improvement of human rights in countries where genocide has become commonplace, and they say that human rights have deteriorated in a country where there are no executions, where torture has been virtually eradicated, where prisoners, including Somocistas, have been located in work centers where they have a continuing relationship with their families and many of them are under a regimen of what we call "open farms," in which there are no sentries other than those of moral preaching and our own confidence in the prisoners. Open farms—without police and without bars. And if this audacious measure raises some doubt, I invite anyone who holds this doubt to visit Nicaragua and observe this beautiful, profoundly humane project in action.

Witnesses of the treatment we grant prisoners are the International Red Cross, the Commission of Human Rights, a group of North American jurists headed by Mr. Ramsey Clark, writers of worldwide prestige such as Julio Cortázar, Carlos Fuentes, Gabriel Garcia Marquez, Gunther Grass and Graham Greene, among others.

Have there been abuses in Nicaragua? In the first weeks after the Triumph, when there were still no police, no judicial system or laws, the people in various cases took justice into their own hands. The accumulated hatred against those who had assassinated, raped women, stolen with impunity was great. But within a few weeks effective control was established throughout the country, putting an end to this type of procedure.

There have been other cases of abuses, of mistreatment of prisoners, of some assassinations, of robberies committed by members of our armed forces. But we have been implacable in judging them. Today there are many Sandinistas completing sentences in our jails . . . and nobody abroad raises a voice in their behalf!

When the Revolution triumphed, the Miskito population of the Atlantic Coast was submerged in centuries of historic backwardness, not only with respect to developed countries, but with respect to the population of the rest of Nicaragua.

The Somoza dictatorship never made the slightest effort to bring education or health to this population. Tuberculosis decimated lives and illiteracy annuled minds. To ignore the Miskitos was Somoza's policy.

We wanted to resolve this historic backwardness, and began with a great deal of will, but with little knowledge.

We committed errors, many errors; many times no account was taken of the cultural particularities of the Miskitos; at other times there was no emphasis on learning their language, and basic aspects of anthropology were unknown. Such errors were committed in good faith; they were taken advantage of by the bad faith of the counterrevolution. Many of the former

Miskito leaders, such as Stedman Fagoth, who had been an agent of Somoza's Security Office, commenced working with the CIA to divide the Miskitos and prevent them from supporting the Revolution. An enormous campaign was launched, including radio broadcasts from Honduras, in which they urged the Miskitos to "flee" to Honduras because "the Sandinistas will kill you," or "they'll send your children to Russia so they will deny their parents," etc.

Many Miskitos were deceived and left, becoming objects for recruitment by the counterrevolution on the Atlantic Coast. There they lived in virtual concentration camps. Many of them stayed there, and others were resettled in zones that a number of you have certainly visited, where they have everything that our scanty resources can provide them.

But since we are conscious that the Miskitos who committed crimes against order and public security were deceived and manipulated, the governing Junta of National Reconstruction recently decreed a total amnesty for them so that all those who are outside the country may return to the bosom of their families as well as those who have been released after having been held in prison by judicial sentence or in the course of police investigations.

SEVENTH THESIS: IN NICARAGUA THERE IS RELIGIOUS PERSECUTION
We have affirmed, and we repeat once more, that the Nicaraguan people are revolutionary and Christian. Numerous priests, pastors, monks and nuns participate fully in the revolutionary process. This participation had its origin in the old nightmare of injustice and exploitation that our people endured; in the renovating ideas of the Second Vatican Council; and in the flexibility and vision of Nicaraguan revolutionary leaders.

Many Christians participated as militants in the Sandinista National Liberation Front. There were Christians who gave their lives for our Revolution, including some priests who fell in combat, such as Fr. Gaspar Garcia Laviana. Various Catholic priests are Ministers of State, others are diplomats. The spiritual guide of Nicaraguan youths is the Jesuit priest Fernando Cardenal.

I will not point out the variety and number of religious people in the intermediate strata of revolutionary power, though it might be well to mention that some Ministers of State, such as those of Education and Housing, are militant Christians. There are institutions such as the Valdivieso Center, the Central American Historical Institute and the Center of Agrarian Studies and Promotion under the responsibility of religious personnel.

Part of the Catholic hierarchy is opposed and politically hostile to the Revolution. They adopt positions that go beyond the religious fields, and in this sense there are contradictions. But on the level of freedom of religion, they have never suffered any interference from our authorities. During the past several weeks we have had a series of dialogues with the bishops, which have served to improve relations with the Episcopal Conference.

EIGHTH THESIS: NICARAGUA FOMENTS AN ARMS RACE IN CENTRAL AMERICA

Let us begin with a real fact: Nicaragua was first threatened and then invaded. We have the right and the obligation to defend ourselves, and we also have the duty to not attack other countries. We do not propose to invade Honduras, and obviously we do not propose to invade the United States. Therefore, our arms and our military doctrine are of a defensive nature.

We must ask who is attacking Nicaragua? Is it not the United States? Did they not recently approve $24 million for what they call "covert operations" against my country? Is it not the United States that presently has 5,145 soldiers in Honduran territory? Is it not the United States that has constructed three airfields in Honduras to facilitate "rapid deployment" against Nicaragua? Is it not the United States that constructs radar bases, that has spy planes intruding into our air space and great fleets navigating along our coasts? Is it not the United States that promotes the reactivation of that union of repressive armies called CONDECA, from which they illegally wish to exclude Nicaragua? They attack us on all sides, then they accuse us of arming because we are preparing for our own defense.

Honduras now has a great quantity of sophisticated armaments: Scorpion tanks, A-37B aircraft, several dozen fighter bombers and helicopters, besides a training program and organization of a clearly offensive character against Nicaragua.

We are not worried by the quantity of arms possessed by Honduras, inasmuch as it has a perfect right to have them so long as they are not used against another country.

We also, naturally, have a perfect right to possess arms, and no one can call this right into question so long as we do not use them against another country. The danger, therefore, lies in the decision to attack, that is to say, in the decision to make war. We are more preoccupied by the enormous military arsenal that the United States has in the Panama Canal Zone, which is a sort of small capital of aggression against Latin America.

We lack airplanes, and we do not have enough weapons for each Nicaraguan to shoulder a rifle. That is to say, our problem is not one of a lack of people willing to fight, but a lack of arms. We are convinced that the problem of other Central American countries is not one of arms, but of men and women.

We know what war is because we have made war in order to achieve peace. We know what war is because we are at war to defend peace. This explains why we arm ourselves, and this explains why we go about the world demanding its intervention on behalf of peace. We grasp the steel of war in our country because no alternative exists, and we have been disposed to come to the United States to engage in a dialogue for peace because it is the best alternative.

Our Revolution continues—despite pressures, despite economic boycotts, despite war—along the road of institutionalization that we have proposed. From the first moment we said that elections would be carried out in 1985 and we are keeping our promise.

On 17 September 1980 the Council of State, by means of Decree 513, approved the inauguration of the electoral period in 1984 and elections in 1985. This was preceded by an official communique of the National Directorate of the FSLN on 23 August 1980 which also proposed the carrying out of the electoral process in 1985. This decision has been reaffirmed again and again by the leaders of the Revolution.

The decisions announced a few days ago reaffirming the inauguration of the electoral process on 31 January 1984 are simply the continuation of a decision made more than three years ago.

Because of this it is paradoxical that these decisions of ours are attributed to pressures and to the covert war against Nicaragua. As it is also paradoxical that the decisions we have taken on different occasions to prevent the Miskito population from becoming the victims of an artificially-imposed war, are likewise interpreted by the Reagan administration as a consequence of the covert war against Nicaragua. Are they perhaps ignorant of the pronouncements made by the FSLN since 1981 in which are affirmed the respect for the traditions, culture and rights of the indigenous population of the Atlantic Coast?

All of that is paradoxical, as we have said. They make war on us—which is the only thing that could make an electoral process difficult—and then they say that, thanks to this war, we are holding elections. They set their millions of dollars and an enormous propaganda apparatus in motion to deceive the Miskitos and use them as cannon fodder in their wide-open "covert war," and then they say that the Revolution's amnesty is a consequence of their war. What a way of falsifying reality!

We granted amnesty because we are strong. We will hold elections because we are strong; we are generous because we are strong. We are strong because we are right; we are strong because here the people have the arms; we are strong because here democracy, justice, respect for human dignity, national dignity and national honor predominate.

Among the peace proposals for the Central American area, we have included the theme of military advisors and that of armaments. We propose the withdrawal of all military advisors in the area and the freezing of armaments in the entire region. Would not this be an effective step toward achieving peace?

The North American people have the right to be well informed; they have the right to demand that their governors present them with real facts rather than lies or half-truths to justify actions against other peoples. They have the right to listen to the victims, they have the obligation to judge the victimizers.

Nicaragua is never going to attack the United States. Nicaragua is attacked by the United States. The North American people have the right and the duty to know this.

The North American administration has two options: either it continues along the belligerent path that only presages an enormous cost in lives, not only of Central Americans, but also of North Americans; or else it decides to engage in dialogue, to understand our peoples, to collaborate with social changes and with the possibility of development.

No Fallout Shelter
Peace Is Our Only Security

FROM *Nuclear Times* 2:6 (April 1984): 20

Photo by Steven Borns

(DON'T) GIMME SHELTER: Fallout shelter signs in some churches are being replaced with signs like the one pictured above, which adorns Unitarian Church of All Souls in New York City. Organizers have found that the conversion process sparks congregational education on civil defense and, often, media attention. The growing roster of noncompliant churches includes the St. Thomas Aquinas Church in Ames, Iowa; New York City's Riverside Church; and every Catholic church in Richmond, Virginia.

The Revo and the U.S.
Health Care in Grenada

FROM *Health/PAC Bulletin* [14:6/15:1] (November–December 1983/January–February 1984): 43–53

Last November an independent fact-finding commission sponsored by the American Medical Student Association, the Black Psychiatrists of America, the Manhattan chapter of the National Medical Association, the Physicians' Forum, and the Committee for Health Rights in Central America and the Caribbean visited Grenada to investigate health conditions in the wake of the October 25th American-led invasion.

The commission consisted of nine experts in health care and an attorney. One member was Grenadian by birth and two others knew the country well from previous visits. All ten spent at least a week on the island and some were there as long as two weeks, visiting hospitals, health centers and stations, and the bombed mental hospital as well as interviewing Grenadian officials, U.S. civilian and military officials, representatives of the International Red Cross and Planned Parenthood, numerous health care workers, and other Grenadian citizens.

These two reports, each written by several members of the commission, describe health care under the Provisional Revolutionary Government led by Prime Minister Maurice Bishop and the situation immediately after the invasion.

HEALTH CARE BEFORE THE INVASION
The New Jewel Movement took power as the Peoples' Revolutionary Government on March 31, 1979, when it overthrew the Gairy dictatorship. The

PRG quickly declared several national priorities, including improved health care for all of the island nation's 110,000 citizens.

"We have acknowledged that it is our duty to provide the population with a health care system which is available, accessible, affordable, and of high quality," Prime Minister Maurice Bishop stated in his opening remarks to a meeting of Caribbean health ministers in July, 1980.[1] Health care was also considered a prerequisite to national development—"Health is Production Too" was a common PRG slogan.

Even before taking power, the new leaders were aware that Grenada's health care system labored under typical vestiges of colonialism and underdevelopment, including a deficiency of many types of health care workers as well as maldistribution and inequities in the provision of services. Among the workers in short supply were physicians, environmental specialists, laboratory technicians, and administrative personnel; those the island did have were often poorly trained. Qualified health workers often emigrated to North America during the Gairy years rather than deal with the substandard conditions at home. In 1979 specialized medical care such as pediatrics, ophthalmology, and orthopedics was virtually nonexistent. Dental care was scarce, and inadequate when available—tooth extraction was the norm, rather than repair.

Data and other health information were inadequate, rendering health needs assessment difficult. During the Gairy regime, three quarters of the health care budget went for hospitals, leaving little for outpatient and rural facilities. Those government facilities which did exist were dilapidated, often lacking running water, incinerators, equipment, and supplies—including medications used to treat common diseases.

There was a heavy emphasis on curative medicine in the Gairy years while preventable illnesses such as measles, rubella, and malnutrition remained rampant, thriving on an outdated and overburdened infrastructure—poor water supplies, inadequate sanitation for liquid waste disposal, lack of a national program for controlling insect and other disease carriers, no public transport system, and roads in desparate need of repair.

Like education, health care was a privilege not a right under Gairy. Richer Grenadians often travelled abroad for comprehensive care. The majority got substandard care, if any—resources and personnel were concentrated in the urban areas, inaccessible to rural Grenadians, and what little the government provided in funding and facilities was often commandeered by the private sector.

The PRG developed both short and long term responses to these daunting problems. In the short term, the country's limited national resources, already bled by Gairy's drain on the national treasury, made international assistance imperative. Numerous appeals were sent. Cuba responded most generously, with a team of health specialists including internists, orthopedic specialists, pediatricians, ophthalmologists, psychiatrists, dentists, and a health planner. They were provided on two year terms of duty, paid by the Cuban government; housing, food,and transportation were the responsibility of Grenada.

The Cubans' arrival immediately increased the number of physicians from 23 to 40. This permitted an overall expansion of the free medical care system introduced by the PRG and made it possible to decentralize services to outlying medical stations on the island of Grenada itself and its smaller sister islands, Petit-Martinique and Cariacou. Health personnel, including physicians, laboratory technicians, and consultants, were also recruited from other Caribbean countries, Europe, and North America.

At the same time, in an effort to meet needs over the long term government health scholarships were increased dramatically. Hundreds of students were sent to the University of the West Indies, Cuba, and Eastern Europe to study medicine and allied health subjects.

Financial and material aid to expand and improve health care facilities were also solicited. Among those who provided assistance were the governments of Canada, West Germany, and Venezuela, and the European Development Bank, the Swedish Save the Children Foundation, and the Pan American Health Organization (PAHO).

The PRG adopted the World Health Organization goal of "Health for all by the year 2000." Its strategy to achieve this included decentralization of the administrative and planning process and involving the community as a whole as well as health care recipients and health workers.

Education assumed a pivotal role. The main thrust was to encourage individuals to assume greater responsibility for their own health and health of their family and community. Campaigns promoting programs such as national immunization drives, prenatal care for all pregnant women, and active family planning by husbands and wives emphasized the importance of preventive health.

The scope of this effort was extraordinary. Planning and implementation involved resource groups from voluntary agencies and the private sector, the National Women's Organization and the National Youth Organization, as well as government agencies such as the ministries of health and agriculture and the Grenada Food and Nutrition Council. Along with efforts to reach individuals already in health facilities, an extensive outreach program was initiated to inform the entire population through their schools, worksites, organizations, and neighborhood associations. Health education was routinely incorporated into programs on the island's radio station, Radio Free Grenada, and into articles in the newspaper, *The Free West Indian*.

While these programs were underway, the PRG was improving the collection of data and statistics to provide a basis for expert analysis and rational planning. The first step was an examination of existing health services. Among the problem areas identified were geriatric and mental health, where services were primitive and little rehabilitation or home care was available.

The second step was community assesessment of health needs. This revealed that over 60 percent of the population was under 25; that there was significant malnutrition; that the teenage pregnancy rate was rising; and that there was a high rate of infectious diseases such as measles, dengue fever, gastroenteritis, and rubella.

Based on the needs assessment, the PRG defined its priority health areas as maternal and child care, health education and promotion, prevention of infectious diseases through immunization and environmental health programs, improved sanitation and water, development of community geriatric and mental health programs, intensive training and retraining of health personnel, diversification of the food supply coupled with education about nutritional preparation of indigenous foods, and community participation on a grassroots level. Special emphasis was placed on prevention.[2]

The proposals for meeting these goals were elaborated in the Three Year Health Plan 1983–85. This was completed in 1982 after several revisions benefiting from the suggestions of international consultants, local experts, and the community at large.

The major focus of the plan was decentralization and expansion of primary health services. The structure envisioned for 1985 was a central health center in each of the six main island parishes plus a seventh for Cariacou and Petit-Martinique. Each would also have a district health team consisting of community health assistants, a public health nurse, nurse midwives, public health specialists, a physician who also functioned as the district medical officer, a family nurse practitioner, a nutritionist, dentists, pediatricians, internists, family planning nurses, a driver, and an environmental specialist. This team would service outlying health stations.

Together with other itinerant specialists the teams would also provide free medical care, including home, school, and workplace visits; take charge of immunization campaigns and health education; and run prenatal and well child care clinics as well as special ones for common medical problems such as diabetes and hypertension. All team leaders would meet regularly at the Ministry of Health to facilitate coordination and planning.

In 1981 a model health center with a complete district health team was opened in the parish of St. David's to serve its 11,000 people. Other parishes and the sister islands were alloted ample staff to provide comprehensive primary care, but some lacked the full complement of team members envisioned—in 1983 several still had no environmental specialist or nutritionist and needed drivers and/or vehicles to transport the sick.

Despite these deficiencies, the PRG's commitment to providing health care as a basic right had come much closer to realization. National investment in health care increased from 12.6 percent of the budget in 1978 to 14.7 percent of a larger budget in 1981. A bigger share was going to the outpatient, rural clinics. A new health complex had been built in Sauterns, six medical stations had been rebuilt, and three centers had been refurbished.

By 1983 no Grenadian lived more than three miles from a health station. Some of the clinics had vehicles to transport the sick.

In the model St. David's district, team members had dramatically increased the number of home visits, dressing changes, immunizations, and health education workshops given at schools and workplaces. Other parishes enjoyed free access to pediatricians, dentists, psychiatrists, internists, and ophthalmologists. Many of the 33 health centers and stations provided specialty clinics for hypertensives, diabetics, and well-child care; a good number offered dental care, including repair and even root canal work.

By 1983 over half the nation's youth had been immunized against measles, diphtheria, tetanus, and polio. While malnutrition remained a problem, the infant mortality rate per thousand had declined from 28.96 in 1978 to 13.88 in 1983—a rate lower than in some areas of the United States. This improvement is even more significant when one considers that the official rates before 1979 probably grossly underestimated the real numbers since data collection was irregular before the revolution.

Under the PRG, health information was collected on all patients treated by the clinic nurse midwives; they kept meticulous records of all births, deaths, home visits, inoculations, dressing changes, infectious diseases, malnutrition cases and chronic illnesses, and submitted reports to the Ministry of Health by phone or in writing on a weekly basis. Follow-up of problem cases was routine and reinforced by a network of community health assistants and aided by appropriate mass organizations such as the National Youth Organization and the National Women's Organization.

Community-based health education had become a critical and vibrant part of the health care system. Two health educators provided printed materials to health centers and community organizations and broadcast on Radio Free Grenada twice weekly. The National Youth Organization participated with other community groups to eliminate dengue fever through a national mobilization to unclog drains, clear refuse, and otherwise destroy mosquito breeding grounds. The Grenada Food and Nutrition Council gave training to improve utilization and preparation of local foods, provided hot school lunches, and supplemented efforts to eradicate malnutrition. The National Women's Organization encouraged breast feeding, prenatal care and nutritional food preparation. Breast feeding became the norm in Grenada. A Pan American Health Organization-sponsored program was established to train community mental health workers to provide improved outpatient follow-up and counselling of patients with mental disorders.

This brief summary documents the expansion of health care under the leadership of the PRG in the years following the Gairy regime. In 1983, Grenada's health care system still had many flaws and deficiencies, but what had already been accomplished and the course outlined in the Three Year Plan 1983–85 demonstrate that the PRG had the vision and the determination to overcome them. Despite the limited national resources available, comprehensive primary care, available to all Grenadians free of charge, was a primary goal: "the PRG maintains as its health policy, that the health of the people of this nation is a basic human right, and that the citizens making use of the health services should not be seen as 'those people,' but 'our people,' our 'extended family.'"[3]

Notes to Part One

1. Maurice Bishop, "Health for All—A Right of Caribbean Masses." Feature address at the Sixth Meeting of CARICOM Conference of Health Ministers in St. George's, July, 1980.
2. Summary of the Three Year Health Plan, 1983–85. Provided to us by the Grenada Ministry of Health, November 1983.
3. *Ibid.*

THE INVASION AND ITS AFTERMATH

The number of Grenadian casualties resulting from the U.S. invasion on October 25, 1983 remains undetermined. Many of the wounded were afraid to go to the hospital; others were treated locally in people's homes; and still others were shipped out to Puerto Rico, Barbados, the U.S.S. Guam, Kings County Hospital in Brooklyn, N.Y., and other facilities for treatment. According to statistics provided by the General Hospital, St. George's, on and after October 25, 203 patients were seen at the casualty unit and 64 admitted. The report states that gunshot wounds were the type of injury in over 90 percent of the cases treated and admitted. Although the numbers of Grenadian casualties from October 25th and immediately following may vary, *they are significantly higher than figures reported in the U.S. press.* It appears to us that there is a conscious effort on the part of the U.S. to withhold information on the extent of Grenadian casualties. *The numbers of Grenadian dead are still unknown.* In addition to the 17 persons killed in the bombing of the mental hospital, press reports indicate that 18 bodies of Grenadians were shipped to Cuba and subsequently returned.

Health personnel. One striking consequence of the invasion was the forced evacuation of the Cuban, European and Caribbean health workers, including doctors and dentists working in the expanded primary care health system developed under the Bishop regime. The ranking U.S. A.I.D. official on the island informed us that approximately 25 of Grenada's total of 45 doctors and dentists were asked to leave Grenada following the U.S. invasion. Most of them worked full-time in the public sector, providing free medical and dental care. The 20 physicians still in the country devoted most of their energies to the provision of private medical care, working only half-time in the public sector at most. Our team was informed that a typical private physician visit costs about $20 Grenadian dollars; a typical weekly income is $50 Grenadian dollars.

The consequences of this deportation of more than half of the doctors and dentists are severe. At the time of our visit, there was neither a single pediatrician (60 percent of Grenada's population is under age 25), nor any psychiatrist to care for the 180 patients in the Richmond Hill Mental Hospital or deliver follow-up care to discharged mental patients. There is now no orthopedic specialist, only one ob-gynecologist and one dentist for the entire population.

During our travels to many of the country's health centers and stations, nursing personnel verified the impact of this abrupt drain.

The Happy Hill Health Station, which serves 3400 patients in the parish of St. George's, has no doctors or dentists.

Dr. Regina Fuchs, a specialist in hypertension and diabetes from the German Democratic Republic, disappeared after questioning by the new authorities shortly after the U.S.-led invasion. She had played a primary role in establishing Grenada's diabetic association, run by and for those who suffered from this disorder, and held specialized clinics for hypertensives and diabetics at the St. George's Health Center. Since her departure, the public health nurse at the St. George's Health Center admitted that she is sorely missed.

Patients have been referred from the St. George's Health Clinic to the St. George's Hospital because there are no physicians available to care for them at the clinic. At the Victoria Station, in the largely rural parish of St. Marks, the nurse midwife in charge told us that a pediatrician, gynecologist and dentist were needed to replace the team of Cuban health workers who had visited this clinic every Tuesday for the past two years. A Cuban pediatrician and surgeon serving 6000–7000 people on Cariacou were forced to leave.

Of the 25 physicians and dentists expelled, 12–15 were Cuban. It was the opinion of the U.S. A.I.D. official in Grenada that, "the Cubans probably made care affordable, accessible and available." We corroborated the opinion in our interviews with Grenadian health workers. At the Victorian Health Station, we were told that the Cuban dentist, psychiatrists, and gynecologist delivered reliable quality care and quickly overcame their language barrier. They came every Tuesday for two years, filling a void in those specialties.

At the Ministry of Health, a public health nurse said that the Cuban dentists repaired teeth, a service previously unavailable to Grenadians. She also commented that they adapted quickly to Grenadian culture and were generally respected and utilized throughout the country. Other nurses and matrons noted that Grenadians preferred indigenous physicians and psychiatrists when they had a choice but added that this preference was based more on cultural affinity than the qualifications or professional standards of these Cubans.

The availability of other health personnel besides doctors, dentists and psychiatrists, was also adversely affected by the invasion. Due to the shortage of physicians to care for patients in the urban health centers and hospitals, public health nurses have found it necessary to curtail their visits to the many outlying substations and health clinics as well as their home visits and outreach activities. A nurse working in the Grand Anse Health Center had not been able to travel to her substation at Caliste, located behind the U.S.-occupied Point Salines airport, for three weeks. A pass issued by the military is required to travel to this area; this quite likely inhibits some of the patients from using the health facility.

Laboratory technicians, health educators, and an environmental specialist from other nations left Grenada following the U.S. intervention. In some cases, they were asked to leave; in others they chose to.

The National Women's Organization and the National Youth Organization had been an integral part of the health system. Members assisted in health education (promoting breast-feeding, for example), immunization campaigns, and insect and other disease-carrier control at the grassroots level, maximizing community outreach and participation in these important public health areas. These organizations were disbanded shortly after the U.S. led invasion. The St. Paul's Health Clinic, housed in a community center built by the New Jewel Movement, was closed following the invasion.

U.S. medical aid. In the period following the invasion, the U.S. military provided an orthopedic surgeon and a nurse anesthetist to the St. George's Hospital, the largest hospital on the island. The U.S. A.I.D. official stated that the U.S. military had sent in preventive medical specialists and physician assistants to assess the health needs of the hospitals and clinics.

The intervention of the U.S. military health professionals appears to have been transient and spotty. They delivered health care at Happy Hill station from November 7 to November 18. The nurse midwife in charge of this health station was told that they would return within a week, but had not seen them again at the time of our visit in late November. At Victoria Health Center, the nurse midwife interviewed stated that she had only seen a military physician once; this physician did not deliver medical care. On the island of Cariacou, which had previously received routine medical care from a Cuban team, a military team of physician's assistants, medics, and one physician visited the hospital for the first time on November 23, accompanied by several members of our team. Members of the military were told that they would be staying there for only three to five days. Some clinics along the western side of Grenada had not even been visited by a physician since the invasion.

Since October 19, two physicians provided by the St. George's Medical School, organized and funded by U.S. investors, had been working part time at the St. George's Hospital in the casualty area. However, the school is a two year, preclinical institution with minimal involvement of its faculty or students in actual health care delivery in Grenada.

The only indication of U.S. intentions to ameliorate the health personnel losses was a statement by the U.S. A.I.D. official that his agency was willing to pay competitive salaries to U.S. physicians for up to five months; however, after May 1984 the Grenadian Ministry of Health would have to rely on its own resources to recruit and pay physicians. In the light of declarations by Ministry of Health officials that they can only afford to pay physicians the equivalent of $8,000 U.S. per year, we doubt that many Western Europeans or U.S. physicians will serve beyond the A.I.D. subsidized 5 month period, or be recruited after that time. Even more disturbing was our followup interview with this same A.I.D. official one week later. He revealed that it was even a question whether Congress would release money for the short-term subsidy of physicians or other health personnel salaries.

The losses may be longterm. We were informed that Grenadian students were currently abroad studying health sciences, including medicine and dentistry, and some were due to graduate this spring. When we asked Ministry of Health officials if Grenadians now studying in Cuba and Eastern European medical schools would be permitted to return to practice, we were told the issue was "under study." We believe that these young health workers are a natural source for the dentists, internists, pediatricians, gynecologists and psychiatrists so direly needed in Grenada at this time. They would bring essential skills in public health, preventive medicine, and tropical/rural medicine. Moreover, they were sent abroad by the Bishop government just for this purpose.

The loss of health personnel following the U.S.-led invasion of Grenada may bring back the ill health of the pre-revolutionary period. Health care will certainly be less accessible, less comprehensive, and less affordable to Grenadians, who had enjoyed a decentralized, free, more comprehensive primary care model for the past three years. We have grave concerns about the longterm impact of this immediate drain of health care providers. How will the infant mortality rate rise in the next year on an island which now has only one obstetrician-gynecologist and no pediatrician? What will be the mortality from hypertensive complications and diabetic complications in the St. George's parish without the intensive follow-up of a professional like Dr. Fuchs? What will be the outcome of mental hospitalization for Grenadians without a psychiatrist? How many more public health or nurse midwife activities will be curtailed by a continued deficit of physicians?

Equipment and supplies. Grenada's health centers, health stations, hospitals, dispensaries and its Ministry of Health are desperate for basic, relatively inexpensive, equipment and supplies. Autoclaves are needed to sterilize instruments. Gas cylinders are needed to operate stoves during the frequent electrical outages. The respirator in St. George's Hospital is outdated. Dispensaries lack spatulas. A Maternity Center in Sauteurs lacks "dipsticks" to test urine, sufficient linen and sterile gauze pads, maternity kits for home deliveries, and an extra pair of forceps. The hospitals need transformers and better dietary equipment. The chief planner at the Ministry of Health pleaded for flip charts and magic markers for his presentations to various audiences and for duplicating facilities. According to the Chairman of the Central Water Commission, Leroy Neckles, several water pumps to deep wells in the southern portion of Grenada were damaged by the U.S. bombing. At the end of our visit these pumps had not been repaired or replaced.

The U.S. Military health assessment team, the U.S. A.I.D. official, and the Ministry of Health officials we interviewed highlighted distribution as a major problem facing the Grenadian health care system. The U.S. military occupation forces appeared to have enormous transportation resources such as helicopters, jeeps, and trucks throughout the island. We feel that these could have been used to distribute basic supplies and equipment to health centers and stations around the island. Road repair is essential. Lack of adequate numbers of ambulances and vehicles to transport the sick and injured was cited as a major problem. The transport of women in labor and the sick is seriously impeded by the poor condition of the roads. At the time of our visit to Grenada, telephones generally worked some of the time but communication was nil in the Grand Anse area, where telephone wires had been damaged by the U.S. bombing. Consequently, Ministry of Health officials had to travel to clinics there to communicate with the public health nurses.

While many of the deficiencies in infrastructure and basic medical supplies likely existed before the U.S. intervention, our team saw evidence that new roads and health centers had been built or refurbished by the Bishop government, that some of these supplies were previously available, and had just run out. We certainly did not see evidence of repair of those things damaged by the U.S. bombing or any longterm commitment by the U.S. A.I.D. to provide supplies, equipment, or improved communication.

While some road workers were paid by the U.S. in one area of Grenada, the U.S. A.I.D. official was uncertain of subsequent funds to continue work on roads, sanitation, water supply or medical supply deficits. The future in these areas was just as hazy as the prognosis for replacing health personnel in Grenada. The undeniable reality is that prior to the U.S. intervention, Grenada was in a state of growth and expansion. The evidence on our visit certainly indicates we must question the integrity of these plans and, consequently, the future health of Grenadians.

The psychiatric institution. The Richmond Hill psychiatric institution suffered serious damage from U.S. bombing on the first day of the invasion. Those in charge of the institution informed us that 17 patients and one staff person were killed and 30 persons were hospitalized with injuries. An additional 68 patients were unaccounted for at first, most of them having escaped. These patients subsequently returned to the hospital or remained home with their families. The building that was demolished by the bombs was called the infirmary and contained 80 beds. It housed the older and weaker patients, as well as those considered more cooperative.

No assistance was made available to the hospital by the U.S. until six days after the bombing, when a stand-by electric generator, food, clothing, beds, and mattresses were provided on an emergency basis. When we visited the institution almost a month after the destruction, there was still an unsightly pile of rubble in which hospital administrative records were strewn about. The U.S. played a supervisory role in the repair work and contracted it out to a local firm.

The Director of Matrons (chief administrative nurse) of the mental hospital recommended that a new facility be built at another, more accessible, location. This recommendation was seconded by Dr. George Mahy, a Grenadian psychiatrist living in Barbados whose consulting work in the field of psychiatry is known and respected throughout the Caribbean. According to a U.S. A.I.D. official *there are no U.S. plans to build a new mental hospital.* We recommend that all necessary funds for the building of a mental hospital on a new site be provided by the U.S., and that Grenadians determine the character of this new institution.

We observed the training of a new category of health worker in Grenada, the community mental health officer. The training was being carried out by a Pan American Health Organization consultant, Dr. Johnathan Bernard, through the Ministry of Health. The community mental health officers will prepare families for the return of patients from the mental hospital, do follow-up care of discharged patients, and institute preventive, community-oriented programs. We believe this is a sound program which ought to be supported.

Richmond Hill Prison. The power structure in the Richmond Hill Prison was brought home to us by our experience in gaining permission to enter. A phone call to Sir Paul Scoon elicited his suggestion that we obtain entry through the Grenadian Police Commissioners, Mr. Pat MacLeish. Mr. MacLeish readily gave us permission over the phone and told us to meet him at the prison at 10 a.m. the next day. He did not show up. Ultimately we learned that Jamaican Colonel Ormsby of the Caribbean "Peacekeeping" Force, and only Colonel Ormsby, could grant permission to see the security detainees.

Since the U.S. invasion, there are two categories of prisoners at Richmond Hill prison: the security detainees and common detainees—persons imprisoned for the perpetration of a crime. Health and sanitary conditions in the section of the prison where the security detainees are incarcerated are primitive.

A local physician was reportedly scheduled to visit the prison three mornings a week. The infirmary area in the prison had been taken over for other purposes because of overcrowding. The physician in charge of the Casualty Department at St. George's Hospital reported that he had examined at least two patients brought from the prison, indicating that there is access to the hospital's facilities. The two men had asked for medical attention following alleged beatings. A hematoma was found on the right thigh of one of these men. The cells of the security detainees are about 10 × 8 feet in area. A covered bucket serves as the toilet. The men are taken out of their cells to shower and use a more conventional toilet each morning. At first blankets were not provided although it is chilly at night in Grenada; they are now.

A U.S. officer and the ranking officer of the Caribbean "Peacekeeping" Force who is in charge of the security detainees, Major Prescod, stated that they are permitted from 30 minutes to 1 hour of exercise each day in a narrow yard in groups of seven. However, the security detainees whom we interviewed in private stated that each prisoner is given only 15 minutes of exercise daily alone, and sometimes only every other day; therefore the prisoners are kept in their cells for 23 and three-quarters hours a day. When we brought this account back to Major Prescod following our visit to the prison, he explained that he could not permit more than one of the detainees to exercise at a time (which would increase the time available for exercise for any single prisoner) because he did not want them to converse, and because guns were used to guard the security detainees.

Major Prescod recognized that the presence of guns within a penal institution presents a serious risk, however the Caribbean "Peacekeeping" Force does not fully trust the Grenadian prison's warders (guards) and therefore keeps its own armed men stationed there. This situation obviously precludes the possibility of several security detainees exercising together. The incarceration of the security detainees may be in violation of international standards for the detention of political prisoners. The common prisoners, in a different section of the prison, are permitted to congregate freely.

Three members of the team were permitted to speak with Mr. Bernard Coard, one of the security detainees, in private in his cell. He alleged that three other security detainees who had been taken from the prison to Fort Rupert had been interrogated and beaten there, and then returned to the prison: Mr. Abdullah, who was beaten 2–3 weeks before our visit on November 24th; Lt. Layne, who was beaten on November 14th and 15th; and a third detainee who was beaten a day or two before our visit and forced to sign a confession which included a statement that the confession was being signed without coercion.

One of us spoke briefly to Mr. Abdullah and Lt. Layne, both of whom affirmed that they had been beaten. We did not have the opportunity to speak to the third detainee. Mr. Coard said he was threatened with the prospect of a beating by an officer of the forces assigned to the prison. The International Red Cross had a team of investigators on the island while we were there and some members of our commission spoke with them.

The International Red Cross physician visited the security detainees daily, without witness, in their cells. Detainees expressed concern that after the IRC's scheduled departure in late November beatings would likely increase, particularly since there was no access to attorneys. The International Red Cross official stated that they planned to return to Grenada in early January.

The U.S. Psychological Operations (PSYOPS). The U.S. Psychological Operations (PSYOPS) battalion under Colonel Ashworth, part of the "noncombatant" forces still on the island, played a significant role in the invasion and occupation. According to the head of the U.S. Civilian-Military Operations Command (of which PSYOPS is a division), within 24 hours of the invasion PSYOPS took over Radio Free Grenada, the major source of mass communication on the island, replacing it with "Spice Island Radio." Colonel Ashworth acknowledged that before the press was allowed on the island PSYOPS implemented a poster and radio propaganda campaign which denounced the New Jewel Movement governmental leaders as criminals and promoted the notion that Grenada had become a puppet of Cuban and external military interests. Placards and banners that had reinforced the peoples' accomplishments and positive experiences in self-determination over the past four years have been pasted over with these PSYOPS posters. Some of the NJM banners have simply been removed from downtown St. George's. Leaflets have been dropped by helicopter over the countryside. (In response to a question about PSYOPS propaganda work elsewhere, Colonel Ashworth told the Commission members that a team was currently working in Nicaragua, but he could not elaborate because this was a sensitive issue.)

All records, minutes, and transactions of the NJM-Peoples Revolutionary Government over the past four years have been confiscated by the U.S. According to one military person, these records reportedly show that the Grenadian government under Maurice Bishop had plans to exterminate all Grenadians over age 60 years. Grenadians interviewed have heard rumors that bombs are found "every Tuesday,"—neutron bombs and missiles in Grenada right under their noses. The intent of this campaign appears to be the reinterpretation and manipulation of the aspirations of the Grenadian people manifested under the Peoples' Revolutionary Government.

The psychological impact of the political and military events. The series of events last October, coming in swift succession, contributed to a general state of shock and numbness, bewilderment, disillusion, and depression observed by members of our team. On "Bloody Wednesday," October 19th, the extremely popular head of state, Prime Minister Maurice Bishop, was executed along with cabinet members and political leaders and many other citizens of Grenada. The guns which the people had been assured were intended solely for their protection were instead turned against them. Children were killed. Many in the crowd jumped over the fort's high walls seeking safety from the murderous gunfire. Americans can perhaps best appreciate the emotional impact of these executions by recalling our own reactions to the assassinations of Martin Luther King, President Kennedy, Robert Kennedy, and Malcolm X.

A 24-hour curfew was immediately imposed by the Revolutionary Military Council. Radio messages warned that anyone venturing from homes would be shot on sight; a freedom-loving people was kept under house arrest. These shocks generated a welter of feelings—fear, helplessness, outrage, loss, confusion, uncertainty.

The U.S.-led invasion of October 25th relieved the uncertainty but imposed new stresses. First, there was the bloodshed and destruction of the military conflict itself, accompanied by the noise of bombs, gunfire, and helicopters. In the immediate aftermath bloated and decomposing corpses were permitted to lie in and around the radio station, where fierce fighting had taken place. The staff of the bombed mental hospital and other civilians had to dig bodies out of its rubble with simple tools.

The occupation, with its heavily armed soldiers on foot and in jeeps patrolling the streets; the recurrent roar of helicopters taking off and returning from search missions; the hoops of barbed wire surrounding beachfront hotels occupied by the military; guns pointed menacingly from in front of the Ross Point Inn, which now houses the U.S. Embassy; the searches of cars and checks on identification papers; the sight of cars and trucks which crashed as a consequence of the heavy vehicular traffic and because Americans are not used to driving on the lefthand side of the road, have created a bittersweet sense of relief coupled with feelings of resentment, powerlessness, loss of dignity, and humiliation.

When Grenadian men apprehended by U.S. soldiers are forced to spread their legs and bend forward; have guns poked into their ears and mouth; are handcuffed with their hands behind their backs, blindfolded, and exposed to the noonday sun or rain; are stripped to the waist in public or photographed in that state of undress; are interrogated in small wooden crates; and dragged through the gravel while being called epithets such as "nigger"—the ugly spector of racism and colonialism is patent.

Social deterioration was already apparent. Juvenile prostitution, which had not been seen during the period of the People's Revolutionary Government, was observed by people we interviewed and the three members of our delegation who knew Grenada well. We suspect that this may contribute to a rise of venereal disease in a now health-underserved country.

We saw and heard evidence of increased alcoholism and drug use by Grenadians. U.S. military personnel were observed smoking marijuana in the open—a practice unheard of in pre-invasion Grenada, where marijuana was illegal. Some estimate as many as 5,000 men and women lost their jobs because of measures in the wake of the U.S.-led invasion, including the dissolution of institutions such as the National Women's Organization and the National Youth Organization, and a halt in the construction of the new airport. We know that unemployment is associated with depression and hopelessness, family conflict, and increased morbidity and mortality.

As experts in public health, we anticipate that these conditions, especially the military occupation, will create problems and jeopardize the physical and mental health of the people of Grenada in the long run. The disruption of social systems and unemployment are both highly correlated with breakdowns in mental health. Furthermore, the techniques of humiliation and intimidation will certainly contribute to loss of self esteem among a proud people. The shortage of physicians which we documented earlier in this report, including the total absence of pediatricians and psychiatrists, means that those Grenadians who succumb to these multiple stresses with physiological or mental symptoms will have less access to treatment.

Because we anticipate a worsening of the health and mental health of the people of Grenada, we call for the careful monitoring of key health indices: rate of premature births, of infant mortality, of malnutrition in the pediatric age-range, of admission to the mental hospital, of teenage pregnancy and venereal disease, and of hospital admissions for diabetics and hypertensives whose disorders are out of control.

CONCLUSION

The on-site observations contained in this report have led us to the conclusion that the U.S.-led invasion and occupation are contrary to the long-term health and social interests of the people of Grenada. They reinforce our position that the invasion is to be condemned and that all aspects of the occupation should be terminated swiftly.

The Commission members were Haywood Burns, Esq.; Blanche Grant; Theresa Horvath, Physician Assistant; Diane Lacey; Beth Lyons; Eli Messinger, M.D.; Marlene Price, M.D.; Steven Robinson, M.D.; Professor Margarita Samad-Matias. For a copy of the complete Grenada Commission Report when it is available, contact Beth Lyons c/o CIR, 386 Park Ave. S., New York, NY 10016.

Resources

(The following list contains some of the best readings on El Salvador, Nicaragua, and Grenada for those who wish to examine the subject intensively.)

Armstrong, Robert, and Shenk, Janet, *El Salvador: The Face of Revolution* (Boston: South End Press, 1982)

Barry, Tom, Wood, Beth, and Preusch, Deb, *Dollars and Dictators: A Guide to Central America* (The Resource Center, PO Box 4726, Albuquerque, NM 87196)

Black, George, "Central America: Crisis in the Backyard," *New Left Review*, No. 135 (Sept.-Oct. 1982)

Black, George, *Triumph of the People: The Sandinista Revolution in Nicaragua* (London: Zed Press, 1981)

Collins, Joseph, Lappe, Francis Moore, and Allen, Nick, *What Difference Could A Revolution Make?* (1982, Institute for Food and Development Policy, 1885 Mission St., San Francisco, CA 94103)

Diskin, Martin, ed., *Central America and the United States in the Eighties*. New York: Pantheon Books, 1984. $9.95 paper.

Dunkerley, James, *The Long War: Dictatorship and Revolution in El Salvador* (London: Junction Books, 1982)

Ecumenical Program for Inter-American Communication and Action, *Grenada: The Peaceful Revolution* ($4.50) and *Grenada: End of A Revolution* ($3.50), from EPICA, 1470 Irving St., NW, Washington, DC 20010. Tel. (202) 332-0292.

Fagen, Richard, and Pellicer, Olga, eds., *The Future of Central America: Policy Choices for the U.S. and Mexico* (Stanford: Stanford University Press, 1983)

Gleijeses, Piero, "The Case for Power Sharing in El Salvador," *Foreign Affairs*, Vol. 61, No. 5 (Summer 1983)

LaFeber, Walter, *Inevitable Revolutions: The United States in Central America* (New York: W. W. Norton & Co., 1983)

Pearce, Jenny, *Under the Eagle: U.S. Intervention in Central America and the Caribbean* (London: Latin America Bureau, 1981)

Policy Alternatives for the Caribbean and Central America (PACCA), *Changing Course: Blueprint for Peace in Central America and the Caribbean* (Washington, DC, 1984—Available from the Institute for Policy Studies, 1901 Q St., N.W., Washington, DC 20009)

Rosset, Peter, and Vandermeer, John, *The Nicaragua Reader* (New York: Grove Press, 1983)

"Science Under Siege: Science and Technology in Nicaragua and El Salvador," *Science for the People*, Vol. 15, No. 6 (Nov./Dec. 1983)

Searle, Chris, *The Struggle Against Destabilization in Grenada* (London—Distributed in the U.S. by W. W. Norton)

Torres-Rivas, Edelberto, "Eight Keys for Understanding the Central America Crisis," *LARU*, Vol. 5, No. 1 (Sept. 1982)

Audiovisuals

"Health Care in Nicaragua: Revolucion es Salud," a 23-minute slide show with tape, available from Medical Aid to Nicaragua, PO Box 796, Astor Station, Boston, MA 02123.

"The Hopeful Revolution: Nicaragua," a 16-minute slide show with cassette commissioned by Oxfam-America. Available from Packard Manse Media Project, PO Box 450, Stoughton, MA 02072.

"Target Nicaragua: Inside a Covert War," a brand-new color film with extraordinary footage of the counterrevolutionaries. Rental $60 from New Time Films, Inc., 74 Varick St., New York, NY 10013.

Guide to Films on Central America describes 40 films, videotapes, and slide shows. Copies are $2 plus 50 cents postage from Media Network, 208 W. 13th St., New York, NY 10011, tel. (212) 620-0877.

Where You Can Offer Support

California
Bay Area Committee for Health Rights in
Central America
1827 Haight St., Box 5
San Francisco, CA 94117

Salvadorean Medical Relief Fund
PO Box 1194
Salindas, CA 93902

Florida
c/o Layon
1518 N.W. 7th Ave.
Gainesville, FL 32603

Illinois
Medical Aid to El Salvador
PO Box 14765
Chicago, IL 60614

Iowa
c/o Kozen-Ohly
658 Hawkeye Ct.
Iowa City, Iowa 52240

Maine
c/o Halperin
West Road
Belgrade, ME 04917

Massachusetts
Boston Committee for Health Rights in
Central America
1151 Massachusetts Ave.
Cambridge, MA 02138
(617) 492-4169

New York
Nicaragua Medical/Material Aid Campaign
c/o Casa Nicaragua
19 W. 21st St., 2nd Fl.
New York, NY 10011
(212) 885-1231 (Hal Osborne)

Committee for Medical Aid to El Salvador
PO Box 384
New York, NY 10024

North Carolina
c/o Fox
1413 N. Magnum St.
Durham, NC 27701

Pennsylvania
c/o Mark Lyons
American Friends Service Committee
1502 Cherry St.
Philadelphia, PA 19102
(215) 241-7000

Texas
c/o John Donahue
Dept. of Sociology
Trinity University
75 Stadium Dr.
San Antonio, TX 78284

Washington, DC
c/o Weiss
1705 Hobart St., NW
Washington, DC 20009

Washington State
Seattle Committee for Health Rights in
Central America
PO Box 22670
Seattle, WA 98122
(206) 523-1060

Wisconsin
c/o Schlenker
620 AS 28th St.
Milwaukee, WI 53215

Canada
Coalition to Aid Nicaragua
2524 Cypress St.
Vancouver, BC V6J 3N2

Let's Pretend We're Voting

by Adam Hochschild

FROM *Mother Jones* 9:6 (July 1984): 56, 58

Demonstration Elections: U.S.-Staged Elections in the Dominican Republic, Vietnam, and El Salvador, by Edward S. Herman and Frank Brodhead. South End Press, 270 pages, $20.00, hardcover; $8.00, paperback.
Trouble in Our Backyard: Central America and the United States in the Eighties, edited by Martin Diskin; foreword by John Womack, Jr.; epilogue by Günter Grass. Pantheon, 266 pages, $20.00, hardcover, $9.95, paperback.
The Morass: United States Intervention in Central America, by Richard Alan White. Harper & Row, 319 pages, $14.95 hardcover; $6.95, paperback.

Running a colonial war these days is hard work. It used to be far easier. When British troops in India battled tribesmen on the northwest frontier they didn't have to worry about anybody back home cutting off appropriations. And when U.S. Marines installed Anastasio Somoza, Sr., in power in Nicaragua in the 1930s, there was no nonsense about human rights certification. "He's a sonofabitch," said Franklin D. Roosevelt, "but he's ours."

Today, however, any aspiring imperialist has to fight a two-front war. Abroad, for example, Ronald Reagan must try to bludgeon the people of Nicaragua or El Salvador into doing what he wants; at home he must try to persuade the American people that all this strong-arming serves the cause of human rights.

Combining the two tasks is no easy trick. The regimes our government supports in Latin America have raised thuggery to levels rarely matched since the Nazis. Indeed, points out Richard Alan White in his useful summary of U.S. entanglement in Central America, the methods that security forces in El Salvador, Guatemala, and elsewhere use to "disappear" their enemies originated in the Third Reich. Field Marshal Wilhelm Keitel (who was later hung at Nuremberg) gave instructions that anti-Nazi prisoners "will vanish without leaving a trace." S.S. men were prohibited from revealing anything about their victims.

Yet, while we pour billions of dollars into propping up Latin governments that are the moral equivalent of the Nazis, encouraging military coups whenever necessary, U.S. rhetoric for the home front paints a radically different picture. What we are trying to do, Reagan's people say, is to build up "the democratic center" in a region tragically divided between the extremes of left and right. And so Flora Lewis, *The New York Times* columnist who can be counted on to voice the Establishment line of the moment, writes of Guatemala. "There is a sinister war going on between the two cold-blooded groups seeking to dominate by terror. There are no white hats. The great bulk of the people are caught between."

In an eloquent introduction to the otherwise uneven anthology *Trouble in Our Backyard*, John Womack, Jr., correctly says, "There never has been a center in Central America. . . . There the center is a dream, or a nightmare, or a lie of artificially sweet reason." The U.S. would find Adolf Hitler "to be a man of the center," Womack declares, if he appeared in Central America today.

By far the most blatant contrast between imperial rhetoric and political reality appears when one compares the U.S. claim that we're protecting "democracy" in Central America with the fact that most countries there seldom have anything remotely resembling a genuine election. Washington had the same awkward problem in Vietnam. What is to be done? The solution is something Edward S. Herman and Frank Brodhead, in their deft and original book, have christened a Demonstration Election.

"In both Vietnam and El Salvador," Herman and Brodhead explain, "the United States actively opposed or was completely indifferent to elections until military occupation and state of siege conditions prevailed. Official observers and media analysts and commentators never note this oddity, nor suggest that elections held in such unpropitious circumstances are meaningless, nor hint—God forbid!—that the elections are held only after military occupation precisely *because* the desired results are thereby assured. On the contrary, the conventional view is one of wonderment that elections can be held at all under such adverse conditions."

The authors' account of the 1982 elections in El Salvador is quite relevant to the similar charade played out in that benighted country this past spring. The point is not the substance of the election, but its appearance. Remember all the televised pictures of Salvadorans standing in long lines to vote, all the editorials about democracy taking root, all the Reagan administration's harsh censure of the rebels for refusing to participate?

One reason why opposition parties didn't take part in the 1982 elections was a law requiring any new political party to submit the names and addresses of 3,000 members—a convenient hit list in a nation that has had tens of thousands of death-squad killings. A few years earlier, during a brief period when the Salvadoran Left *was* trying to participate in above-ground politics, scores of their leaders were kidnapped, mutilated, and killed. And what about those long lines of people standing at the polls, voting with their feet for democracy and against the guerrillas? In El Salvador, voting is compulsory. As proof that you've voted, you get a stamp on your identity documents—the papers police demand to see at the roadblocks and spot checks that some Salvadorans endure several times daily.

The ballotting itself, Brodhead and Herman go on to say, had little resemblance to anything in civics textbooks. Voters signed to acknowledge receipt of a *numbered* ballot, which they deposited in a ballot box of transparent plastic. Then there were the 250,000 new sets of identity papers mysteriously issued in San Salvador just before the election, and the 700,000 additional ballots suddenly discovered after the total number of voters was announced.

How do people in the U.S. get hoodwinked into believing that such sham elections are the real thing? One factor, explain Brodhead and Herman, is our government's adroit use of "observers": groups of senators, academics, and other luminaries, who are brought in for a few days to helicopter around between polling places and give the appropriate testimony afterward.

"The observers invariably find demonstration elections good, whether held in Rhodesia under conditions of intense civil warfare [or] in Vietnam under the rule of generals openly admitting no popular base whatsoever. . . . There has even emerged a body of professional observers, associated mainly with establishment and right-wing propaganda agencies like Freedom House and the American Enterprise Institute, who travel from one demonstration election to the next to give their approval." *Demonstration Elections* shows a picture of Notre Dame University's president, the Reverend Theodore Hesburgh—who should know better—standing in front of one of El Salvador's transparent ballot boxes. He apparently found nothing awry, and issued an enthusiastic report later.

The other force that sells demonstration elections to the U.S. public is this country's mass media. *The New York Times* coverage of El Salvador in 1982 was far better than that of most papers. Yet, during the months before the election, 67 percent of the pre-election stories that the *Times* chose to put on its front page relied primarily or exclusively on government sources. And, according to Brodhead and Herman, *not one* U.S. media outlet reported a broadcast two weeks before the election by Salvadoran Defense Minister Jose Guillermo Garcia, under whose rule the death squads flourished as never before, in which he declared that anyone not voting would be guilty of "an act of treason."

The civics texts are right about one thing: real elections—where people have a choice that means something, know what the alternatives are, and don't get shot for doing the choosing—are a pretty good thing. Whatever their limitations, no one has yet devised a better defense against tyranny. But a demonstration election is held not to provide anyone with a genuine choice—it is held to provide a media event, for consumption thousands of miles away. Staging such events is an essential part of fighting a colonial war in an age of home-front skepticism and mass communications.

As a final fillip to their sharp and impressive analysis, Brodhead and Herman look at a Soviet-sponsored demonstration election in Poland in 1947. Then, as now, the population of Poland was heavily nationalist and Catholic and had no love for the Russians. The Russians staged elections designed to confirm their puppet regime in power. The elections had all the hallmarks of those in El Salvador and South Vietnam: the mass media were largely in pro-government hands, hundreds of opposition candidates were not permitted to run, 170,000 Soviet-trained security police patrolled the country, and anti-Soviet political figures were arrested and beaten. The only difference between this election and those under our sponsorship in Latin America is that all its flaws were brilliantly exposed in the U.S. press. Nobody in the West was fooled by the Soviet charade. If you want to make sure an injustice gets exposed, the moral is clear: make sure that it happens in *their* backyard, not in your own.

A Pledge of Resistance
A Contingency Plan in the Event of a U.S. Invasion of Nicaragua

by Jim Wallis

FROM *Sojourners* 13:7 (August 1984): 10–11

BACKGROUND

The plan began to emerge during a retreat. On November 2 to 4, 1983, representatives of the Christian peace movement met at the Kirkridge retreat center in northeastern Pennsylvania for Bible study, prayer, and political discernment. The Kirkridge retreat has become an annual event drawing together those from major denominations and churches, religious orders, national organizations, communities, campaigns, and local action groups that are providing leadership for peacemaking in the churches.

We met in the aftermath of the Grenada invasion. Some of us were in frequent contact with Nicaraguan churchpeople who were expressing great fear that their country would also be invaded. Our deep concern and friendship with the Nicaraguan brothers and sisters set the tone for our prayer and discussion.

Witness for Peace, a grassroots effort to keep a continuous, nonviolent presence of U.S. Christians in Nicaragua's war zones, was to be publicly launched in December and was already attracting a great deal of support and enthusiasm. We all committed ourselves to that bold initiative and together drew up a statement pledging ourselves to a plan of action in the event of a United States invasion of Nicaragua (see "A Promise of Resistance," Sojourners, December 1983). That "contingency plan" was subsequently presented to each of our constituencies in the churches and sent to every member of Congress, to the Departments of State and Defense, to the CIA, and to the president, informing them of our intentions should they undertake direct military action against Nicaragua.

Witness for Peace has now become a strong, grassroots movement involving thousands of U.S. citizens from the churches, religious community, and beyond in direct, non-violent opposition to the CIA's not-so-secret "covert" war against Nicaragua. Meanwhile the contingency plan has undergone more discussion and refinement. Conversations have taken place within Witness for Peace, with the Inter-Religious Task Force on Central America, among the Christian peace groups that planned the Kirkridge retreat, in local church, peace, and action groups across the country, and with many churchpeople and groups in Nicaragua, including North Americans who live and work there.

The response has been enormously positive, and feedback has shaped the evolving plan. As people and groups have heard of the plan, they have enthusiastically committed themselves to it. At the national level, a number of groups are now involved: Witness for Peace, the Inter-Religious Task Force on Central America, Southern Christian Leadership Conference, Fellowship of Reconciliation, Pax Christi, New Call to Peacemaking, World Peacemakers, Clergy and Laity Concerned, American Friends Service Committee, SANE, and Sojourners. Church and denominational networks are also rapidly becoming involved.

We all believe, along with friends in Nicaragua, that it is time to concretize the contingency plan and be ready to implement it as soon as possible.

PURPOSE

We hope either to prevent a direct U.S. invasion of Nicaragua or to make such military action so politically costly it will have to be halted. By announcing a credible and coordinated plan of massive public resistance, we hope to forestall an expanded war against Nicaragua. If the U.S. military undertakes direct action against Nicaragua, we will undertake nonviolent direct action against it on the largest scale possible. In so doing we hope to bring the issue before the American people, pressure Congress to act, and demand an immediate end to the invasion and the withdrawal of U.S. forces from Nicaragua.

THE PLAN

In the event of a U.S. invasion of Nicaragua, the following will happen:

1. A signal for action will go out to regional, state, and local contact people and groups.

2. People across the country will gather at a previously designated church in their local community (at least one in every congressional dis-

trict). These churches will be the gathering points for receiving and sharing information, for prayer and mutual support, for preparing and commissioning one another for action.

3. A nonviolent vigil will be established at the congressional field offices of each U.S. senator and representative. Each office will be peacefully occupied until that congressperson votes to end the invasion.

4. A large number of people will come to Washington, D.C. (in delegations from every area of the country) to engage in nonviolent civil disobedience at the White House to demand an end to the invasion.

5. The United States citizens in Nicaragua who are in active partnership with us (Witness for Peace, Maryknoll, the Committee of U.S. Citizens in Nicaragua, etc.) will launch their own plan of action in Nicaragua in concert with us. Depending on the political situation, the timing of the invasion, and the possibility of getting into Nicaragua before or during an invasion, we will send other people to Nicaragua to join in the actions of the United States citizens already there, if our partners in Nicaragua feel such an action would be advisable.

IMPLEMENTATION

The contingency plan will be carried out by a number of local groups acting together (the local networks, chapters, and contacts of the supporting national organizations and other local groups). In each local area, an ad hoc committee should be created to formulate and carry out the plan locally. The following activities will be the responsibility of the local committees:

1. Designating the churches in each local area where people will gather.

2. Planning a service of prayer, preparation, and commissioning for action.

3. Establishing a local scenario for action, consistent with the national plan, in each congressional district.

4. Carrying out the preparations and training necessary for each local action.

5. Selecting a delegation to go to Washington, D.C., for civil disobedience.

6. Gathering pledges from the largest possible number of people in each local area who will commit themselves to act in the event of a U.S. invasion of Nicaragua. The list of those pledged to action will stay at the local level, but the number of those pledged to action will be sent to Washington to announce to the government and to the press.

COMMUNICATION

Witness for Peace regional offices have agreed to serve as contact points for the communication system of the contingency plan. When they receive information or signals for action, they will pass the word on to contingency plan state coordinators, who will then contact local coordinators. The Witness for Peace regional coordinators will also help to facilitate establishment of the communication network in each of the regions. The Witness for Peace regional coordinators are listed below.

West Coast: Mary Kurt-Mason, 515 Broadway, Santa Cruz, CA 95060; (408) 425-3733. **Southwest**: Buddy Summers or Lynn Holmes, 4220 S.P.I.D. #212, Corpus Christi, TX 78411; (512) 852-8755. **Northern Midwest**: Betty Wolcott, 3221 S. Lake Dr., Milwaukee, WI 53207; (414) 744-1160. **Central Midwest**: Grace Gyori, 3913 N. St. Louis, Chicago, IL 60618; (312) 267-7881. **New England**: Bob Bonthius or Fran Truitt, RD 2, Box 422A, Ellsworth, ME 04605; (207) 422-9007. **Mid Atlantic**: John Collins or Bill Webber, 198 Broadway, New York, NY 10038; (212) 964-6730. **Southeast**: Betsy Crites or Josefina Tiryakian, 1414 Woodland Dr., Durham, NC 27701; (919) 688-5400.

Because of both regular contact with Nicaragua and proximity to Washington decision making and press, the Witness for Peace Washington office and Sojourners have agreed to be the points from which information and the signal for action will be given. A consultative process of decision making involving others is being established to decide when the signal for action should be given. This U.S. contingency plan is being coordinated with the plans being developed by our U.S. friends in Nicaragua, who will determine the feasibility and advisability of more U.S. citizens joining them in Nicaragua in the event of an invasion.

CONCLUSION

Given the urgent situation in Nicaragua and the possibilities of further United States escalation, the contingency plan should be ready for implementation as soon as possible. This call will go out from the various organizations, groups, and constituencies involved. The contingency plan will subsequently be announced to the government and to the press in the hope that a pledge of resistance on such a large scale will help deter the possibility of a United States invasion. Discussions are under way about how this or similar plans might be useful in opposing U.S. military escalation elsewhere in Central America.

The work on this effort has already brought people and groups together. We all hope that will continue. To succeed, the plan needs a broad base of support. Making this promise of resistance and doing the work to make the promise credible will surely deepen our understanding and experience of the things that make for peace. If the armies of the United States are mobilized to wage war on Nicaragua, may a mighty nonviolent army of U.S. citizens also be mobilized to wage peace.

Women Against the Occupation

FROM *Connexions: An International Woman's Quarterly* 11 (Winter 1984): 9–10

In response to an inquiry to the Israeli group Women Against Occupation about their activities, Connexions *received the following reply dated October 10, 1983.*

Our group does not have a clear cut position about each issue that exists here, for example, the question of Zionism. There are women in our group who are anti-Zionist (myself included) and support the establishment of a democratic and secular state in all of Palestine. Others support the establishment of an independent Palestinian state in the occupied territories, either as a minimum program or as a permanent solution. Since all positions are decided on by consensus, we have not gone on record as supporting any defined political solution and do not exclude Zionist women from joining our group. Actually the only positions one has to agree upon when joining are women's liberation (broadly defined), Israel out of Lebanon and the occupied territories, and self-determination for the Palestinians. I see this as the broadest possible political basis on which women can organize as feminists, since I see the state of war between Israel and our Arab neighbors and the oppression of Palestinian rights as the main issue blocking women's emancipation in Israel and that of Palestinian women.

I think it is really astounding that such a group emerged, since I've been politically active for some years and the feminist movement here has always been small, limited and crippled by elitism and has refused to take political positions.

Right now we are involved in several projects. The main ones are support for the strike of women Palestinian political prisoners. We held a second demonstration last week with the participation of the prisoners' families and members of women's groups in the West Bank. It looks as if this is going to be a long and bitter struggle since both sides are determined to win and we need all the international support we can get.

Another project is establishing ties and permanent relations with women's groups in the West Bank. We have already met with them and will continue in order to work together on all relevant issues.

The following is compiled from a statement published by Women Against Occupation in April 1983 and from an article especially written for Connexions in October 1983.

In June 1982, the group Women Against Occupation [originally called Woman Against the Invasion of Lebanon] was formed in Israel as a direct response to the war in Lebanon. With its massive destruction of a civilian population, this war quickly lifted the facade of Israel's higher moral status for those who still clung to that antiquated belief. Using the excuse that the PLO was storing arms in southern Lebanon, the Israeli Army bombed hospitals and schools there. Cluster bombs and phosphorous bombs, two particularly barbaric types of weapons supplied courtesy of the United States, rained upon southern Lebanon. Electricity was cut off and food supplies were not allowed to enter Beirut for days. The massacres in the Sabra and Shattila refugee camps, horrifying as they were, were but symbols of the greater destruction wrought upon Lebanon by the Israelis. As the days, months and now year drag on, it becomes increasingly clear that this is a war of terror designed to liquidate as many Palestinians as possible and to petrify into submission those who are left alive.

In addition to being highly critical of the invasion, many Israeli Jews have begun to reexamine their own society and to discuss the role of war in their lives. Beyond its dubious military aims, war serves as a smoke screen to cover up many of Israel's internal problems. How convenient to conduct a war financed by the USA, which at the same time deflects attention from Israel's continued occupation of Arab land from the 1967 war, from the 130% yearly inflation rate, from the increasing conflict between Sephardic and Ashkenazi Jews, and from the continuing oppression of women.

Women Against Occupation was organized both to protest the war and to expose the links between militarism and the subjugation of women. Although many anti-war groups sprang up following the invasion, we felt that it was important to organize specifically as women. When a heckler at one of our demonstrations told us that we "would be better off baking cakes for the soldiers," it was evident that the attitude is that it is a woman's duty to support the men at war, and if there was to be anything said or done, it should be by men.

Yet it was precisely the anticipation of this attitude which caused our group to raise the slogan "Silence means approval," which embodies our position that it is our right and duty to protest against the war for several reasons: women should be perceived as equal members of society and should take part in and responsibility for any decision made by the society they live in; we believe that since women do not (as a rule) initiate wars or take an active part in them, they have every right to protest against this situation which has been imposed upon them; the fact that society traditionally demands women to reproduce, take care of the home and children, suffer violence, and support the men from behind the lines, provides the very grounds for women's rights to object to war.

In a militaristic society one's worth comes from having served in the army, from having been on the front lines. Those who have not served are considered unworthy of speaking out and of participating fully in the nation. Such a claim is raised against Israeli Arabs, whose non-service in the army is often used to legitimize their oppression and to silence them. Although Jewish women do serve in the army, they do so in primarily supportive and servile roles (teaching, secretarial, etc.) and are thus excluded from full national participation. Issues which relate specifically to women such as battery, abortion, and reform of divorce laws are given short shrift. Even within the anti-war movement our views are not taken seriously, because we have not seen "action."

The repercussions of this action have been acutely felt by Palestinian and Lebanese women since the invasion. In this war, directed as it is at a civilian population, women and children suffer heavier casualties than men, who are mobile. To the women who are not killed or injured are left the daily pressures of looking for food and water when there is little to be had, of taking care of the wounded, and of searching for male friends and relatives who have been dragged off by Israeli soldiers into "detention camps."

The effects of war, however, extend much further than its direct physical consequences. They serve to reinforce the entire social structure, particularly the role delegated to women. First, women are used as alibis for war, "it is waged for our protection and for the security of our families." Later, we are expected to be grateful and nurturing toward those who risked their lives our our behalf. Yet, the hypocrisy of the vanquishing army toward women is clear: to its own women it projects a sentimental glorification of the home and family, to enemy women there is overt hatred and an attempt to destroy these same institutions.

The recent debate in Israel over abortion and the new tax law, which will give more aid to large Jewish families, exposes the reactionary way in which a militaristic society views women. Several months ago a $50 surcharge was

NOGA

Signs read left to right: silence means consent; women against the invasion of Lebanon; we won't be alibis for murder.

imposed on all Israeli citizens leaving the country. The added revenue is to be allocated to all families with four or more children in which the father has either served in the army or has been exempt from military service due to religious reasons. More recently the government changed a law, which gave a sum of money to every mother at every birth enabling poor families to buy needed equipment, clothing, etc. for the child, to a law giving subsidies only to women bearing their fourth child, and again only to those belonging to families meeting the above-mentioned stipulations. In short, these laws apply to Jews only.

Hand in hand with increased aid to large families is a restrictive abortion law. In 1979 a clause in the abortion law enabling women to abort on socio-economic grounds was repealed, making abortion legal (but not free of charge) only in cases of incest, rape, religious reasons, severe physical damage to the mother or child, and other extreme cases.

It is not a coincidence that the issue of abortion comes up in the midst of war. Dr. Haim Sadan, advisor to the Minister of Health, said in an interview that "abortions have resulted in the loss of 20 [army] divisions since the creation of the state." The sexual division of Jewish labor is thus clearly laid out: men are drafted into the army to kill Palestinians, while women's wombs are mobilized to produce more soldiers and to solve the demographic problem. How is the Jewish state to remain in existence if the Jewish birth rate declines? Former Prime Minister Golda Meir is on record as having declared that she couldn't sleep nights thinking of all the Arab babies born.

On the other hand, it is unofficially reported by some persons that Arab women in Israel (1948 borders) can have abortions on demand, are indeed encouraged to use contraceptives and abort, in total contrast to the situation of Jewish Israeli women.

The Jewish woman is thus viewed as a machine of reproduction. Her ability to reproduce is her most valued asset. Consequently, to struggle for abortion rights challenges the state in a fundamental way. Women Against Occupation is currently involved in this struggle—a change in direction from when we first started. In the beginning, we organized women-only demonstrations against the war and were concerned specifically with the war's destruction. We wrote pamphlets linking feminism and the anti-war movement and we participated in the Fifth National Feminist Conference in Haifa, where our workshops on the war and on Arab women were the most heavily attended.

During the debates on abortion, we focused our attention on that issue while continuing to participate as a distinct group in anti-war demonstrations. We printed a poster that illustrates the role of women in Israel. It shows a woman as a mechanical baby maker. To her womb are connected two umbilical cords. One is connected to a group of identical boys dressed in soldiers' uniforms, and the other to a group of miniaturized baby machine women.

At this point our group is predominantly Jewish, although Palestinian women have participated in our various activities. Recently, we have been making contact with Palestinian women outside of our group in Arab villages and on the West Bank. We have begun to visit Palestinian women who have been imprisoned for being politically active. We feel this is a first step toward closer communication with Palestinian women.

In the above statement, we have raised a few points which we believe can throw some light on the correlation between the permanent state of war which exists in our region and the oppression of Jewish and Palestinian women. We believe that ending this state of war by establishing an independent Palestinian state and guaranteeing all Palestinians human and democratic rights is a major issue in our struggle for women's emancipation.

Further reading

"Israeli Response to War: An Israeli Feminist Account," in American Friends Service Committee Women's Newsletter, Volume 4, Number 1, 1501 Cherry Street, Philadelphia, PA 19102.

Poem for El Salvador

by Rob Brezsny

FROM *The Sun: A Magazine of Ideas* 100 (March 1984): 20–22

[Sung]
> I want all the children
> to have enough to eat
> I want to believe
> in a world without end
> I want everybody
> to be safe and happy
> I want everyone
> to be loved

[Spoken]
> Poem for El Salvador
> Poem for Lebanon
> Poem for Cambodia and Chile and Northern Ireland and Grenada
> Poem for South Africa and Namibia and Angola and Poland and
> Afghanistan and all of Southeast Asia
> Poem for the millions and millions of words
> written for the millions and millions of strong angry fighting men
>
> Poem for the bleeding gums of 50,000 women refugees in Somalia
> and for the broken ribs of Cambodian nurses raped by Vietnamese
> soldiers
> Poem for the breasts of Argentinians hooked to electric shock
> torture machines
> and for the ashes of Palestinian mothers exterminated by
> Israeli bombs

Poem for the hands and knees of the maids who scrub the floors
    of the Salvadorian ruling class palaces
    and for the hair of Spanish midwives hacked off by the
        medical police
Poem for the cracked skulls of the battered wives of San Francisco
    and Dallas and Philadelphia and Chicago

Poem for the wombs of all mothers
    birthing more and more men
    who invent new diseases
    and cut off the heads of children with bayonets
    and worship and torture
    for the greater glory
    of the Cult of Personality

Poem for cancer in the hearts
    of all strong angry men who hate life

Strong angry men keep coming up to me and saying
"Why don't you write more poems about the armed struggle for
    liberation in El Salvador and the Philippines and Namibia
    and Angola"

So I wrote a poem
    about the son of a Russian Communist Party official
    who begged me to smuggle him in some "good American pornography"

    and the wild stag parties of the Red Brigade
    on the night before they go out and shoot off the kneecaps
    of another Italian judge

    and sitting with macho Marxists
    at a disco in downtown San Salvador
    looking all the pretty ladies up and down

    and making love with the daughter of a white collar criminal
        from Exxon
    while she was on an Irish vacation
    and I was living with real wife-beating soldiers
    of the Irish Republican Army

    and hearing the same dumb joke about the slut who couldn't
        get enough
    as told by Yassir Arafat and Henry Kissinger
    and Colonel Khadafy and the Dallas Cowboy football team

Poem for the starving women artists in Somalia
    and the bleeding women geniuses in El Salvador

Poem to burn all criminally innocent entertainment
    and the bad fatherly poetry of Mao Tse-Tung
    and the naked pictures that remind us who we're here to serve
    and the pamphlets of right-wing assassins
    plagiarizing the slogans of left-wing assassins
    and the literature of all strong angry men who hate life

The problem isn't overpopulation
It's overpopulation by the wrong people

The problem isn't overpopulation
It's overpopulation by the wrong people

Poem for the wrong people
Poem for the strong and angry capitalist, marxist, Christian,
Islamic, Jewish, caucasian, black, arab, and asian
woman-haters

[Chanted]
 2-4-6-8
 Organize and smash the state
 2-4-6-8
 Organize and smash the state
 Kick the ass of the ruling class
 Kick the ass of the ruling class
 Push 'em back
 Push 'em back
 Way back
 Push 'em back
 Push 'em back
 Way back
 Push 'em back
 Push 'em back
 Way back

[Shouted]
 Use the food as a weapon
 Use the medicine as a weapon
 Use the soul as a weapon
 Use emotions, use words, use laws, use love
 Use it all up
 Throw it all away
 The thing we dreaded most
 has already happened
 We're already living
 after the end of the world

[Sung]
 I want to go back
 to the simple life with you
 I want to believe
 in a world without end
 I want to be strong and tender
 Be in love with my life like you
 I want to go back to the source
 I want all the children
 to have enough to eat
 I want all the children
 to give up the fight
 I want everyone to be happy
 and warm and safe and strong
 I want everybody to be loved

Section 4

FREEDOM IS NOT SLAVERY

Anti-Feminism Pervades Coverage of Big Dan's Trial

by Stephanie Poggi

FROM *Sojourner: The Women's Forum* 9 : 8 (April 1984): 11

Hundreds of people competed for seats in the courtroom at the Big Dan pool-table rape trials in Fall River, Massachusetts. Thousands more tuned in for live, literally blow-by-blow testimony on their radios and TVs. Newspapers all across the country have provided large photographs of the defendants, witnesses and attorneys, and have obsessively reported every minute detail of the rape on their front pages, day after day. A Boston radio station actually aired a dramatic re-enactment of the rape. And Colony Communications, a Massachusetts cable TV company, defended its broadcast of the woman's name, saying that it wanted viewers "to see and hear everything they would see and hear if they attended the trial." Too bad they missed the rape.

In addition to promoting mass voyeurism, the media have collaborated with the trial prosecution to bring us some of the most outrageous examples of anti-feminism in recent history. Below are some choice items from the *Boston Globe.*

> . . . The Committee for Justice . . . has been monitoring the Big Dan's rape trial for bias against the six Portuguese defendants charged in the case. (March 3)

Stephanie Poggi is a lesbian journalist living in the Boston area.

The fact that the defendants are Portuguese has been stressed over and over in trial coverage. This has the dual effect of increasing the titillation for racist onlookers and of making even the *Globe* look sensitive to racism. But the raped woman is also Portuguese—an item that appears in the press far less often and which seems irrelevant to the Committee for Justice. It's just as likely, if not more so, for a Portuguese woman to be judged a liar and a slut as for Portuguese men to be judged natural rapists. Racism *is* blatantly at work here, but it operates against the raped woman and the witnesses, as well as against the defendants.

> Silva said he "couldn't get an erection." (March 4)

> Silva said he "was physically unable to have sex with the woman that night. . . ." Raposo said he "did not have sex with the girl. . . ." He said he "couldn't." (March 15)

Despite the sperm that was found during a hospital examination several hours after the woman "complained [sic] she was raped," newspaper accounts report that the men charged "couldn't" do it. This focus on the men's failure to have erections not only suggests that a rape did not, could not, take place, but also encourages us to excuse and pity them, explain and forget about "it."

> First [she] told police she had been raped by six men, and in testimony [she] said it was two. (March 6)

How many men raped the woman has emerged as a key question—not just as a determinant of her credibility, but as a point of fact, too. Massachusetts law, like other states', defines rape according to a traditional model of heterosexual male pleasure, i.e., as penetration or oral sex without consent. Thus, the men who tried to penetrate the woman but were physically unable to are not rapists. In other words, if he doesn't get off, no matter how much he tries, you weren't raped. The issue should be her consent, her violation, not his orgasm.

> Confusion still surrounds . . . how friendly she was with the men *before* the attack began. (March 4, my emphasis)

> [Jurors will weigh] how the woman acted when she *first* came in contact with Silva. (March 13, my emphasis)

> The woman [in the Holbrook Five] case went to an all-male bar, like Big Dan's, and that's a situation she should've known was dangerous. She could've left at any time. Perhaps there did come a time when she didn't want to go any further, but she had *already* given her consent. (From one of the women on the Holbrook Five jury which last July acquitted five men charged with gang rape, my emphasis)

What if she actually did flirt, kiss one man (or all of them), have a drink (or two or ten drinks), act the way a "sexually liberated," "not uptight" woman is supposed to? Why should the word "no," so easily understood in other circumstances, suddenly become meaningless in these? What if she did consent to sex with one of the men? Why should that mean she wants sex with all of his friends?

> . . . Defense attorneys probed into details of her relationship with her boyfriend, how much she was drinking the night of the attack, and how *actively* she resisted having sexual relations. (February 28, my emphasis)

Incredibly, the question here is not *if* she resisted, but how actively. Once again, what is "normal" sex if rape means *active* resistance? If you want it, then you only resist for ten minutes or so; if you don't, then you kick, yell, get beaten, bruised and maybe killed to prove you *really* meant "no"? And if the woman was drunk, it only means the men attacked a drunk woman—a particularly vulnerable person.

> The defense has also raised questions about the woman's credibility by introducing a hospital report which says the woman claimed she was raped in 1981–a report the woman denied in court. (March 4)

Ironically, the defendants' statements to police immediately after their arrest are inadmissable to the jury, while the woman's past has been laid bare, crawled over and exploited by the defense. So much for the "rape shield" law, which supposedly prevents introduction of personal and sexual history. Of course, she lied about the previous rape: to admit you have been raped before is to make yourself a total fraud, a "repeat offender" in the eyes of the jury and public. To say we *haven't* been raped, for most of us, is to pretend we have lived on some other planet as some other gender. The denial of a previous rape should be seen as an indictment of our society, not of the woman.

> I don't believe it's enough for a woman just to say "no," I believe a woman has to act "no" with her behavior. It's called signals. (Judith Lindhal, Victor Raposo's defense attorney, March 8)

The *Globe* has called Judith Lindhal "the other woman of the Big Dan's rape trial," suggesting that she is somehow in competition with the raped woman for the attention of the defendants. Unlike the raped woman, Lindhal knows all the "right signals"—we're told she wears "no-nonsense suits," her hair in a "severe bun." (Needless to say, we're still waiting for a report on the male attorneys' wardrobes and hairstyles.) Judith Lindhal has, in fact, become the other woman of the case: she is the other public female victim. Her presence cleverly legitimizes the rape, all of the defendants, and the full-scale attack on the raped woman's credibility. Lindhal is a pawn here, a tool for setting women against each other, rather than against the rapists or the judicial system.

> I don't believe her story one bit and I don't feel sorry for her, either. . . . I was raped and I can tell you, I know I was asking for it and I think this lady was, too. (18-year-old trial observer, March 1)

This statement, one of the saddest reported in the *Globe*, attempts to demonstrate that no loyalty whatsoever exists among us, that not even women who have been raped will support their sisters who are attacked. Such misogyny from other women can only increase a raped woman's sense of powerlessness and isolation. A counselor at the Boston Area Rape Crisis Center says that the Big Dan trials have already caused a third of the women she counsels to change their minds about pressing charges.

Regardless of the verdicts and appeal outcomes in the case, this antifeminist backlash in media and rape trial procedures deserves our anger. We need to raise our voices to use the trial and the attention it has received to reach out to a wider audience and to each other.

Ed. Note: Sojourner *hopes that other women will share their feelings about the Big Dan trials; the deadline for all May material is April 6.*

Women's Health Hindered by Hippocratic Oafs

by Judith Galas

FROM *Womanews: N.Y.C. Feminist Newspaper and Calendar*
5:4 (April 1984): 11

"Close your eyes. For the next few moments I want you to repeat silently to yourself, 'My body is mine and I cannot be violated.'" More than 200 women inwardly repeated Dr. Michelle Harrison's words and silence gathered in the crowded room.

Harrison's voice broke the stillness. "I want you to feel what it is like to be in a community where that is the truth, even for a moment."

The medical community routinely violates women's bodies. Intrusive, even dangerous, birthing procedures, unnecessary or deforming surgery on our reproductive systems and breasts, health-threatening contraceptive pills and devices are so routine as to go unchallenged by most women.

At Outlook '84—A Women's Health Conference, held last March in Bethlehem, at Lehigh University, Harrison exposed the medical system and challenged her audience to be aware of the violation, to be informed medical consumers and to make an absence of violation more than a moment's truth at a conference.

Author of *A Woman in Residence*, a poignant depiction of her seven-month ordeal in an OB/GYN residency program, Harrison is a dedicated proponent of justice and dignity in women's health care and the health care system. Already a licensed psychiatrist and family practitioner when she entered the residency program, Harrison found the four-year program unbearable.

A small woman, with a full, open smile, she is younger than her salt-and-pepper hair first indicates. She admitted with a wise smile that her book was the first ever written by a failure, someone who did not make it.

"I was torn between the system and my moral choices," she said. "I could not cut into a woman's body without reason; I could not tolerate the pain of knowing about the violation and abuse."

"I wrote the book as an apology to the women I cared for, to warn women about what happens in a hospital."

DANGEROUS DOCTORS

Her visit to Lehigh, she said, was an extension of her book, an opportunity to warn women and spread awareness.

She cautioned the women never to go to a doctor alone. "Take a friend with you and be an informed consumer."

"Know whom you are dealing with." She told the women to be aware that medical training is one of systematic abuse, humiliation and exhaustion and that abused medical students become abusive physicians.

"The medical system is like a cult. It violates a young student's most important ethical values and ideals and replaces those values with the group's values," she said. "Patients, especially women patients, are seen as outsiders."

Birth control pills and intra-uterine devices have been widely used since the late '60s, but Harrison said physicians did not prescribe them for their wives and daughters because the methods were dangerous. Their women used diaphragms.

"They are still putting IUDs into women. They are still not warning about infections, and, in fact, tell women the infections do not exist."

Harrison regards childbirth as an issue of power-medicine's control over women's bodies.

"I know women should walk while they are in labor, but doctors certainly don't want to see women marching through labor," she laughed.

As to lesbians, Harrison said with a smile, "most physicians I know insist they have never seen one."

PREMENSTRUAL PIONEER

In 1981, shortly after she wrote her book, Harrison began work at the first clinic for premenstrual syndrome (PMS).

The phenomenon, experienced by millions of women, exemplifies the disturbing combination of patient knowledge and doctors' refusal to see an illness they are not prepared to accept, much less treat.

Harrison's newest book, *Self-Help for Premenstrual Syndrome*, is just that, a tool for self-diagnosis and treatment.

She claims PMS has been used to justify discrimination against women and to support the assumption that women cannot be trusted because of their raging hormones.

"Remember," Harrison said, "ninety percent of violent crimes are still committed by men, and no one tells them men cannot be president because they are too violent."

Harrison suggested that if women charted the emotional behaviors of their husbands and bosses, they would find that men have hormonal cycles as well. Unfortunately, the anger, demands, impatience and rudeness with which men treat their wives and secretaries are simply accepted as normal.

Harrison's speech and PMS workshop were the highlights of a conference that included tips on nutrition, depression, fitness and self-awareness.

A young woman, perhaps frightened by Harrison's image of a harmful or callous medical community, perhaps confused by the conflict between physician as healer and physician as abuser, chose to attack Harrison.

"She's so bitter. She's just a man-hater," she was overheard to have said.

Unable to face the fearful reality that women's spirits and lives are in jeopardy, she found it easier, even necessary, to dismiss the messenger, rather than to accept her warnings.

The Civil Rights Pornography Ordinance

by Catharine MacKinnon

FROM *Feminist Connection* 5:2 (October/November 1984): 8–9

These are excerpts from an address given at the symposium: Pornography, Through the Eyes of Women, held at Madison, Wisconsin, September 15, 1984.

In speaking about pornography through the eyes of women I want to begin talking about the situation of women, the realities. Then I will move into a discussion of those realities through the eyes of pornography.

THE SITUATION OF WOMEN

Women are systematically raped. The latest study shows that 44% of all women have been raped at least once in our lives. It doesn't say how many more than once; that does not include marital rape.

It is increasingly well-known that a quarter to a third at minimum of young girls are the victims of incest and child sexual abuse. At least that many have their initial sexual encounter forceably, and in connection with a typically older man whom they trusted and certainly whom they knew.

Women are systematically battered in homes. Even the FBI, that is learning to redo its scales and measures on the basis of things feminists say are true, estimates that it is the most unreported crime.

A federal study shows that 85% of women have been sexually harassed at some point in their working lives. If you ask: How many of you have been sexually harassed in the last two years, 15% to 20% will say yes in forms that are physical, not just "Fuck me or you're fired."

The best estimates that we have are between 12% and 15% of all American women are or have been prostitutes at some point in their lives meaning that they make their living or existence from their sexuality expressly.

A major part of what it is to be a woman is to be targeted for sexual abuse. Realize that most of those crimes were not known until very recently, and even now most of those are never reported.

If you further look and see what happens to those women who do report those things, you find conviction rates for rape are lower than for any comparable crime of violence. You realize a huge quantity of battery cases are screened out as are rape reports as what they call "unfounded."

You start to understand there's something that might be termed "a conspiracy of silence." What we've got here is something huge, major, abusive, violent that is not even recognized as existing, and that the victims of these do not feel they can speak about it in public. When you talk to victims you find out why. We all know. Because we will not be believed.

What I found when I first started looking at pornography was this: Everything that has taken women all this energy to attempt to uncover, speak out about, break silence on, that it has taken us incredible effort to speak about the rape, to talk about the child sexual abuse, to articulate the battery, is there in the pornography. There you see it all. There you see the rape. The harassment. The child sexual abuse. You see the prostitution.

Except what it is in there is sex. What it particularly is is rape presented as sex, celebrated as sex. It is child sexual abuse presented as the nature of the child, infantile sexuality. It is prostitution in the sense that it is the sale of women's sexuality, presented as just who we really are. Pornography also presents women as whores by nature. It presents battery, however, it calls it at most "sado-masochism." It presents sexual harassment as what we really want in the workforce, what we're really there for.

In pornography women desire to have all these things done to us; it is our freedom, it is our liberation. It is equal to men's desire to do it to us.

Looking into the pornography, what I understood is that pornography presents what we have come to understand as the subordination of women.

DESIGNING THE LAW
When Andrea Dworkin and I designed a law on pornography for the Minneapolis City Council at its request, we said that pornography is a violation of women's civil rights, among other reasons because of its role in maintaining and creating sex as a basis for discrimination. Pornography is a way to condition the way women are seen and treated, so that when we are abused

it is seen to be legitimate, when we are violated it is seen to be our nature, when we are discriminated against it is seen to be equality.

We define pornography as sex discrimination also because of our understanding that this is done to women as a group.

What it is to have something done to you as a member of a group is that some of you may be selected out as the victims of it, on what is essentially a random basis. For instance, what woman gets raped is like roulette. What child gets sexually abused is like roulette. What woman winds up a prostitute is like roulette. There are so many empty chambers, you just spin it and you pull the trigger and maybe you happen to be in front of it, the chamber that's full. But there is something entirely non-roulette-like about the fact that the gun is pointed at women. It is a woman when someone is hit.

And that's why we have designed it as a civil rights violation. The fundamental approach that we take to pornography situates it within the systematic violation of women as a group, based on a comprehension that pornography works like all forms of systematic terrorism work. That means that women as a whole are a terrorized population.

Women, I think, deal with that as much by denial—which is perceived as a survival strategy—as by fear. We are also now attempting to deal with it through political action.

In our definition of pornography, Andrea Dworkin and I define it really for the first time for what it is. That is, part of the institutionalization of the second-class status of women as a group.

We define pornography as "The sexually explicit subordination of women through pictures and words." We add that it must also include a number of specific and concrete things. These include: Women presented as sexual objects who enjoy rape. Women presented as sexual objects who enjoy pain or humiliation. Primarily it must include women as dehumanized, as objects or things or commodities, or it can include women being penetrated by objects or animals. Women being tied up, mutilated, bruised, physically hurt, in a context that makes those things sexual, and a number of other concrete elements.

Those concrete elements are designed as an empirical description of what is actually in the pornography. They are also designed on the basis of an understanding of pornography's connection in hundreds of ways to the actual concrete abuse of women.

SUBORDINATION
We understand that is an active process. It includes acts like rape, battery, sexual harassment, enforced prostitution. It is an activity in the way the second-class civil status of women is enforced. What we have done is define pornography in an active way. We do not say—as you have undoubtedly read in the paper—that pornography is everything that depicts or describes

the subordination of women. We say pornography is the graphic sexually explicit subordination of women.

The active role that pornography takes in defining women as subordinate beings happens in a number of different ways. Subordination has to do first of all with *objectification*.

Objectification means when you look at a woman you see a thing. Pornography does that. It teaches, it conditions its viewers so that what we're looking at is a thing, when in fact it is a woman we're looking at. If you think this hasn't worked on you, you might think how you regard the women in the pornography. Are they women like you? They're cut. Do they hurt? When you hear them scream, are you turned on by it? Do you think they are turned on by it too? What I'm suggesting is the process of objectification has to do with conditioning how you see. It works for us all.

Another element of subordination is *hierarchy*. It has to do with a person being a thing who is then on the bottom. In our analysis, the erotization of hierarchy is the key dynamic in keeping women down.

The next category is *forced submission*, another part of subordination, which is to say once you've made a woman into a thing, and you've put her on the bottom of the hierarchy, you can tell her what to do.

Finally, *violence*. This is a term I've learned not to use very much, through understanding its elusive gender neutrality. It's sort of a word like humanism or androgyny. It acts as though things are all equal that aren't. In other words, when one says pornography is violence, not sex, it exempts the sexual enjoyment of violence. If violence is practiced as sex, it is sex. When one says that pornography includes violence, I want to make clear that pornography includes violence that is in many ways not seen as violence. It's seen as passion. It's seen as, you know, 'He loves me so much that's why he beats me.' It's seen as sado-masochism—that is, the woman's specific sexual pleasure derives from being tortured.

FOUR ACTIONABLE INJURIES

We did not define pornography as a civil rights violation for any other reason than that it is one.

We also define four acts in our laws, that are injuries that are actionable. What that means is just the existence up in the sky someplace of pornography is not enough that someone would be able to do something about it.

What we wanted to do was define pornography for what it is, and then to place power in the hands of women to do something about it, by making clear on the basis of all the testimony and evidence principally from women of the ways pornography hurts women in our lives. To put the power in the hands of those women who have been hurt by it to do something about it. Women spoke to us about their injuries, they talked about how pornography was used against them, how they were used in it. We designed the ordinance on the basis of that, in addition to what is really a simple empirical research method of walking into the pornography store and seeing what is there. This is a feminist law in that process sense of the word. It is congealed out of women's pain.

The four acts that are actionable in our law are:

1. Coercion into pornography performances.

We learned the most about this initially from Linda Marchiano, who was coerced into making the movie 'Deep Throat.' I also learned the most about it from the fact that no one *believes* she was coerced into making 'Deep Throat.'

In this part of the law we allow a woman who was coerced into pornography to sue the people who did this to her for damages, and also to stop what was made off of her performance.

2. Our second injury is having pornography forced on a person. We are making it a legal violation that if anyone forces pornography on anyone, including a child, in a home, or a place of work, or in a public place, or in education, that the person who did that can be stopped, and can also be sued for damages. The pornography that they use nothing can be done about, under this injury.

3. We are also allowing people to sue who have been assaulted in a way that is directly caused by specific pornography. We have had a lot of reports by women who are assaulted, forcing the pornography on them as in 'Here you stupid bitch, this is what I want you to do.' 'Read this: Look it says here you don't necessarily enjoy it at the beginning but if you keep trying you start to like it. If you love me, you'll try.' That is the marriage testimony that we've received.

What then occurs often is that the pornography is put up on the wall. The woman is put next to it. She's posed and then she's raped. It's used in gang-rape. It's used in incest. Little children are shown pornography and then treated the way the children in the pornography are treated. Pictures are also taken of them doing that, and those pictures are used to keep them doing it.

Children or women are told 'Here's the pictures of the people enjoying it. What's the matter with you?' Then they're told 'Look like you enjoy it.' The pictures are taken, and when they say, 'I don't want to do this anymore,' the people who take the pictures will say, 'I will use the pictures and show it to your parents or your boss and it will show you enjoying it so no one will believe you when you say you were forced.'

The specific assault provision I think is going to be very hard for people to prove, particularly as against the pornography itself. It's written to say that assault or wrongful injury directly caused by specific pornography is actionable. For instance, we had a Native American woman testify who was raped while the men were screaming, 'This is a lot more fun than Custer's Revenge,' continually talking about the video game while raping her.

4. Finally we made actionable trafficking in pornography. Trafficking is defined as the activity of sale, production, exhibition or distribution. This is based on the mountain of evidence that connects pornography with the second-class citizen status of women. Our law allows any woman to sue a trafficker for the violation of women's civil rights, which the trafficking constitutes, both for damages, if it can be shown that he knew what he was selling was pornography, and also for an injunction regardless of knowledge. An injunction means you can make him stop doing it, which is the main point.

NO OBSCENITY

I'd like to say a couple of things about why this is not obscenity. Obscenity law has been designed by a specific group of men to attempt to keep out of the sight of the victims, women and children, material that those particular members of the male power establishment don't want us to see. Sometimes I think it's because they don't want us to see what they really want, even though they then go do it to us.

Sometimes I think it's to, in part, keep it sexy. That is, all this taboo business that surrounds obscenity has a lot to do with keeping it off-limits, ineffective and a kick to get. If sex isn't sexy unless it's a violation, how will we keep the pornography sexy, when there's so much of it and it's everywhere! One of the ways is to have it be violent. Another way is to have it be a violation to get it. It also has a real function in making child pornography sexy. To put it crassly, in many respects without having male power, which is real, define the violation of a child as a violation, then it would feel about as sexy as taking candy from a baby.

I'm also against obscenity law content. Obscenity law is an *idea* of what some people are offended by. It's a way to impress some people's morality on other people, particularly their sexual morality. It is that which appeals to the prurient interest—who knows what that is? I guess we know pornography gives men erections but that's never been the same as what appeals to the prurient interest, because obscenity law is now the law and pornography is out there.

Obscenity law is worried about things like nudity and excessive candor, it's worried about presentations of forms of sexuality that some people don't like, such as homosexuality. It's worried about perversity. It's concerned about community standards. Again, who knows what they might be? Although of course we do, because pornography's out there.

Finally, obscenity law exempts those things which are seen to have literary, political, artistic or scientific value. Think about the history of the sub-

THOSE WOMEN AGAINST PORNOGRAPHY...
ARE ANTI-SEX.

ordinations of women, the silencing of women, in creating the standards, our lack of voice in defining what's politically valuable, our lack of voice in defining what's artistically valuable. We've been their great art; we haven't said what is great in art. Similarly in literature, they make the text; we're their vocabulary of the pornography: cunt, pussy, all that stuff.

The concepts of obscenity law are not like what we're doing. The definition of the problem is not the same. The dynamic of the use of the law is not the same. Obscenity is a criminal law. It's seen to violate good order and morality. What we're interested in trying to do is to make a civil law to further the equality of women.

The reason we are viewing this as a civil law and not as a criminal law is first of all because we do not want to empower the state. We want to empower women. We think the state has a very bad record in vindicating our rights.

I'm in a daily rage about Minneapolis (and obscenity). They asked us to do this about pornography for them. We did it. We got all of these women to come and speak in public about their violation and pain. They trusted that city council. They gave them this knowledge for the first time in history. We showed it in public—we don't go around saying we want this stuff put underground! We're the ones who go around showing it to people! I think we made it not very sexy. It is what you call "de-tumescence." Not only do they defeat the ordinance, but they went and passed an obscenity law off of it! And an opaque covers law! Yes! What do they have to do? They have to make it "sexy" all over again, prohibit it, make it bad, say women's bodies are dirty and off limits, put it in the hands of the prosecutor, and make it sexy again.

FIRST AMENDMENT

The First Amendment prohibits what's understood as censorship. In my opinion, even though it is not a legal fact, obscenity is a lot like censorship.

Obscenity law is an idea; it can mean anything to any number of people. It is designed for that purpose; it is recognized as that. That means it is extremely subject to abuse. It is a criminal law. It puts power in the hands of the state to decide what can be written, read and seen, on the basis of what the state thinks is good for people. What I think it actually does is make those decisions on the basis of what particular people wielding the power of the state at that time think is good for the maintenance of male dominance.

Our law on the other hand is a civil law. It is concrete. It describes a thing, it doesn't describe an idea, it describes an actual practice in the world. And it is only actionable through activity. It isn't actionable through its mere existence. It's only actionable through the practices, the doing of the coercion, the doing of the force, the doing of the assault, and the doing of the trafficking. We didn't just have an idea. It is making, selling, distributing and exhibiting. Those are things you do, they're actions.

The First Amendment makes exceptions now for a lot of things that are seen as causing harm. It makes exceptions for its otherwise clear prohibition on laws that restrict speech.

It makes exceptions for libel in which the words are understood as the injury. The words hurt someone. Even though they are words you can make a law against them so the person who is hurt can do something about them, stop them, get damages for them. And it doesn't violate the First Amendment.

There are laws against obscenity. The Supreme Court designed the law against obscenity. They said obscenity was not speech. That's how they made it consistent with the First Amendment. It has escaped the notice of few that obscenity is words and pictures like other words and pictures. What the Supreme Court seemed to understand—and I think it's the one thing they understood and got straight on obscenity—is that when they looked at this stuff they saw that it did something. It isn't just *about* something.

Anyone who's ever heard Andrea Dworkin speak, for instance, should understand that speech *does* something.

Similarly there is an exception under the First Amendment for child pornography. It's a recent one. The Supreme Court has recognized that child pornography, although not obscene, can be banned.

Our law is not a ban in the sense that what a ban means is a criminal law that is passed on a certain day, after which everything that it covers is illegal. A ban allows things like cops going in and sweeping things off shelves.

When people tell you our law is a ban they are saying *relief* for the proven violation of the civil rights of women as a group is a "ban." We "ban" segregation, which is to say there's a law that says you've done it and you can't do it anymore.

A TOOL FOR CHANGE

I don't understand all the whys of pornography, like why there have to be a million more pictures. When there are already millions, why do they need more and more and more of it? I don't know. But I do know pornography tells me why it is that someone who was born not enjoying my pain can become someone who does.

It is because he is told that is what a man is, that is what a man is entitled to, that is what masculinity means. When you get an erection from it, it means you want to go do it to a real one. It's a systematic conditioning process where men's deepest pleasures are being conditioned to our violation. So when we are violated in the world it is no longer something for which we have no explanation. You can't just say pornography is this mirror anymore, that it just reflects what is already there.

I think the ordinance is something that organizes women. It changes women, including women who always thought sex discrimination meant nothing other than some young educated woman's right to go have a job like a man. It's moving women. As segregation was found to be the engine of the definition of black people as different and therefore inferior, pornography is the dynamic of sexism that defines us as different and therefore inferior, that makes discrimination sexy. The ordinance is a tool for change.

A Homophobia Workshop

FROM *Off Our Backs* 14:1 (January 1984): 12–14

The following workshop was developed by Suzanne Pharr, the Lesbian Task Force of the National Coalition Against Domestic Violence, and many good women, all of whom are much more than friends. . . .

PHOBIA

Phobia, from the Greek, means fear, dread, hatred; and for our purposes when we talk about homophobia, we are talking about that particular blend of all of these things that works to keep homosexuals as a hidden (closeted) underclass of society, discriminated against, treated as deviants, sinners, maliciously perverted, sick and abnormal.

From those who hate us most, we receive the messages that we should be cured or killed; from those who are liberal and tolerant, we receive the messages that we must be quiet and invisible.

This workshop is designed for use with the second group, those people who do not call for our physical deaths but kill us bit by bit with their demands for our invisibility, for our public denial of who we are and how we live.

It is they who accept our outstanding work for social change in organizations for women, for peace, for the environment, within organizations for social workers, teachers, psychologists, and then tell us in return that they do not want our visible presence, especially when we organize to work against our own lesbian oppression, because they say that our lesbian visibility will hurt the organization's funding, credibility, and effectiveness in the community it serves.

For us as lesbian/feminists, such attitudes have been the source of much pain and confusion and anger. Clearly, it has been sometimes easier for us to

Reprinted by permission of the author, Suzanne Pharr.

take the brutality of the greater world than the subtle oppression of non-lesbian feminists, well-meaning in their sincerity when they say to us that we must consider the greater good, that the particular social change project, so endangered anyway, must be saved above all else.

These are the women we love as sisters, these are the social change projects *we* helped create, that we bravely led, these are the only places where we thought there was a chance for us to flourish and grow, uncloseted and visible, and supported by loving women struggling for the transformation of the world.

So, this workshop is for those people who say to us, "We don't see why you would want to endanger our work with your need to be so obvious. It's only a bedroom issue, and we don't care who you sleep with. All we ask is that you be discreet."

And our answer is this: WHAT YOU SEE AS ONLY A BEDROOM ISSUE IS ALL OF OUR LIVES, WHO WE ARE, AND WHAT WE LIVE AND DIE BY, AND WE CANNOT LIVE WITHOUT OUR LIVES.

The Lesbian Task Force of the National Coalition Against Domestic Violence has felt a need for a homophobia workshop that could be used to address the homophobia in battered women's projects—among staff, volunteers, battered women, boards—and state coalitions and feminist organizations.

Over and over we have heard stories from lesbians working in these organizations who were forced, upon loss of job, to be completely closeted, or, at best, so discreet about their lives that at every moment some decision had to be made about how much of one's real life could be shown.

Also there were stories of discrimination toward battered lesbians coming to shelter for safety and finding it was not a safe place for them.

Lesbians have told us stories of how their work is invalidated, of how they are kept from advancement, of the many, many subtleties of discrimination and oppression.

These are the stories of brave women who have stayed with their work, even when psychologically battered and unsupported, and these are the stories of lesbians who have been fired, usually for some smokescreen reason, and have grieved for the loss of their life's work. We honor these many women through this workshop.

The design of this workshop is drawn from the experiences of many women who have worked to eliminate homophobia in the workplace, in schools, in feminist organizations, and we are indebted to them for their work and great courage.

With some modifications, this workshop can be used for any group, though what is presented here is created mainly for the battered women's movement. It falls into two parts: the first is consciousness-raising about what it feels like, what it means to be a lesbian, and what forms discrimination takes; the second is more specific, seeking strategies for dealing with homophobia within the workplace or organization. Ideally, an entire day is necessary for the workshop; however, it can be squeezed into 2½ or 3 hours.

One final note: this workshop deals primarily with homophobia as it affects lesbians and our lives; it does not treat the subject of gay men. This is a conscious choice on my part, for I feel that even though we share some common problems, nevertheless there are great differences, and for the sake of clarity as well as politics, the focus in this instance should be kept on lesbians.

PART ONE

I. The Power/Privilege Chart
It is important to begin with a discussion of how oppressions are connected, of how homophobia is not isolated in its development, and of how similar it is to other forms of oppression. I usually begin with this chart on a blackboard:

Power/Privilege The Norm	The Unempowered The Other
Men	Women
Rich	Poor
White	People of Color
Christian	Jews, Moslems, Atheists, all others
Heterosexual	Homosexual
Temporarily able-bodied	Differently abled
Young	Long-lived
Traditionally educated	Self-educated
Owners, managers	Workers
Adults	Children

This chart can be used in many ways to show how those in the left-hand column hold power or dominance over those in the right-hand side. For instance:

1. Those who are considered the Norm set the standards, make the rules, written and unwritten, which control the life of the Other. Those who clearly belong to the Norm consider themselves right, and this rightness, this privilege gives them another right: to control the other.

2. Those who have power enforce these rules and standards with economics, morals, laws, and always in the end, violence.

3. The Other is mysterious, unknown, lumped into groups and controlled by stereotyping: "All women are emotional. . . . Blacks like to live with their own. . . . Jews are always top in their class."

4. The Other, in many cases, is said to have the power to corrupt the Norm: Women are seductive, people of color are dirty and carry diseases,

homosexuals recruit children, the poor are draining the country's financial resources. Lies and myths are created to justify the actions necessary to protect the Norm.

5. There are more people who belong (globally) to the Other than to the Norm. It is clear that identification with each other and coalition among members of the Other would change the balance of power/privilege distribution. It is for that reason that it is so much in the interest of those who have power to control those who do not.

6. And finally, those who are in the lefthand column rarely, if ever, willingly yield up power to those on the righthand side. Power and rights have to be won or taken. For instance, very few people were concerned about the differently abled in this country, about how people in wheelchairs could not enter public buildings, go to public schools, or use public bathrooms, until a strong coalition was built and legislators got the experience of spending a day strapped to their wheelchairs. White people felt little concern about the lack of civil rights of Blacks until people bonded together to form a movement and, among other things, whites felt the potential economic impact.

Others participating in the workshop will draw many more ideas from this chart, and they may add other categories of power and dominance.

II. Names
Ask the group to give all the names they have ever heard homosexuals called, and list them for the group to see. This is a good ice-breaker, for it gives people a chance to say the unspeakable, and to get out some of their homophobia in an acceptable way. There is usually a sense of the ridiculous and lots of laughter. This is also a time that names gay men are called can be included and general homophobia discussed. Here are some of the names people may give:

Butch	Femme	Amazon
Dyke	Diesel-Dyke	Sissy
Faggot	Bulldagger	Fairy
Queer	Pervert	Witch
Man-Hater	Feminist	

A short discussion is sufficient here. Take a couple of the terms and talk about them; for example, show how so many terms describe not being the Norm (queer, pervert) or not fitting into a role (butch, sissy, fairy, Amazon, diesel-dyke). Hold a short discussion of how roles (masculine and feminine) are used to control. And finally, point out how some of the words (faggot, witch) keep alive our memories of one of the ultimate means of control: the burning of people who are different—faggots and witches at the stake,

Jews in concentration camp ovens, Blacks in their homes with crosses ablaze outside. The words are used to remind us what will happen to us if we step out of line, if we are too vocal, if we demand our rights, if we forget to be quiet, to pass, to be invisible.

III. Myths and Stereotypes

Ask the groups to give all the myths and stereotypes they have heard about lesbians. Here are a few:

Lesbians look like men.
They all play softball.
Lesbians seduce children.
All they need is a good lay.
All lesbians are either butch or femme.
Lesbians want to do men's jobs.
Women become lesbians because they have had bad experiences with men.
Lesbians have had bad childhood experiences with their fathers.
Lesbians have had bad childhood experiences with their mothers.
Lesbians want other people's children because they can't have any of their
   own.
Lesbians socialize only in dark and dirty bars.
All lesbians are alcoholics.
Lesbians hate themselves.
All lesbians are strong and powerful.

You will get a long working list of these. I choose only a few of my favorites to talk about, usually beginning with "Lesbians seduce children," because this gives me an opportunity to get into a discussion of violence against women and children right away. First, ask the group who it is in the majority of cases who abuses children. Ask them to raise their hands if they have ever personally known a lesbian who assaulted a child in school. Ask them if they ever knew a man who did this. Who created this myth about homosexuals when the great majority of all child sexual abuse is done by heterosexual men? And for what purpose was the myth created? (It is diversionary and helps protect the true abusers.) Make a strong statement here about the abuse of children—that we in the movement to end violence against women and children do not believe in the sexual abuse of children by *anyone.*

Next I go on to talk about "Lesbians want to do men's jobs" and once again point out that homophobia is not a system of discrimination created to control just lesbians but *all* women. Why are we in our organizations supposed to be so terrorized when someone says, "All of you working there are just a bunch of lesbians?" Why are we told it isn't "womanly" to do non-traditional jobs that pay higher salaries?

And finally, to end on a light note: "Women become lesbians because they have had bad experiences with men." To which I say, if that were the case, then all women would be lesbians.

IV. Invisibility Role Play

Ask for one brave woman who clearly defines herself as a nonlesbian to do this one; if you can't get a volunteer, ask the entire group to imagine along with you and then discuss it afterwards. Here is the situation: Imagine that you as a non-lesbian are part of a group that is only 10% of the population and you are heterosexual; nonlesbian activity is illegal, and your lifestyle must be kept hidden from the public lest it reveal your sexual proclivity.

Assume now that a family holiday such as Christmas has just finished, and I, your lesbian supervisor at work, ask you casually (for it means little to me) what you did over the holidays. How will you, the non-lesbian, describe the events of the holidays without giving me any clues that you spent any part in intimate ways with members (non-related by blood, that is) of the opposite sex, and how will you keep me from knowing that you did anything connected with heterosexual institutions, rules, traditions? Will you change pronouns? Will you lie by omission? And how will you feel about yourself?

And now, in this switched-about world, I decide to give a January party for the office crew and ask all of you to bring your partners. Will you dare to bring the man you have lived secretly with for the past five years, thereby letting us all suspect/know you are abnormal, sick, illegal? And if you don't, what will you tell him as you leave him home and go out as this pretended single woman that the world takes you to be? And what will you tell him when you get home at night? Once at the party, will you speak to other suspected non-lesbians or will you be afraid that being friendly with them might make people suspect you? And what will you do when I, your host, turn down the lights and put on slow-dance music—who will you dance with? And by what signals will you recognize the other non-lesbians there? Will you ask one of them to dance? Will that be too dangerous?

And when your male partner of five years, with whom you have no legal ties because there are none available to you, gets sick and goes to the hospital, how will you get to see him, how will you deal with his family that has all rights sanctioned by law, how will you keep from exposing yourself in your love for him? And when he dies in that hospital and you have no right to the body, to burial, to recognition of your relationship, to public grief or support, what will you do? Where will you turn?

This role-play can be taken along many lines. I recommend that you be fairly relentless with it, pushing it until everyone in the room *feels* what it means to be so in fear of the loss of one's job, one's children, one's church, one's community, that a lesbian would feel forced to live a double life, to change the gender pronouns, to lie about her life outside work, to keep quiet about her feelings (even when in excruciating pain about the loss/ death of a partner). Push it until everyone understands the stress that lesbians live with every minute if they are closeted at all, the stress that their relationships suffer because of closeting and the absence of societal sanctions, the terrible struggle with integrity at every turn. Help non-lesbians to understand that when a lesbian is suffering from homophobic oppression and has to choose partial or complete invisibility, she feels like a six-foot person forced to walk around in a room with a five foot ceiling.

It is absolutely essential that participants understand why so many lesbians choose invisibility as their only means of survival, even though we all know that invisibility keeps us divided from each other and unable to speak against our own oppression and keeps us from having support of sympathetic non-lesbians. At a workshop in Pennsylvania, a non-lesbian was having trouble seeing why our sexual preference was more than a bedroom issue, why it was so dangerous, and a very fine and brave woman whom everyone had thought to be a non-lesbian for years came out and said, "Because when I tell you that I am a lesbian, as I do at this moment, I give you the power to destroy my life."

PART TWO

I. How Lesbians Are Battered Women/Why Lesbians Are in the Battered Women's Movement

It is at this point that the connection between battering, rape, incest, and homophobia is to be made. Each of these is a violence against women, each is about power over women, and each is about *controlling* women. Each is not so much related to sexuality as to the use of power and control. As Bernice Reagon once said, we women all remember somewhere in our cells what happened to us in former days when we stepped out of line—we were burned as witches—and for that reason many women are afraid to show strength and independence today. Instead of burning, today our activity, strength, and independence are kept limited by violence and the threat of violence. Lesbians are committed to work to end violence in the lives of women because we understand these connections and suffer from all of these forms of control.

Some similarities between lesbians and battered women are that: 1) lesbians, like battered women, risk loss of community if they tell their experiences; 2) they risk the loss of their children; 3) they are kept isolated and silenced; 4) they are frequently blamed for their experiences and told if they would only change, then they would be accepted; 5) they are very often emotionally battered; 6) they are sometimes physically battered.

II. Lesbian Baiting

Lesbian baiting is a conscious action, often subtle, to get lesbians out of organizations and to control the work of women. It can take the form of firing lesbians outright on trumped-up charges, of threatening lesbians about the damage their visibility is causing the organization, and of generally making lesbians' worklives miserable by coolness, indifference, lack of support, exclusion, low pay, few rewards, no advancement. Lesbian-baiting from women from within an organization usually comes from fear. When lesbian baiting comes from outside—"we can't in good faith refer clients to you anymore because we know that there are lesbians on your staff"—it is a way of controlling all women, women's expression and freedom. Please tell me how any women anywhere can ever prove she is *not* a lesbian? And to what extremes does she have to go in the attempt to prove her acceptability in a male-defined world? When non-lesbian staff are confronted, they almost always speak of the good of the organization, or the best of them simply say they don't know what to do to protect both the lesbians and the organization. The problem-solving and strategy sessions are designed to help those who mean well and just don't know what to do.

III. Problem Solving
Break the large group up into small groups (6–8 people each) and give them one of these problems (written on a piece of paper) to talk about and solve together. Allow at least 15–20 minutes, and then have each group report back to the large group.
Examples:

1. You overhear two kids calling each other "Queer" and "Faggot" in the shelter. What do you as a staff person do?

2. Before the group starts, a resident tells a queer joke, and most of the women laugh. You, however, know there is a closeted lesbian in the group. What do you do?

3. A battered woman in the shelter suspects that a staff member is a lesbian and goes to the director, saying she won't stay in the same shelter with a lesbian. How do you as director handle this?

4. Your child advocate is a lesbian. Two mothers come to you and say they don't want this woman touching their children. What do you do?

5. Someone from your primary referral group calls and says he doesn't feel he can refer any more women to the shelter because it is common knowledge around town that the shelter has lesbians on the staff. What do you as a director do?

6. A lesbian separates from her lover of eight years and is despondent and distracted for weeks. Her distress is evident to everyone in the shelter. How do you deal with this with everyone in the shelter? How do you support her?

IV. Strategies
For this session it is helpful to do brainstorming with the entire group. Deal with each essential category: battered women in shelter, staff, volunteers, board, funders, community. Get people to seek realistic measures and to begin with small, realizable steps. For example, a seemingly small step is to begin with using the word *lesbian* easily and effortlessly in talks with different groups. For instance, in a talk with the board or funders, include les-

bians in the list of women you serve and hire, along with older women and women of color, etc. The reason for this small step is to rob the word of its potency. If everyone in the organization is afraid to use the word lesbian and if it isn't spoken, then it holds a terrible power. Put it out in the public into common acceptance, both in talks and written work. Then the organization will be in a less defensive place when the word lesbian is used negatively against it. Many other strategies will come from the group, but keep each concrete and reality-based.

V. Non-Lesbian Support of Lesbians

Divide into small groups again and discuss concrete ways non-lesbians can support and do anti-homophobic work. Allow 20–30 minutes, and then report back to the large group. (Important note: in this session, and throughout the workshop, it is important not to expose invisible lesbians in the group. Be sensitive to this, and also seek ways to validate them and their work by talking about the examples of fine lesbian leadership in social change work, in women's publications and music, the poetry of Adrienne Rich and Audre Lorde, etc. The very fact that an out lesbian is leading this workshop and that the subject of homophobia is being discussed will be validation in itself.)

And finally: this workshop is only a beginning, a piece of work waiting to be changed and improved upon, for that is the way the world is transformed, piece by piece, improvement by improvement. Its goal is to provide enough information for people to *begin* a dialogue about lesbian existence and lesbian issues in the movement. It recognizes that it is a hard, slow and often painful journey for human rights, but that if we are to work for women, then we must recognize the importance of lesbian existence and the interconnectedness of our lives, our work, and our freedom.

Pornography and the Doubleness of Sex for Women

by Joanna Russ

FROM *13th Moon: A Feminist Literary Magazine* 8 : 1/2 (1984):
19–30

Remember Uncle Max? Every woman I know has an Uncle Max. Say you're fourteen, at a family Passover celebration in a room so crowded that changing seats is almost impossible, and Uncle Max (who's your great-uncle, really, in his sixties) has suddenly begun telling you how much he loves you (he's never had two words for you before), how wonderful you are, how you're his favorite niece, and meanwhile he keeps kissing you sloppily on the cheek (or the mouth) and holding the back of your neck with one hand while he strokes your forearm with the other. You manage to get up and make your way to the kitchen, where you indignantly tell your mother what's happened and she says, looking past you with unfocused eyes, "I'm sure you must be mistaken, dear." You (angrily): I'm fourteen, not a baby, and I know what's happening, &c.

Mother: Well, I'm sure it's only your imagination, but if it bothers you, just sit somewhere else.

Once I had remembered Uncle Max (he came up in a discussion between me and a friend in which we finally realized we were talking past each other) all sorts of memories began to come back, like the fifteen-year-old male stranger at a party when I was twelve who had grabbed my wrist hard

Reprinted by permission of *13th Moon*.

enough to leave bruises, dragged me to a couch, and sat there kissing me while his fingers dug into my flesh, like the boy (he must have been four-teen) who said to twelve-year-old me in high school, "Hey, baby, your pants are showing," like my mother's telling me in a strangely embarrassed voice when I was going to summer camp, "Remember, boys can't get pregnant." Or my friend's mother who, upon hearing on the radio that a woman had been beaten up in the subway at three a.m., said, "No decent woman would be out there alone at that hour."

Are there more? Oh, yes, lots more, from the constant obbligato of Don't go out alone after dark, Don't go into "bad" parts of town, Don't let boys go too far, Don't get "in trouble," Don't "get caught," Don't ever visit a boy's apartment, Don't stay out after midnight, Don't go to a local doctor for con-traception or you'll be expelled (this was in college), to another male fifteen-year-old who at camp said as he passed the counselors' bungalows, "Meno-pause Alley," to the girl friends who kept worrying aloud if "he" would re-spect them if they went "all the way" and the friend with whom I conducted a little theater in our twenties who came out of the women's room saying in tones of intense relief, "Thank God it's come." When I was twelve or thir-teen at my parents' New Year's Eve party I was pulled out on the living-room floor by our family dentist, to dance. Mind you, *nobody* likes a dentist, but this one (a friend of the family) never completed a filling in less than an hour, and didn't ever let me know about novocaine. (I was sixteen before I found out that there was such a thing as local anaesthesia.) This was the detestable, incompetent boob who insisted on dancing with me. I hated it and I hated him so I shrunk away. He pulled me ostentatiously close and grinned.

And everybody laughed.

My mother laughed. My father laughed. The guests laughed. And in my head a voice said: *Come on now, this isn't serious, you're oversensitive; after all, he didn't rape you, did he? It's all in fun. Don't be a prude* (and so on).

I hear this voice still. I suspect most women do. It chided me in college when I was facing the conflict between being an artist and being a woman, when the choices presented to me and my friends were: 1) Marry so you can have sex in safety, and thereby prove your inferiority and vulnerability; 2) stay celibate and go crazy (it was an article of faith then that all spinsters were "sexually repressed" and therefore diseased); 3) have sex outside mar-riage and die of an illegal abortion, or 4) become a lesbian—a state so un-thinkable and unspeakable, so utterly absent from anyone's view of reality that it probably didn't exist—but was, of course, unutterably criminal, in-sane and destructive at the same time.

Shall I go on? Shall I mention the movies and plays in which "non-sexy" women were ridiculed? Or the ones in which ultra-"sexy" Marilyn Monroe was ridiculed? (My, some folks are hard to please!) Or what Erica Jong calls the King Kong school of art? As late as the mid-seventies a young male poet swaggered on the stage at a university where I taught, and prefaced his first poem by grinning and saying, "Women don't like this one." Earlier, in the late sixties, at the same institution, poetry readings inevitably included hairy young men who exclaimed, "Fuck you, America! I want to ram my cock up your asshole!" At which several women students whom I had carefully encouraged to attend, got up and left, surmising quite correctly that their own poetry—and their presences—were not welcome.

I remember a discussion in the mid-seventies in which all the group (including me) said that their parents had been liberal and honest about sex, whereupon the group leader said, "Did they ever tell you about your clitoris?" and we all looked at one another and were struck dumb. A close friend of mine was dragged (at age eleven) into the boys' bathroom by a group of boys; they handled her breasts, and when she started to cry, they told her she had to like it because she had big boobs and women with big boobs "liked it." And there were the exquisitely sensitive young men of my teens, artists all, who chided us young women for not being free, beautiful, and spontaneous, by which they meant putting out for them—this in an era when abortion was illegal!—and one who said to me scornfully only a few years ago when I asked for his company to the subway (in New York), at 2 a.m., "I didn't think you were like all those *other* women."

If I stop now, don't believe there isn't more. There's much more, like the psychoanalyst of my twenties telling a woman who had almost been raped, "But you must have known there was something wrong with him. Why did you want to punish yourself?" (This was a woman who'd attended the singles dance, where she met this man, at the psychoanalyst's express suggestion.)

If I cite so much from my own life, it's because my life has been in no way exceptionally or spectacularly bad. I wasn't battered as a child, wasn't raped by father, stepfather, or mother's boyfriend, didn't have an illegal abortion, didn't run away from home to find that the only way I could keep eating was street hustling, didn't get pregnant while unmarried (or while married either) and never went through the pressures of outright rebellion against gender norms. I wasn't seduced or abandoned or beaten up, and I wasn't even caught masturbating—except once, come to think of it, when my parents told me I might "hurt myself" (I knew this was a lie)—and oh yes, they caught me playing doctor with friends at the age of five and solemnly gave me the same warning. And my word, I've forgotten the psychoanalyst I saw in my twenties (for symptoms of a chronic physical disease which was diagnosed fifteen years later) who told me that I envied the male penis. (I was willing to believe this, but hadn't the faintest notion of what to do about it.)

Perhaps the worst thing about our sexual training as women (if I've been citing heterosexual incidents it's because the vast majority of women, lesbian or not, are brought up in heterosexual families and learn their lessons about sex from heterosexual standards and situations) is the enormous social pressure not to see or name the kinds of incidents I've been describing: To view them as trivial, to discount them, to accept them "tolerantly," to pretend to enjoy them or find them funny or simply to deny that they exist or existed or, worst of all, to deny that they are painful and out of our control.

Take a woman raised like this (and we are all raised like this, more or less) and expose her to arguments about "sexual liberation" and her response is likely to be that men are taking too many liberties with women as it is. What I need (she is likely to say) is safety and respect, not any more "liberation." Expose such a woman to pictures of women meant to turn men on, and she will—quite simply—become enraged. Show her *anything* designed to titillate men sexually, whether violent or not, and you will rouse the envy and rage of a whole lifetime—and it *is* utterly enraging, although the envy is not at all the envy of concrete sexual acts. Rather it's the envy of men's freedom, the envy of those who've been battered into choicelessness and silence for those who are entitled to speak and make choices.

Sexuality for men (including gay men, as far as I can see) is by and large a realm of free choice, limited to be sure by practical considerations, but not limited by the very fact of being male. Men are "entitled" to sex.

Sexuality for women is a realm of helplessness and unpleasantness, in which bad and painful things are done to you that you can't control, in which you must "go along" with male behavior even when you dislike it, in which you are not entitled to your own wishes and your own enjoyment, and haven't even the privilege of seeing or naming the above facts. In the light of this truth, the anti-pornography movement is not only understandable; it's absolutely necessary. A society that claims that women's real trouble is "sexual repression" (whatever that is) badly needs to be enlightened. We aren't sexually repressed; we've been sexually battered and sexually brutalized. It's about time this particular vileness were exposed for what it is, once and for all.

But that's not the whole truth.

I also remember passionate "friendships" with girls and women, especially the friend who wanted me to kiss her and hold her. I remember necking in the front seat of a car at sixteen with a young man I'd lusted after for weeks, and being gloriously, sexually high for days. I remember endless crushes on movie stars, mostly male. I remember (with enormous pleasure) Mae West's *She Done Him Wrong*, and some blazingly incandescent experiments with masturbation in my twenties. I remember coming out of a Gay Liberation Front lecture at thirty-three into the most luminously beautiful June twilight I've ever seen, and saying to myself over and over that lesbianism was real, that people really did it, and that I wasn't the only one and I hadn't invented it. I remember desire so pure and intense that it was almost enough just to feel it. I remember touching the delicate and precise helmet of bone under a beloved's fair, fluffy hair. I remember a New Year's

Eve party where grown-up women went about playing wonderful kissing games, like kids. I remember, years later, another car (cars seem to be some kind of adolescent American theme) and a curly-haired young man with a delicious amber moustache.

I think that for most women sexuality is inescapably double. Even women whose sexual education has been horrendous (for example, those who are raped repeatedly by an adult male relative) have also to deal with some positive feeling, much of it sexual; even women whose experiences have been much more positive than they were typical cannot entirely escape this culture's negatives. I suspect that even lesbians who've never had so much as a heterosexual thought must still deal in some fashion with the tangled mess sexism makes of sex.[1] Not to mention the male side of this equation, that is, the glamorization of male power and violence and the sentimentality about women and "family" which is the obverse of the violence. Sex is ecstatic, autonomous, and lovely for women. Sex is violent, dangerous, and unpleasant for women. I don't mean a dichotomy (i.e. two kinds of women or even two kinds of sex) but rather a continuum in which no one's experience is wholly positive or negative, and to which different women will give very different weightings.

I think this doubleness of experience may explain the bitterness of the fight against pornography (to which I've contributed as much as anyone, I'm afraid) and the phenomenon of the sides being so very horrified by each other because they are perpetually talking past each other. When A attacks violence and B hears her attacking sexual freedom, B will defend sexual freedom—and A will hear her defending violence. You see how it goes, round and round and louder each time, though A doesn't intend to attack sexual freedom *per se*, and B doesn't mean to defend violence.

I think a woman's position on this continuum (which can change even from week to week) will determine on which side of the pornography issue she finds herself. The more your life has had to do with the violence and cruelty of (male) sexuality, the more salient these are to you, the more you will attack (male) sexuality as violent, callous, and cruel. And you will be perfectly correct. The more your life has had to do with the autonomy and joy of sexual expression, whether you have had to work your way through to this joy or not, the more sensitive you will be to issues of sexual suppression, and the more you will tend to defend sexuality *per se* as a valuable good. And you will be perfectly correct.

To make the whole business even worse, on the anti side there's not only sensitivity to the violence of patriarchal sex, but also *some* women who perceive any kind of open expression of sex as dangerous and brutal. And the other side has *some* women who perceive sexual expression as so important and valuable that any kind of sexual expression, no matter what it is, is fine. There are, indeed, *some* women who do get off on power, *some* who proselytize. (I suspect that they've simply felt really sexual for the first time in their lives, and are treating sexual pleasure as their own exclusive property.)

I am now more sensitive to the issue of sexual repression than I was five years ago, when I was more sensitive to the issue of sexual dangers and pains; *therefore* I've been perceiving the opposite side as inexplicably crazy. No doubt they've perceived me the same way. We're both right—not about the craziness, I mean, but about sex. It is inescapably double. Depending on the kind of attention we pay to it (which may even vary from day to day or mood to mood) we will stress one side or the other—and mishear our opposite numbers on the other side. Each will perceive the other as having gone mad and we'll end up with just what's been going on for the past few years, with me passionately denouncing Andrea Dworkin, for example (for which I'm very sorry and wish to apologize publicly), and Robin Morgan, in her new book, not only denouncing Pat Califia (which I rather expected, considering the whole mess-up that's been going on) but also wasting invective on Deirdre English, of all people! I suspect that Morgan has gotten her information second hand (she cites the sloppy and sensational *San Francisco Chronicle* for some important figures and ignores *For Her Own Good*, a fine piece of work by Deirdre English and Barbara Ehrenreich) or is simply so caught up in the whole mishearing, misperceiving mess that she's as bitter and quick to denounce as everyone else. Something of the same kind happens when an anti-porn activist describes with horror the photograph of a woman in a sex magazine who's lying on her back with her knees up and spread and is spreading her labia apart with her fingers. I have heard this position called degrading and humiliating, though as far as I can see the position indicates only that the woman wants to be penetrated, which certainly isn't in itself degrading or humiliating. And yet in the context of the whole sexist treatment of women by men, the picture is another assertion of men's property in women and men's control over women.

Meanwhile, I hear that in this city, some woman tried fist-fucking another and caused permanent physical damage, hospitalization, and surgery in her victim. But what about a friend of mine who did S&M (she's a very good person) who described it to me as mostly play-acting? The fantasies involved were fantasies of violence, true, but nobody she knew wanted anything like that to happen in reality. And surely there's nothing wrong with that—except that fantasies like those, acted out by men *and sold to the public as depictions of reality*, are among the things that create a cultural atmosphere in which rape and property in women are seen by men as "glamorous" and promoted as "natural."

Is there any way of establishing that we are not at each others' throats? That what's driving us all crazy is that women's experience of sexuality under sexism is inescapably double? I think only c.r. groups have a chance of succeeding in this matter and then only if the groups absolutely outlaw statements about women in general and any judgment of particular women's practices and everybody's political positions about everything. We must start with our own experiences—not judgments or opinions—and then we may have a chance of undoing the wickedness done to us by this violent and anti-sexual society. The con game that's been practiced on all of us has been the equation of sex with violence, as if we have to choose between being sexual and victims of violence on the one hand or no-violence-therefore-no-sex on the other. If we detest the violence inherent in our sexual experiences in the world as it is, the culture gives us to understand that we are denying sexuality itself; if we choose the positive good of sexuality itself (and I certainly believe that sexual expression is *per se* a very valuable and important thing) the culture then insists that we must also choose violence. If some of us go a little gaga and talk as if any exhibition of sexuality (especially male sexuality) were humiliating and coercive, it's no wonder. Meanwhile others of us are going out of our gourds in the other direction, insisting that even obviously hostile books and pictures are redeemed because they have sex in them at all.

Trouble is, we're both right—and both wrong.

Meanwhile, nobody has bothered to define pornography or S&M or even prostitution (sometimes) in any precise and objective manner, so that we can begin to talk about them in a reasonably analytical and nonjudgmental way. After all, before you can judge something as good or bad, you do have to know what it is. And we need to stop calling "obscene" anything we don't like. We also need, I think, to find out a lot more about prostitutes and the only way to do this is to talk to the prostitutes themselves. (An early conference on prostitution, I am told, was an embarrassing flop precisely because this wasn't done.) I also think—and here I do disagree with a good many women—that psychoanalyzing somebody else's experience or fantasies (especially without listening to their account of it) is necessarily ineffective, however passionately you may feel about the subject. The only people capable of analyzing what fantasies really mean are those to whom the fantasies appeal.[2] I have heard feminists explain the horrible psychic depths of S&M'ers to me and S&M'ers describe with relish the twisted puritanism of anybody who doesn't like them. This is very much like hearing monogamists decry the revoltingly neurotic motivations and moral degradation of the promiscuous—not that they know anyone like that, of course, nor have they—Heaven forbid!—been promiscuous themselves. And so on and so on. Is it necessary to point out that these "explanations" and "analyses" are worth exactly zero? They are passionate self-defenses, not analyses of phenomena or people. In the first issue of *Trivia: a Journal of Ideas*, in an essay called "Sadomasochism," Kathleen Barry states that condemnation of the feminist anti-pornography movement "can threaten the very existence of feminism" and that when Gayle Rubin (in *Coming to Power*) asks for a repeal of all sex laws "except those dealing with actual, not statutory, coercion" what she really means is that threats of death are not coercion. Clearly, we are talking past each other!

When c.r. groups first formed, what we brought to them were those areas in which we felt most crazy, most weak, most wrong, most defeated. I believe that knowledge of our real sexual histories (that is, not our political opinions) may be similarly difficult to feel and express. Such a task, considering our own tangled feelings and the inescapable contradictions built into female sexual experience by this culture, demands an honesty that will, at times, produce intense shame and (I would expect) feelings of defeat and self-condemnation. These must be listened to, not short-circuited by shoulds and oughts. What we need is the gritty reality of what we really feel, what we really want (however "disgusting" or "wrong" it seems to be) or how "anti-feminist." These feelings are very painful.

They are also messages.

Before we can know what something means, we must allow it to enter consciousness in full force. Is horror at something "fear swollen by a hidden wish" (as one psychologist, writing about something completely different, once said)? Is bravado merely hiding self-hatred? And so on.

I hope I won't be misunderstood here to be saying that our troubles with sexuality are "merely psychological" or due to our training in the past but not to constant pressures today. Any message our sexuality or feelings about it gives us is bound to be about us *and* our society; if there's any piece of crucial feminist knowledge, this is it.

If only we can do this, what an enormous gain it will be for the whole women's movement! I think we all feel right now that sexuality is a crucial issue for feminism—nobody would be so upset if it weren't. I don't think we'll be in shape to take on sexuality as an issue without a lot of consciousness-raising about female sexuality and female sexual fantasy.

Even so, pornography seems to me a very tricky issue merely from the point of view of tactics, and we might do well to direct our anger elsewhere, at least for a while. Not only is feeling about this issue very divided in the women's community, it's an issue that is bound to be misperceived by the culture at large as anti-sexual no matter how many declarations we make to the contrary. *Some* women talk as if pornography were the one single cause, or the most important single cause, of misogyny in this society—and this is, I think, plainly untrue. (One limited issue after another has been proclaimed—by *some* feminists—to be "the" cause of patriarchy, a view that's ahistorical and much too simple. Something as longstanding as woman-hating can hardly be caused by a phenomenon so relatively new as pornography.) I've also heard—I may be wrong—that pornography is an issue which will enable us to reach right-wing women, an idea I find very self-destructively dramatic rather than politically practical. The right is organized and wealthy, remember, and far more apt to use us than vice versa.

And what good is it to reach women who disagree with *all* our other issues? Why the dickens are we not trying to reach the millions of women who are already inclined our way? I remember a c.r. group, the very young members of which spent an enormous amount of time and energy working with one battered woman, only to have her finally return to the man who battered her. Battering is, goodness knows, an emotionally gripping issue, but as Virginia Woolf says, a battle that wastes time and energy is as ill-advised as one that wastes lives.

And why, if what we're against is the glamorization of male violence, don't we direct our fire at Hollywood's ostensibly "realistic" depictions of life, like *Apocalypse Now* or *A Clockwork Orange*? Or those endless cop shows on TV? Or all those women so terrified on primetime TV because they are menaced by one man and need another man to protect them? Or the "family" shows which glorify traditional values (traditional ever since the 1950s) at the expense of our autonomy, humanness, and self-respect?

Surely this sort of stuff pollutes the cultural atmosphere far more than commercial fantasies made for male masturbation. Movies and TV affect many more people (like women and children) that specialized, commercial, male fuck-books or films don't reach. More than that, the pornography I've seen—I have fifteen S&M books in my closet at the moment—seems to be aimed at specific sub-groups of male buyers. (The books advertised on the backs of the books I have come in clusters, i.e., monks-and-nuns books, Nazi-slave books, teenage-girls'-school books, and so on. The settings seem to matter, though they are sketchily limp; the sex scenes are just about identical from book to book.) As for the men's magazines, surely heterosexual men's desire to look at women's bodies is in itself perfectly acceptable. What's not acceptable is that the images sold to men are plastic and unreal, and that such sale takes place as part of a deeply sex-hating and woman-hating society. But to attack pornography seems to be going in the wrong direction. Sexual fantasies—to judge from women's—don't make much sense if taken at face value. Moreover, those fifteen books (chosen by a friend of mine for the horribleness of their covers) are much more concerned with fucking than they are with violence. It's not pornography *but the mainstream culture* which delivers violence *as a substitute for sexual pleasure.* I think the mainstream culture is much more dangerous than specialized-for-sex stuff, which has at least gotten to a sort of halfway position on the matter. It's true that if the Holocaust is of personal importance to you, and you read, say, *Nazi Love-Slave*, and lend it your own reality, you will be disgusted and frightened. That doesn't mean that the book is the cause of woman-hating or even an important cause. I find many of the things we take for granted much, much worse—like the sentimentality of "Little House on the Prairie," the TV tape of which I would very much enjoy burning with my own hands.

Several essays on pornography have stressed that the Nazis used it to flood occupied countries in order to corrupt the population thereof, but the fact that they did it doesn't mean that it worked or that they knew what they were doing. They allowed no such stuff in Germany itself; instead, the kind of propaganda made for home consumption was very much like what we're getting now from the right: For women, motherhood and "femininity" glorified, and for German youth, in general, the Virgin Mary as an ideal. For young men the ideal was the fervent love of comrades (some of these artifacts look very homosexual today) along with rigid sexual purity. The classic union of sexual repression with violence can't occur in pornography, which has sexual expression as its raison d'etre; as far as my experience goes, it's in supposedly nonsexual material that the viciousness gets really bad. Nothing in *Hard Knocks for Honey* or *The Sadistic Sisters of Saxony* (honest, I'm not making up these titles) comes close in vividness, realism, or loving attention to detail of the commercial for Hitchcock's TV program which was made up of a montage of different women screaming in terror. I would not mind too much rereading the S&M titles (above) for the only hazard there is boredom, but I walked out of *A Clockwork Orange* a few years ago, shaking with anger, and would do so again.

That's the sort of stuff we should be attacking.

I've tried to find an inspirational ending to this essay and can't. The doubleness of sexuality will certainly continue. For years I hated myself for still having any affection for my father (who had become very ill when I was about eight, and used to assuage his own fear by bullying my mother, and, later, me). I thought I must be crazy to keep on feeling anything positive about someone who had so obviously hurt me. It took a long time to decide that I had not been defeated and that his misbehavior was far less humane than my continuing affection. When you live in a badly sexist world and continue to have some positive feelings for those who are oppressing you, it's all too easy to become horrified at yourself and try to wipe away all positive emotion towards the oppressors. Since that is not entirely possible, many of us are left with an entirely understandable terror at ever expressing these feelings—it feels like total defeat—and a lot of energy must be taken up denying that these positive feelings exist. I have even heard of rape victims who were aroused sexually by the situation of rape—mind you, this does not make rape less godawful; on the contrary, to my mind, such an impossible-to-deal-with contradiction makes the whole business infinitely more horrible.

Well, I am talking only about my own experience; this is the kind of thing I would say in a c.r. group. Double situations are not only painful but terribly confusing. If dancing with my dentist was sex, I certainly didn't want any; and yet—

Two other speculations: I don't think we should expect gay men's experience with pornography to be anything like ours. For many gay men, gay male pornography was the first (and sometimes the only) validation of their sexuality they could find. Nor—I'm convinced—is the issue of pedophilia identical with what little girls experience with adult men. For one thing, the major emphasis of this society is that women are passive or childlike with men. Contacts between adult males and boys are not harmonious with the major emphases of the society. Boys are brought up (once into adolescence) to be entitled to sexual feelings and experimentation as girls are not, and are therefore probably more capable (certainly in adolescence) of refusing and choosing sexually than girls are. (I'm not saying that this is the whole truth about male teenagers/adult male relationships, but that they are different from teenage female/adult male ones.[3])

How to stop Uncle Max? I think an anecdote a friend of mine told me lately is instructive. She has a fourteen-year-old son whose friends have taken to hanging around her house, in part because she's willing to give them straightforward information about sex and smoking and so on, and accepts the fact that they are sexually active without accepting dishonesty or coercion or manipulativeness as O.K. because "anything goes." Recently one of the girls, at the age of twelve, decided to have intercourse (for the first time) with her thirteen-year-old boyfriend. "She said that it hurt at first but after that she liked it a lot." This same little girl (she's under five feet tall) was recently grabbed from behind by a neighborhood rapist who'd already made attempts on two other pubescent girls. Lily (not her name) stamped backwards on the rapist's instep, crunching it heavily, and then screamed as she ran away. What was striking to both me and my friend was what Lily did *not* do: She didn't panic, wasn't helpless, and above all (says my friend) was enraged but without feeling the slightest guilt. When something like that happened to me at the same age, I felt that I must have invited it or colluded with it, or liked it somehow. I suspect that the two incidents are related and the more open and autonomously chosen sexual pleasure a woman has, the better she's equipped to deal with this culture's substitution of violence for sexuality and the sexual repression that makes such very bad things possible.

Perhaps a word about "sexual repression." As far as I know, the only radical male authority who does not think that anything goes in sex is Wilhelm Reich—one of those clunky Germans who know only one thing (but one good thing) and keep repeating it ad infinitum. When I speak—as Reich does—about sexual "liberation" I do not mean (as he didn't either) any kind of sexual outlet of any quality, and the only superiority of this to that being which one happens more often. What Reich (and I think very perceptively, for a man) understood was that when classic forms of sexual suppression—like the Nazis' in their own country—first begin to disappear, what you get is not freedom but a lot of very nasty behavior in which the preexisting violence begins to be visible, *along with* some genuinely progressive behavior and events. I don't know what Reich's opinion of S&M would be since he never mentions it. What he does call "sadism" is what we would call simply cruelty and viciousness—like (he says) getting a woman drunk so that she can't resist when several men fuck her, a practice that used to be common in college fraternities when I went to school twenty years ago, and may be still.

"Sexual liberation" does *not* mean, when I use the phrase, joylessness, furtiveness, compulsion, threats, or the kind of behavior Phyllis Chesler notes in *About Men* in which she asked men whether they enjoyed sex with women and got the answer, "I like orgasm, of course; who wouldn't?" This kind of partial and miserable activity is a sign of repression, not freedom. We are surrounded today by plastic images of "sexuality," of beautiful models with painted faces and blow-dried hair cavorting in stylized situations of glee, by endless stupid chatter about "sexiness" and "freedom," of endless exhortations that we must be (hetero) sexual—but with the partner of the right race and age and class and capped teeth and advertisers' clothing, and seminaked bodies shown in titillating poses without any (God forbid) real nudity or vulnerability or real touching. Anyone who thinks this society is anywhere near "sexual liberation" should try sitting in a bus with her hand on a friend's genitals, and watch the faces around her. Unfortunately we are caught today between two lies, not one: The still powerful beliefs of the right and the "you *must* be sexual and any way is O.K." which involves the utter unreality of, say, *Playboy* pictures—are women born airbrushed?—and any damned thing at all, from the pleasures of shared fantasy (which do promote intimacy) to the acting out of power fantasies *against* others.

And, just to make it even more confusing, sexual situations (as defined by the culture) and the contact of warm bodies does indeed rouse some minimal response—which explains the man in *About Men* who has to fantasize a baseball game to come to orgasm, and me and my dentist; I had responded, after all, and not knowing that this minimal, reluctant response, very much mixed with loathing, was not "sex"—how could I? I had no genuinely free sexual experiences to use as a comparison—believed that this sort of contact *was* "sex"—and I had somehow colluded in the whole business.

The best cure for pornography is sex—I mean autonomously chosen activity, freely engaged in for the sake of real pleasure, intense, and unmistakably the real thing. The more we have experiences like this, the less we will be taken in by the confusions and lies and messes all around us.

Sexuality is a personal issue for everyone, and an extremely painful one for many of us. Let me stress again that the early c.r. groups did not deal with the kind of things that made us feel strong and free. In fact, the strength and freedom came directly from expressing the things that made us feel hopeless and crazy.

Let us begin—please!

—January 1983

Notes

1. Women who've been exclusively lesbian from an early age probably face a different set of problems growing up. It would be interesting to know how much of the anti-pornography movement such women make up. My impression is that most of those active in the anti-pornography movement are either heterosexual or lesbian feminist—that is, women who have spent a good part of their lives as heterosexuals.

2. This doesn't mean that they inevitably will analyze them, or that their analyses will be accurate; it means only that they can know the context of such fantasies, and therefore have a chance of making a correct analysis.

3. I'm not talking about children.

Men Stopping Rape

FROM *M: Gentle Men for Gender Justice* 13 (Fall 1984): 46

Men Stopping Rape, formed last October, following Andrea Dworkin's speech in Minneapolis. Thousands of leaflets with the following informa- tion have been distributed to men in Madison. Comments are invited and permission to reprint is given.

Every day there are opportunities to interrupt the sexist behaviors, includ- ing our own, which support rape:

• Confront men who use sexist language or make "jokes" degrading women. (Much slang obviously gets used this way.)

• Challenge institutions that profit from sexist advertising, depicting women as willing victims of violence and promoting sexual objectification of women. (Boycott products using exploitative advertising and picket movies which, for example, depict women enjoying being raped.)

• Become familiar with the history of women so that you can better chal- lenge male supremacist beliefs about rape.

• Join with other men in helping you to develop an anti-sexist awareness. (For example, join a men's consciousness-raising group at your men's center, a Men Stopping Rape group or a man's childcare collective.)

• Stand up to other men about what rape really is (a criminal exercise of power over and control of another person, acted out through sexual viola- tion of another) and how they are supporting rapist energy by their behav- ior. Be prepared to lose their support by building new support networks for yourself (for example, at your men's center).

• Be aware of your own behavior which may be threatening to women. For

Reprinted by permission of Richard Cote, editor, and the journal, now titled *Changing Men*.

222 · *Freedom Is Not Slavery*

example, on a quiet street at night, instead of walking behind a woman, cross to the other side. When approaching a woman on the street, keep your hands visible. Walk so that women have a clear path. Be aware that every man is a potential rapist/killer to all women. Avoid fast sudden moves or jerky body movements.

• Be alert to signs of women (*and* men) who may be suffering physical or verbal assault. Notice acts of violence and be willing to confront potential rape scenes in any way you can. (Your noticing or involvement may give the woman time to escape if she's in danger. Do not expect her to trust you any more than her assailant.)

• Do not confuse friendliness with sexual invitation. ("No" means *no*, and if you are confused or think you are getting a "mixed message," it is your obligation to ask her.)

• Confront homophobia and explore male-male friendship. The more emotional and physical connections that a man develops with caring men friends, the less unwarranted pressure will fall on his relationships with women as his only emotional outlet.

• Confront the fear and hatred of that which is "female identified." For example, wearing clothes that are female-identified, e.g., a skirt, earrings, or carrying a purse, is one of the best ways to experience something of the objectification or assault that a woman is often subjected to.

• Support women's efforts to end sexual assault. For example, form or join a men's childcare collective to provide childcare and support services for "Take Back the Night" marches, battered women's shelters, rape crisis centers and women's community events.

• As men, demand better police action on rape. Demand police/court/public support for rape victims.

• Be willing to examine your male ego defensiveness when listening to the expression of feminist ideas and your resistance to change.

The statistics are grim. Every 18 seconds another woman is abused. Every 2 minutes another woman is raped. One out of three women will be sexually assaulted in her lifetime, with 75% of these attacks by someone she knows. One out of four women is sexually abused before she is 18 years old.

Women have ample reason to fear every strange (and many familiar) men they pass on the street—especially when it's dark, poorly lit, and there are few people around. We need to become aware of what women feel walking down the street or at home with us, and then act out of that knowledge to diminish their fears.

Thank you, Seattle Men Against Rape and Louisiana Sisters in Struggle for supplying most of the information on this sheet.—Men Stopping Rape, Box 305, 306 N. Brooks, Madison, WI 53715.

Sonia: War is the Only Word for Women's Lives

by Sonia Johnson

FROM *Sojourner: The Women's Forum* 9:10 (June 1984): 11

I have agreed to run for the Citizens Party presidential nomination because, as one glance at the present line-up of males so loudly proclaims, the two major parties are still slamming the Old Boys' clubhouse door shut in women's faces.

Sixty-three years after winning the vote, twenty years after *The Feminine Mystique*, for women still to be so shut up, and so shut out of the mainstream of American politics, is incredible. It is also unacceptable—to me, to the Citizens Party and to a growing number of Americans. It is unacceptable not only because it is blatantly undemocratic, but because the imbalance of power between men and women in this country and the world is dangerous and potentially lethal. Men with their monopoly on power are not just nudging us, they are hurtling us toward planetary annihilation.

Women's voices, particularly feminist voices—the least co-opted women's voices—must be heard over the gunfire of wars raging around the globe and the mounting chains and terror. To restore the balance necessary for survival, women's voices must be heard *and attended to* in the decision-making councils of the world. Clearly, we cannot wait for men to get around to granting us permission to speak. There is too little time and too much at stake. Everything depends on the courage women summon to say what must be said and on our willingness to take risks to do what must be done— right now.

Reprinted by permission of *Sojourner: The Women's Forum* and the photographer.

We must first have the courage to say that women's issues—the hazards of being female which are regarded as so peripheral and trivial to the men in power—are in fact the axis upon which all other issues of life and death turn.

We must make clear to the world that the oppression of women lies at the core of our present dilemma, that it is the archetypical oppression upon which all other oppressions—racism, imperialism, colonialism, war—are modelled. Men raped and subdued women before they conquered neighboring tribes. In learning to dominate women, they developed a conquistador mentality: if it is reasonable and justifiable and necessary (and sanctioned by God) for men to rule women, then it follows that it is justifiable and reasonable and necessary (and sanctioned by God) for one nation to rule another, the strong to rule the weak, people of one color to rule people of another color, the rich to rule the poor. And every time this happens, balance critical to the world is lost.

What this means is that, despite clamor for peace, as long as we continue to wage war against the dignity of women in our homes and streets and offices, our churches, schools, and courts, we cannot expect to understand even the nature of peace, to say nothing of what is necessary to achieve it. If we cannot stop rape in the microcosm of the streets of one U.S. city, we cannot expect to stop violence in the macrocosm of other nations and the planet.

War is the only appropriate word for women's lives.

More than two thousand women are raped in this country every day, fifty percent of women are beaten by the men they live with, sometimes beaten to death, incest is an epidemic—one out of four females will be incestuously assaulted before age eighteen. Thousands of Black and Hispanic women are sterilized every year against their will.

Not only physical violence but economic violence against women is woven implacably into the fabric of our society. Eighty-nine percent of Americans living in poverty are women and our children; by the year 2000 we will comprise the entire poverty population. To be born female on a patriarchal planet is to be born behind enemy lines.

Sexism, the polite term for this war, is the model for racism, classism, ageism—all the other wars we are waging at this moment on our own soil against our own people. Each of them is a grim struggle made desperate by government leaders who pour out the lifeblood of our economy into non-productive, non-recyclable weapons of destruction.

I have agreed to run for president because someone must say that only in a massive global revolution in the status of women is there hope for the survival of the planet and the human species. Such a revolution would signal the death of the conquistador mentality, the rapist mind, which is destroying us all.

Sonia Johnson

Everywhere I go in this country, I see the ravages of this mentality. And I am outraged by what I see. While the Pentagon spends three-quarters of a billion dollars every day on intimidating, terrorizing, and killing, I see people out of work—ten million citizens now without jobs, people without homes, without enough to eat, who cannot afford health care or education. And I remember that our forefathers spoke of the common welfare as well as the common defense. Things are dangerously out of balance.

We clamor for peace, but peace means more than the absence of outright, shooting war. Peace means being safe from assault in our homes, workplaces, and streets. It means being able to work at a decent job for fair wages. It means being able to go to school, have adequate housing, enough nutritious food to eat, good health care. Peace means having a safe environment, having a say in the policies that affect our lives, being able to turn on the heat in the winter. Peace means having hope. It means living without terror of nuclear holocaust.

I am running to say that there cannot be peace in the world without justice, without compassion, without mercy at home.

When I ponder what can be done about a global network of warlords who spend enough in one day preparing for and waging war to feed the entire human family for one year, I am reminded of the ancient Israelites who were advised to beat their swords into ploughshares and their spears into pruning hooks—a creative military conversion plan, and still very sound economic policy.

Our obscenely obese military budget, which enriches a very few and, by creating a $900 billion national debt, impoverishes all the rest of us, could be cut in half *at once* without posing any threat at all to defense. With that first liberated $125 billion, we could begin learning how to wage peace in the United States.

On my first day as president, I would announce a national emergency plan to eradicate the conquistador mentality from our culture. I would see to it that we work as diligently at reversing the evil and ancient belief in the legitimacy of power imbalance as we had formerly worked at dominating the world.

My second day in the oval office would be spent sitting in a circle of nonpatriarchal women from every country, planning how to bring arms immediately and globally under female control.

Men have never made weapons they have not used, and there is every indication that this trend will continue until women intervene. Two of the very few virtues of oppression are that the oppressed are conditioned *not* to use force, and have no "face" to lose. The human family is therefore much safer with weapons in the hands of the average woman than of the average man.

Having most of the $125 billion still in hand on my third day in office, I would see to it that Congress re-fund the programs so disastrously cut by

Reagan in favor of warheads. Programs which save people's lives and dignity and restore their hope are inseparable from peace.

And at this time in history, the only appropriate—the only possible—role for a nation which wishes to be the greatest in the world and live to enjoy its reputation, is to be the peacemaker, the mediator—the signal of hope to a troubled world that we *can* lift ourselves out of barbarism, we *can* take an evolutionary step into an age of genuine humanity.

To be the peacemakers, the facilitators of empowerment for other nations, and the champions of global harmony means withdrawing all arms, advisors, troops and agents provocateur from countries such as El Salvador, Nicaragua, Honduras, and Lebanon. It means listening to the voices of the people and scrapping plans for deployment of missiles in western Europe. It means exporting, instead, a commitment to genuine democracy and human rights, affirming the right of every nation to choose its own destiny.

Like us, the Soviets are saddled with leaders who would rather blow us all to Kingdom Come than lose face in the absurd game of King of the Mountain. Despite the fact that the majority of Americans and Europeans polled oppose deployment of the Cruise and Pershing II missiles in Europe (and there is evidence from Soviet feminists that the Soviet people are also fed up with the insane macho of their leaders), deployment [has gone] forward as planned.

Leaders who do not listen to our overwhelming consensus, leaders who have broken the contract they made with us to represent us, are renegades and criminals and should be arrested immediately.

Our leaders say that a strong defense is the road to peace. But we are not deceived. I was taught as a child that those who sow the wind reap the whirlwind—an imaginative way of saying that preparing for war is the surest way to have war, that violence breeds violence, that the means *are* the ends.

The men in power would also like us to believe that a world without war is not possible, that war springs from human nature. But we do not believe this either. War is created by a rapist habit of mind and like any other bad habit, it can be broken—*must* be broken. And there is genuine hope that it can be broken. Because, unlike other animals, we humans ourselves decide what our nature is. We, not our genetic programming, are in control of our fate.

But the fact remains that believing the rationalization that war is intrinsic to human nature and therefore inevitable has brought us to the tightest spot the human race has ever got itself into. Because neither Democrat nor Republican leaders are willing to face the terror they feel in their hearts, they cannot see clearly that we actually teeter on the brink of doom at this moment. While they choose comfortable blindness, many of the rest of us are deeply in the pain of "foresuffering" (to use T. S. Eliot's word) the horrors that are unavoidable if we continue to allow grown men to act like irresponsible little boys.

Our fear has taught us what we value most—we value our lives and the lives of our children. We are grieving for the children we brought, in all innocence, into a most terrible world. My sons and daughter have not deserved this legacy. Neither have yours.

I would do anything to give my children the kind of world I knew as a child, a world I could trust to stick around, to be there long enough for me to grow up in it.

So for my children's sake, I am running for President. I want them to know that, having inadvertently brought them into the world at its most terrifying and dangerous, I am now doing everything I can to save their lives.

Ed. Note: Sonia Johnson is seeking contributions and other assistance in her Presidential campaign, which will continue until November regardless of whether she receives federal matching funds by June 1. In the Boston area, contact Women for Sonia, 91 Bristol Rd., Somerville, MA 02144 (776-5662); elsewhere, contact Sonia Johnson, Citizen for President, 3318 Second St., South, Arlington, VA 22204 (703-553-9114).

Sonia Gets Funds

FROM *Sojourner: The Women's Forum* 10:1 (September 1984): 9

Citizens Party presidential candidate Sonia Johnson qualified for $140,000 in primary matching funds from the Federal Election Commission. Johnson is the first third-party candidate ever to receive federal primary matching funds.

Johnson has also filed a petition with the Federal Communications Commission asking to take part in any televised presidential debates. "To exclude anyone from television now is to exclude them from the election," she said.

Reprinted by permission of *Sojourner: The Women's Forum.*

WATCH OUT, BIG BROTHER!

The Taming of Nestlé
A Boycott Success Story

by Fred Clarkson

FROM *Multinational Monitor* 5:4 (April 1984): 14–17

On January 26, 1984, Doug Johnson, one of the key organizers behind the boycott of Nestlé products, ended six and a half years of abstinence when he shared a Nestlé chocolate bar with Nestlé executive Neils Christiansen. Though a suspension of the boycott had just been announced, this action told the roomful of boycott organizers, corporate officials, and media representatives that the Nestlé boycott was really, truly over. The historic occasion followed six weeks of secret negotiations between the Nestlé corporation, and American and Canadian boycott leaders.

The concessions made by Nestlé, the world's largest food corporation, were called "stunning" by boycott leaders, who believe the agreement may have turned Nestlé from an adversary into an ally. "If Nestlé abides by the agreement, it will do a lot to contribute to the lives of children," says Doug Johnson, who is National Chair of the Infant Formula Action Coalition (INFACT), the principal organizer of the boycott. "We now share with Nestlé a mutual interest in seeing other infant formula companies bring their marketing practices into line with Nestlé's."

The international boycott had called on the Switzerland-based company

Fred Clarkson is a freelance journalist based in Washington, D.C. He was a member of INFACT's advisory board for two years.

to halt the aggressive promotion of infant formula in the Third World. The campaign eventually moblized some 100 groups in 65 countries, including ten nationally organized Nestlé boycotts. Such extensive international organizing grew out of women's, consumer, and health activists' common concerns about the hazards of bottle feeding.

The well-documented health problems associated with bottle feeding in developing countries result in an estimated one million infant deaths annually, according to the United Nation's Children's Fund (UNICEF). Following a 1978 U.S. Senate hearing, Senator Edward Kennedy (D-Massachusetts) defined the problem this way: "Can a product which requires clean water, good sanitation, adequate family income, and a literate parent to follow printed instructions be properly and safely used in areas where water is contaminated, sewage runs in the streets, poverty is severe, and illiteracy is high?"

Among the high-powered sales tactics at issue in the campaign were mass media advertising and the use of "milk nurses"—company sales agents dressed in nursing uniforms who pushed formula use to new mothers at home and in the hospital.

The boycott agreement is based on Nestlé's compliance with the World Health Organization/UNICEF Code of Marketing of Breastmilk Substitutes, the first international marketing code in history. Four remaining issues were resolved by the two sides during the secret negotiations, which were mediated in part by UNICEF.

The boycotters and the company have agreed to accept UNICEF's final word while they work out details of the agreement. Meanwhile, the International Nestlé Boycott Committee (INBC), the umbrella organization of boycott supporting groups in North America, has suspended the boycott, pending a final evaluation of Nestlé's progress in mid-August.

The agreement has been widely recognized as a major victory for the international consumer movement. "Business theorists will keep alive the memory of the Nestlé boycott as a classic case history of marketing a good product, then ignoring the ensuing problem, and finally mismanaging the inevitable crisis," the trade journal *Advertising Age* commented recently. "The lesson to be learned here is that the absence of sophisticated regulatory mechanisms in the Third World should not be misconstrued as an open invitation to free-wheeling marketing behavior."

In the early 1970s, the devastating impact of decades of accelerating commercial promotion of infant formula and bottle feeding in the Third World began to be understood by the international medical community. The emotionally charged issue caught on in 1974 when *The New Internationalist*, a British journal concerned with Third World issues, ran an expose. This was followed by a more detailed monograph published by the British development organization War on Want which identified Nestlé as the major company involved. The issue captured the attention of the popular press in Europe when Nestlé sued a Swiss group for translating the War on Want report into German under a new title, "Nestlé Kills Babies."

In the U.S., the churches took up the formula issue with American companies in which they owned stock. Since 1974, Protestant denominations and Catholic orders have investigated and worked for reform of company sales practices through the Interfaith Center on Corporate Responsibility. But the limited effectiveness of filing minority shareholder resolutions at annual meetings, and the need to challenge the industry leader—Nestlé has 40 to 50 percent of the Third World formula market—led to the formation of the Infant Formula Action Coalition (INFACT) in 1977 to organize grassroots education and action in the U.S. At the first INFACT national conference in November 1977, 55 religious anti-hunger activists, students, and health workers, launched the Nestlé boycott, primarily because of Nestlé's refusal to meet with critics or acknowledge the seriousness of the problem.

The connection between corporate marketing practices and sick and dying infants struck a chord of conscience during a relatively non-political decade. "Everybody can identify with small children. Nobody's anti-baby," points out Cynthia Kokis of the Lane County, Oregon chapter of Clergy and Laity Concerned. "We just had to confront the tragic fact that one in ten Third World babies dies by the age of five, and that many were sick because of misuse of a product." Kokis adds that the documentation of the problem provided by the church and medical communities profoundly affected "people who just couldn't imagine that corporations would lie or do anything wrong."

Another reason for the campaign's success was the universal appeal of the issue. There "wasn't a vested interest of common people siding with the corporations," says Kokis. Labor campaigns like the grape and lettuce boycotts in support of the United Farm Workers, or the more recent J. P. Stevens campaign, she adds, touch on "previous decisions people have made. People either say 'I'm a union man,' or 'I'll never be a union man.' But nobody wants a sick baby."

The basic demand of the boycott was to "halt sales promotion of infant formula in developing countries." This was to be a sticking point in the final negotiations, because the WHO Code called for application in both developed and underdeveloped countries to protect mothers and children from undue commercial pressure. Ultimately, the boycotters felt that to preserve the integrity of their campaign, they could not hold out for application of the code to developed countries and stuck to their original demand that Nestlé follow the code in the Third World.

Along with organizing the boycott, INFACT aimed a letter writing campaign at Congress, which led to a dramatic Senate hearing in May 1978. Chaired by Senator Kennedy, the hearing brought Third World health workers, church activists, medical experts, and company executives to Washington, D.C. to present their cases. The hearing attracted tremendous media attention, and catapulted the issue into the national arena.

Kennedy and the industry later asked WHO and UNICEF to take up the issue at their upcoming conference on infant and young child feeding in 1979. Ultimately, that meeting produced a document that called on the industry to curtail various sales tactics, and urged health professionals to support breastfeeding through hospitals and to avoid acting as indirect sales agents for the industry. This became the basis of the WHO/UNICEF Code of Marketing of Breastmilk Substitutes, which was passed by the World Health Assembly in May 1981. The only negative vote on the code was cast by the U.S. delegate, under orders from the Reagan administration.

Around the time of the WHO/UNICEF meeting in the fall of 1979, two key campaign coalitions were formed to lead and organize the burgeoning infant formula movement. The International Nestlé Boycott Committee was

INFACT

In March 1983, INFACT singled out Taster's Choice coffee—Nestlé's best-selling product in the U.S.—for a concerted boycott effort, prompting rallies like this one in Minneapolis in March 1983.

created, mainly to promote solidarity and set up the unified negotiating team which ultimately settled the boycott. The International Baby Food Action Network (IBFAN) was established as the coalition of all the groups in the international campaign primarily aimed at the WHO Code development process.

CODE vs. BOYCOTT

The shift of the center of activity from the U.S. to the U.N. seemed a coup for Nestlé. The company told potential boycott endorsers that there was no need for a boycott because the WHO was handling the matter.

After the WHO/UNICEF Code was passed, however, activists decided to use the boycott as the vehicle for enforcement of Nestlé compliance with the code. Nestlé still had a long way to go, they believed, though the company had made incremental changes in policy over the years. In 1978, Nestlé pledged to stop mass media advertising in the Third World. In 1979, Nestlé pledged to abide by the WHO/UNICEF statement and the "code process." In 1981, after bitterly fighting the code and the boycott, Nestlé agreed to abide by the "aim" of the code, and in 1982, Nestlé adopted the whole code as company policy, but instructed its field staff on how to interpret the code. Several sets of revisions followed under pressure from consumer activists and Nestlé's own "audit commission" chaired by former Secretary of State Edmund Muskie.

But throughout this period Nestlé's practices in the field routinely violated stated company policy. "We needed field data to see if Nestlé was really putting the code into practice," says Doug Johnson, "So we did guerrilla research. We sent people on intensive trips through several countries to visit hospitals, clinics, and homes to investigate the real field practices." This campaign documented violations which were then released to the press.

Nevertheless, since 1982, Nestlé did make steady progress. At the same time, public understanding of the boycott and the WHO code was getting lost in a morass of obscure details about the code, and charges and countercharges about code violations. Some boycott supporters defected during this period, notably the American Federation of Teachers and the Church of the Brethren, who were apparently convinced that Nestlé was abiding by the code.

The remaining 87 members of the INBC analyzed Nestlé's progress to date, and decided to continue the boycott over four remaining issues: limiting free supplies of formula to those who cannot breastfeed; stopping all personal gifts to health workers; revising misleading literature for mothers and health workers; and including clear warnings on infant formula labels about the hazards of bottle feeding and the benefits of breastfeeding.

A few days before the December 1983 press conference that announced these four demands, Doug Johnson happened to meet Neils Christiansen, a

Washington-based Nestlé executive, on an AMTRAK train between New York and Washington. Johnson explained the four demands to Christiansen, who took them back to Nestlé. Thus began a critical series of 12 meetings primarily between Johnson and Christiansen, which were conducted with pledges of binding secrecy: both parties agreed that if details of the talks were leaked, the talks would be terminated. In six weeks, an agreement was reached.

To Christiansen, the two key elements of the agreement were the role of the churches, and the mediating role of UNICEF. "The termination of the boycott by the Church of the Brethren and most of the Methodists had a profound effect," he says. "The churches recognized Nestlé's progress and recognized what we were doing to implement the code," Christiansen says that UNICEF's "willingness to negotiate" was the catalyst of the agreement. "When we sat down with UNICEF," he says, "both of our ideas changed to some extent. They helped us to reach consensus." The boycott, he says, "was not an issue" for Nestlé. "Our sales figures never showed any impact of the boycott."

Doug Johnson disagrees with this explanation, however. He believes the key factors were: the pressure of the boycott; boycott organizers' public acknowledgement of Nestlé's progress over time; and the willingness of Nestlé to make the necessary changes to end the controversy. "Nestlé finally did what many company ideologues didn't want them to do: go forward with face-to-face negotiations," he says. "This was an enormous breakthrough that allowed those of us most intimately involved to engage in a give-and-take exchange." Johnson also believes that changes in Nestlé's top management may have permitted a more "pragmatic" approach.

Johnson stresses the role of the big city "campaign centers" developed over the past year, where boycott volunteers have been systematically trained and organized to make a measurable dent in Nestlé's sales. The first such centers in Chicago and Boston succeeded in getting Nestlé's Taster's Choice coffee off the shelves of a number of stores, and at the time of the agreement, were putting pressure on the larger supermarket chains. Nestlé was aware, says Johnson, that two more centers were to open soon. The centers are continuing operation, and gearing up for the next campaign.

Despite Nestlé's dismissal of the economic impact of the boycott, a look at articles about Nestlé in the business press makes a strong case for the effectiveness of the boycott tactic. In 1978, *Fortune Magazine* reported that Nestlé, which at the time was selling almost $2 billion worth of food products a year in the U.S., hoped to double that figure and increase the U.S. share of its global sales from 18 to 30 percent by 1982. To reach this goal, the company launched a multimillion dollar advertising campaign.

In 1981, *Business Week* reported that Nestlé's "U.S. sales and earnings were down slightly," adding that the company had revised its timetable for the 30 percent market share to 1985.

And a recent article in the *Wall Street Journal* suggests that it may have been the boycott that thwarted Nestlé's strategy of trying to expand its North American market. "Weak" U.S. sales of $2.4 billion last year, says the *Journal*, "account for only 19 percent of world sales." "The end of a boycott against Nestlé may . . . help" the company's efforts to increase their U.S. market share, the article states.

WHAT'S NEXT FOR THE BOYCOTT

While the end of the boycott may well be a boost for Nestlé, IBFAN—the international coalition of groups active in the formula movement—almost came apart at the seams after the suspension was announced. In early February, about 125 IBFAN activists held a strategy conference in Mexico City. Although most delegates were from North America, people came from as far away as Bangladesh, Thailand, India, Swaziland, Kenya, Zimbabwe, Western Europe, and Latin America.

Most delegates were pleased with the concessions gained through the Nestlé agreement, but there were two problems voiced at the meetings.

The first was that IBFAN leaders believed they had not been adequately consulted on the boycott suspension—a major decision in which they felt they should have played a role. Secondly, the Europeans felt that the North American agreement effectively made a separate peace with Nestlé, and undercut their boycott efforts in Europe. In several countries with no tradition of boycotts, the Nestlé boycott had only caught on in the past year. They had also hoped to persuade Nestlé to apply the WHO code in all countries, not just developing countries, as the already concluded agreement had specified.

But as the North American delegates from INBC explained to the conference, they felt constrained to not go beyond the original boycott demand in their negotiations with Nestlé, largely for the sake of the integrity of the campaign in gaining enforceable agreements with other companies. The INBC agrees that the code should apply universally, and plans to help the European groups to gain an agreement with Nestlé through all means short of boycotting.

In the end, the conference agreed that if Nestlé fails to live up to its agreement, the boycott may be reopened and the stakes raised to include universal application of the code.

To head off future communications and decision-making gaps, the European boycott groups are being integrated into the INBC decision-making structure. IBFAN is tightening up its communications process, and for the first time, a North American IBFAN is being organized. This will allow the many groups with domestic agendas related to such areas as women's reproductive health, childbirth education, and women in the workplace to participate in the infant formula campaign in ways more central to their organizational goals, without a sole focus on boycotting. Thus there will be a broadened coalition to take up the struggle when INBC's reason for existence—the boycott—is no more.

Johnson believes that Nestlé may now help lobby national governments into making the WHO code national policy so that all infant formula companies will have to play by the same rules. "Now that the infant formula giant is following the code," Johnson argues, "the others will have no excuse, other than greed, not to change their practices too."

Phyllis Gabriel of the Interfaith Center for Corporate Responsibility says that all three American manufacturers of infant formula are "giving lip service" to the code, but that so far have given no firm commitments to following the code. The companies are also concerned, however, about being "the next Nestlé," and campaign activists plan to keep them guessing about upcoming strategies in hopes of gaining an industry-wide commitment to the code.

In assessing the impact of the boycott, Gabriel observes that "while the boycott didn't affect Nestlé's corporate strategy, which is to make money, it did bring about significant changes in the company's marketing strategy. Also, the WHO Code was a significant victory in itself. Similar codes could be developed for other products. Finally, the network of health workers and consumers built up over the years could serve as the basis for another campaign."

To Richard Barnet, co-author of *Global Reach: The Power of the Multinational Corporation*, "The boycott demonstrates how effective people can be when they analyze the power of multinationals and call them to accountability. Nestlé's agreement to change its practices represents a considerable victory and a model for other kinds of campaigns for consumers.

"The Nestlé campaign was also successful," he adds, "because it was a clear-cut issue—it violated a very elementary sense of decency—and because of the great energy and tenacity of its organizers, who didn't give up even when it looked like the campaign might fail."

For the thousands of people who participated in the Nestlé boycott, the campaign will have a profound and long-lasting impact—especially on their perception of corporate behavior and accountability. "Corporations have a more difficult time now," says Cynthia Kokis of Clergy and Laity Concerned. "People have started asking me for material on what corporations are doing well. Nestlé did that."

Nuclear Free Zones Proliferate

by G. S.

FROM *Not Man Apart* 14:7 (September 1984): 6

On July 13 there were 1,481 cities worldwide that had declared themselves "Nuclear Free Zones." One day later the number soared over the 2,000 mark as New Zealand, a country of more than 3 million souls, declared itself "nuclear free."

At least that's one reasonable interpretation of the election held there on July 14. On that day, New Zealand voters gave the Labour Party a majority in Parliament and put its leader, David Lange, into the Prime Minister's job. Labour had campaigned on a platform that included a promise to make New Zealand nuclear-free. If Labour sticks to its campaign promise, it will become the world's second nuclear-free nation. The small Pacific island nation of Palau became the first denuclearized nation in 1979. A few years later Palau sent shock waves from the South Seas to the Tidal Basin in Washington, DC, when it refused harbor privileges to a US Navy ship suspected of carrying nuclear weapons.

New Zealand's decision has also sent temblors of window-rattling proportions thundering through the thickets of State Department and Pentagon planners. Secretary of State George Schultz, in the midst of an Asian-nation shuttle, was suddenly faced with the chore of pleading for an accommodation with the no-nukes Labour government. In the meantime the US has ordered its nuclear navy to stay well clear of New Zealand's waters—in effect, recognizing New Zealand's claim to be a nuclear-free zone.

DO WE FEAR OUR

ENEMIES MORE THAN

WE LOVE OUR CHILDREN

Closer to home, the US Navy is encountering growing resistance in Hawaii, where the Maui County Council has declared the islands of Maui, Molokai, Lani, and Kahoolawe off-limits to nuclear weapons and materials. The council also voted to prohibit development of nuclear facilities and banned the dumping, storage, and transportation of nuclear materials either on land or in the waters between the islands. The council's ordinances could also put an end to the Navy tradition of anchoring off Maui for shore leaves.

On the US mainland the NFZ movement continues to expand. In the last three years 57 communities have voted to ban nuclear activities. Nearly a million Americans now live in nuclear-free zones, from Hawaii to New Hampshire. Ninety-one more cities are considering initiatives that would proclaim their neighborhoods and downtowns nuclear-free. On a much grander scale, citizens groups in Alaska, California, North Dakota, and Oregon are seeking NFZ status statewide. (If these campaigns succeed, more than one-tenth of the entire US population would be living in declared nuclear-free zones.)

Existing NFZs

It was 26 years ago that the United Nations proposed the concept of nuclear-free zones and Poland became the first nation to call for the creation of a nuclear-free Central Europe. Since then several treaties have been negotiated designating four regions as nuclear-free zones. The largest are the nations of Latin America and the continent of Antarctica. Nuclear-free pacts have also been proposed for Scandinavia, Africa, the Middle East, and, in January 1984, the Balkans.

Definitions of nuclear-free zones vary. Some, like most of the resolutions, adopted by individual American cities, exclude all radioactive materials except medical supplies. Others, like the treaties concerning Latin America and Antarctica, ban nuclear weapons but permit nuclear powerplants.

As a practical matter the nuclear weapons race may be more fundamentally derailed by the kind of grassroots campaigns taking place in a few critical American cities.

In 1983 the Nuclear Free Cambridge Campaign lost a hard-fought battle to ban nuclear weapons activities within city precincts. Cambridge was not your average American city. Residing along its tree-lined avenues were such defense giants as General Dynamics, Sperry, Northrop, Rockwell International, Martin-Marietta, Honeywell, Avco, and Draper Laboratories. The initiative was defeated by the most expensive per-vote election campaign in US history. The opposition invested $17.50 per vote.

This year's critical race will take place in Santa Monica, California, where a nuclear-free resolution would compel four local industries—Lear Siegler, Puroflow, G&H Technology, and the Rand Corporation—to phase out their weapons contracts within two years.

"The initiative would neither force any of the affected companies to relocate nor require them to shut down," explains campaign director Kelly Hayes-Raitt. It would only require the firms "to redirect some of their activities."

"The legal justification for this campaign," according to legal advisor Michael Brush, "is that health and safety issues are in the jurisdiction of local communities." While Hayes-Raitt admits that the power to determine national defense policy rests in Washington, "the United States Constitution does not grant our lawmakers the authority to engage in a policy that may lead toward national suicide."

For further information contact: Citizens for a Nuclear Free Santa Monica, 2434 Fifth Street, 106, Santa Monica, CA 90450 (213) 392-8715.

Gathering Strength
Worker Ownership and Control in the 80s

by Len Krimerman

FROM Changing Work: A Magazine About Liberating Worklife 1
(Fall 1984): 18–25

A DECADE OF DEVELOPMENT

The maps tell a good bit of the story. In the mid-seventies, many of the editors of Changing Work took part in what we now see as the first stage of a new and exciting movement to transform the American workplace. In those days, our vision of cooperatively-owned and managed work, work in which those who labored shared equally in the benefits and decision-making of productive enterprises, frequently outran reality. Progress (as Map 1 illustrates) was rare and meager; in addition, as the map doesn't reveal, it was very often temporary. Thus, Colonial Cooperative Press and International Poultry, Inc., two New England worker cooperatives established in 1977, both lasted less than three years.

By the mid-eighties, however, the situation had begun to change—a second, more evolved phase of what can be called the "worker control" or "worker ownership" movement had emerged. This movement takes a wide variety of forms: from one-person, one-vote (self-managing) cooperatives which are owned and controlled equally by their entire workforces, to businesses owned by their employees but in which democratic control over, or selection of, management has not yet been achieved, to joint management-

Reprinted by permission of Changing Work and the author.

Gatherin

WORKER OWNERSHIP AND CONTROL:
EARLY 1970'S

Plywood
Co-ops

Hoedads
(Reforestation)

Milwaukee Journal

Gray Ba
Electric

Scavenger
Refuse
Collection Co-ops

Consumers
United Group

Assocation
for Self Management (T)

Federation of
Southern Cooperatives (N) (T)

American Cast Iron
Pipe Co.

NOTES	SYMBOLS
1. The maps are designed to be panoramic, rather than comprehensive, to give the main contours of each period, rather than a complete picture.	N: NETWORK
	U: UNION INVOLVEMENT
2. Many related phenomena have been left out, e.g., consumer co-ops, housing co-ops, self-governing communities, participatory management programs, small-sized collectives. We invite additions and corrections.	T: TECHNICAL ASSISTANCE/EDUC AL ORGANIZATION (for ad phones, see "Resources, page 3 Numbers in states (1, 2, 9...) refer to worker co-ops or firms in which em own a majority of the stock.
3. In preparing these maps, reference was made to the National Center for Employee Ownership's list of "Majority Employee-Owned Companies." The Center, of course, is not responsible for any errors or omissions the maps may contain.	

trength

WORKER OWNERSHIP AND CONTROL:
CURRENT STAGE

Earth Bank Assocation (T)

9

North West Foresters
Association (U) (N)

7

kers Trust (N)

akland
lant Closing
roject (T)

Action
Resources, Inc. (T)

Community Economic
Adjustment Dept. (T)

Mid-Peninsula
Conversion Project (T)

26

Waterhouse
and Associates (T)

Michigan Employee
Ownership Center (T)

New Hampshire
College (T)

Rath
Meating Packing Co. (U)

Atlas
Chain (U)

PACE (T)

Hyatt-Clark (U)

MidWest Center
for Labor Research
(T) (U)

O&O (U) (N)

Co-op America (T) (N)

Weirton
Steel (U)

MACED (T)

FSC (N) (T)

MASSACHUSETTS	NEW YORK	D.C.	NORTH CAROLINA
ial Cooperative ation (T)	Program On Employment and Work Systems (T)	Association for Workplace Democracy (T)	Guilford College (T)
e for Community nics (T)	Alternative Fund (T)	National Center for Employee Ownership (T)	Twin Streams Educational Center (T)
eship Institute (T)	Community Center for Economic Development (T)	National Consumer Co-op Bank (T)	Center for Community Self-Help (T)
(T)	NYC-Metro AWD (T)	Campaign for Human Development (T)	Cooperative Research and Development Group (T)
acher Institute (T)	l/Econ (T)	Center for Economic Organizing (T)	

labor programs which leave traditional ownership intact but require that workers and management agree on all matters concerning how work is to get done, e.g., its organization, scheduling, quality control, safety conditions, etc. What unites all of these is the common aim of providing workers with substantial and increasing control over their workplaces and worklives.

Seen in this light, the "worker control movement" (WCM), as shown by our second map, has now become a visible and growing presence in the American economy. There is virtually no section of the country that has not been witness to a worker buyout of a shutdown plant, the conversion of a successful privately-owned business to employee ownership, a network of locally-run cooperatives or collectives, a labor-management agreement to democratize the organization of production or improve the "quality of work-life," none that is without access to a "technical assistance organization" which provides aid of various kinds to workers seeking to start and manage their own businesses or to gain more control over their present work. More-over, by now many of these innovations and transformations have begun to withstand the test of time. Consumers United Group is a group insurance firm in Washington, D.C. owned and managed by its 250 workers, and well into its second decade. It continues to experiment with new forms of floor level democratization, personalized work schedules, and department coun-cils, and has begun to help finance other worker-owned enterprises. The In-dustrial Cooperative Association of Somerville, Massachusetts entered its sixth year as a technical assistance organization by opening a revolving loan fund of $1 million to support worker cooperatives, by expanding its staff, and by opening up two new departments devoted to "public policy assis-tance to city and state governments" and "cooperative conversions and new venture start-ups." (Quoted from *ICA Bulletin*, March, 1984.) Workers Owned Sewing Company, a cooperative formed in the wake of a plant clos-ing in Windsor, North Carolina in 1978, has held on through difficult times to move from sub-contracting to direct manufacturing (including a contract to produce jogging shorts for Sears, Roebuck, and Co.) Last year, WOSC doubled its original workforce to approximately sixty worker-owners.

Each year brings further confirmation of the expansion and increasing strength of WCM. Thus in 1983, to mention just a few highlights:

• A *steel mill in Weirton, West Virginia* was bought by its workers from National Steel, Inc. and became the largest (6,000) 100% employee-owned plant in the United States;

• The *New York Times Magazine* printed a full-length article describing growing trends in democratic worker-ownership;

• The *state of New Hampshire* created a publicly-funded Community De-velopment Finance Authority empowered to provide financing to employee-owned businesses, thus following precedents set in prior years by Wisconsin and Massachusetts;

• *People's Express Airlines* (33% employee-owned and highly democratized) was joined by several major airlines which introduced employee stock ownership plans (some with voting rights) in exchange for wage concessions;

• *US Sugar*, the nation's largest sugar producer (2,500 employees), moved to 53% employee ownership; so did Transcom, the 10th largest truck carrier;

• *Hyatt-Clark*, a 1981 worker buyout from General Motors, introduced substantial and well-received programs in shop-level democratization in 75% of its departments, and developed job advancement and educational enrichment programs;

• *Atlas Chain*, a United Auto Workers Plant (as is Hyatt-Clark), started production as an employee buyout, assisted by an infusion of capital from the Consumers Union Group of Washington, D.C.

QUALITATIVE NOT JUST QUANTITATIVE

Progress within WCM has been qualitative as well as quantitative. That is, not only are there more worker cooperatives, employee buyouts, conversions to employee ownership every year, and more that survive for longer periods, but the kind being formed now contrast sharply with those that struggled for existence a decade or so ago. This *qualitative development* is shown by three features, designated as *N*, *U*, and *T* on our maps, which mark these contemporary efforts to transform work as unique in the history of democratized or cooperative enterprise in America.

Attempts to bring democracy into the workplace are not altogether unknown in American history; witness the Plywood cooperatives that formed in Washington and Oregon during the Great Depression or the cooperative agrarian enterprises that played an important role in the economies of Minnesota and Wisconsin during the prior decade. But these ventures have mostly been short-lived, or have survived at the cost of compromising their democratic ideals (e.g., by hiring second-class wage labor who were denied any share in decision-making or surplus revenues). Further, these earlier cooperatives existed largely in isolation from one another, and in isolation from other established or progressive segments of American society, in particular, the labor movement, local and state governments, and grass roots organizations. Often, the skills and resources necessary to keep businesses alive and well were in short supply; undercapitalization, inexperienced management, gaps in marketing, technological, and financial expertise were typical shortcomings.

Today's wave of cooperative and democratically-run enterprises presents a much different picture. Far from developing in isolation, one at a time, the concept of "network" has become paramount. When the O&O workers took over two stores from a closed down A&P chain in Philadelphia, they established an Investment Fund to loan start-up capital to other worker cooperatives. The Center for Community Self-Help in Durham, North Carolina has recently launched a community development credit union for the same purpose. And the worker-owned enterprises in North Carolina, some ten at last count, including WOSC, a bakery, a casket-making cooperative, a statewide newspaper, a building collective and others, have formed a loose regional federation for mutual support. Through this federation they hold an annual worker ownership conference shaped by the needs of their democratic enterprises, exchange resources and the lessons of experience, and build marketing and other agreements with cooperatives in Central America and Canada. Furthermore, any democratically-managed workplace that comes to life today is immediately eligible for membership in, and a panoply of services from, Co-op America and Workers Trust—from group health insurance to computerized marketing assistance. Networking—the linking of one's resources, experience, and struggles with those of others—is becoming the rule in this new period of changing work.

Union involvement is another distinguishing feature of today's WCM. Traditionally, and as recently as a decade ago, organized labor viewed producer cooperatives as inconsequential or with some suspicion. From the union perspective, these enterprises operated at the margins of our economy (e.g., during severe recessions) or turned workers into small-time capitalists, bent on protecting their own private profit even at the expense of workers or wage-levels outside their own businesses. Besides, where workers become owners, what useful role is left for unions or collective bargaining? A glance at Map 2 will underscore the shift in union attitudes that is taking place: such ventures into workplace democracy as the O&O Supermarkets, Hyatt-Clark, and Rath Meatpacking, would not have been possible without critical and continuing union involvement. Further, a leading role has been played by the United Steel Workers in the formation of the Tri-State Commission on Steel: this commission has called for a "locally accountable and democratically controlled regional planning authority" to manage the re-industrialization of Pennsylvania's Monongahela Valley, an area which had been exploited, and has now been abandoned, by such major private steel firms as US Steel and Bethlehem Steel.

Certainly, not all unions have endorsed worker control or even shop-floor democratization or participatory management; in subsequent issues, *Changing Work* will examine in detail the scope of union involvement in WCM and the role(s) that unions can play (and are playing) in recreating worklife. But it remains clear that attitudes have already altered: there is now an historically unique openness, within the labor movement, to ideas like employee ownership, worker cooperatives, economic conversion, and democratic management and a willingness to explore ways to make these useful both to union organizations and to their individual members.

"Technical Assistance" is itself a made-up, technical term which has gained currency only in the past six or eight years. There was little of it available in the mid-70s, and what there was often proved difficult for workers to comprehend or turned out to be of minimal use in coping with the complexities and time-pressures involved in creating new and democratically-organized businesses. In retrospect, this was understandable: no one had tried to gather and distribute information on how to start a co-op or keep one going, on where and how to secure financing, on the legal structure and by-laws best adapted to such businesses, on the internal procedures and committees essential for keeping a democratic enterprise healthy, on the new skills, resources, and relationships workers would need to develop in order to gain real and not just formal control over their work. Starting a new business of any sort is tough enough: some 50% fail before the end of their second year. Starting a cooperative or liberated workplace—and keeping it alive—was not only difficult, but involved utterly unmapped terrain. For the most part, technical assistance for worker-owned and democratically-managed enterprises had to be invented from scratch.

Amazingly, this happened. First came the Association for Workplace Democracy (1974), then the Industrial Cooperative Association (1977), the Philadelphia Association for Cooperative Enterprise (PACE), the National Center for Employee Ownership . . . now there are at least 45 organizations which specialize in developing or supporting worker-owned enterprises. What they can offer varies: some provide only educational materials such as case studies, how-to manuals, or directories of resource people and organizations; others primarily furnish funding assistance through loans, loan guarantees, or grants. But many offer a wide spectrum of client services ranging from *business guidance* (preparation of feasibility studies, financial plans and marketing projections) and *legal assistance* (development of by-laws and help with incorporation and tax regulations) to *educational* and *organizational development* (imparting technical business skills, help in establishing grievance and communication procedures, and in building self-confidence, mutual trust, and responsibility-sharing.

Several technical assistance groups have recently developed at least some independent financing capacity, among others the ICA, the Center for Community Self-Help, and community development finance authorities in several states. But most intriguing, perhaps, many groups offering technical support have recently expanded their role, and their relationships to clients, in a very imaginative way. Throughout the seventies, technical assistance providers were mainly "reactive": they waited for and responded to clients in distress situations, especially those faced with plant closings. Today, this somewhat passive or limited approach is giving way to what is called a "pro-active" or "developmental" strategy. Rick Surpin is the Director of the Center for Community Economic Development in New York City, a component of the Community Services Society, one of the oldest social work organizations in the country. According to Rick, the Center's responsibility is an *entrepreneurial* one: that of locating viable business opportunities, bringing them to potential clients such as Tenant Councils or church groups, and then working with those clients to help develop the businesses on a secure basis.

This "pro-active" or "entrepreneurial" turn means that technical assistance providers are no longer rigidly bound to distress situations or to their clients' prior work situations or business plans. If your factory shuts down, they might propose ways of making the old business viable under worker ownership. But they might instead suggest other product lines or wholly new business ventures whose feasibility they had already established. Further, this new flexibility enables these support groups to do long-term planning and entrepreneurial development for an entire community or municipality, rather than concentrating on dramatic but isolated plant closings. In short, technical assistance is not only one illustration of qualitative development within the WCM, but is itself evolving qualitatively, taking on new and expanded objectives. (A model for much of this development in technical assistance has been the Mondragon network of cooperatives in the Basque region of Spain, in particular their "Empresarial" strategies.)

TO WHERE DOES THIS ALL LEAD?

Looking at the two maps, and at the qualitative changes we've just sketched, it seems fair to conclude that WCM has made real progress in the last decade; that—in the words of a song written by Maggie Cherry, a North Carolina worker-owner—"We Come a Long Way." But this, though certainly true, is not the whole truth.

It is a sobering fact that, despite all of these promising signs, the yearly budget of the entire WCM (to paraphrase Steve Dawson, director of ICA) is spent in less than an afternoon by any one of the Fortune 500 companies. "We still got a much longer way to go" before the promising changes in worklife just described can flower in a permanent way and are within the reach of most working Americans.

Furthermore, the fledgling worker control movement, though growing and gathering strength, is still weak and disunified in important ways. When interviewed during 1982 and 1983, veteran activists in this movement conceded, for example, that there was still too little business and management expertise within their ranks; that credibility with established institutions, though on the rise, still had to be cultivated (e.g., top union leadership and major party candidates have yet to endorse or encourage democratic ownership or worker cooperatives); that communication, collaboration, and solidarity among the various elements of the movement were often fragmentary (e.g., there is virtually no collective planning or strategizing within WCM); and that workplaces in the public (and nonprofit) sectors had been largely overlooked as appropriate environments for democratized or liberating work. Specifically, many of those interviewed spoke of discords and disagreements with WCM that had been persistently avoided or downplayed, or on which positions had been advanced in the absence of sustained dialogue. One example of this is the split between advocates of self-managing cooperatives and proponents of employee ownership.

For the first group, the ideal enterprise is a Mondragon-type cooperative, one which is worker-managed and democratically-owned. Thus, (i) its ultimate priorities and policies are shaped either by all workers collectively or by a democratically-elected body (e.g., a Workers Council) responsible to, and replaceable by, the entire working membership; and (ii) ownership in such an enterprise is democratically revised, in that only working members can own shares, each member owns one and only one share of the firm, and shares cannot be sold or transferred but, if members exit, revert back to the co-op. Those who promote employee ownership, on the other hand, adopt a more diverse model: they accept worker-owned and managed cooperatives as one, *but only one*, worthwhile form of enterprise organization. In addition, they also accept, apparently on an equal footing, employee-owned firms which provide workers with some participation in management-level decisions but not control (e.g., where workers do not elect most of the governing Board) and/or which retain the currently entrenched notion of ownership and thus permit shares to be unequally distributed and to be sold outside the workforce.

Beyond this employee ownership-worker cooperative dispute, there are other key issues on which frank discussion within the WCM has been, at best, intermittent. One of these echoes the previously mentioned and longtime union suspicion of worker owned enterprises. In an article published in 1982, Lance Compa, who works for an international union in Washington, D.C., put the case about "The Dangers of Worker Control" as follows:

> From the standpoint of the labor movement, adopting the objective of greater worker control is bad policy because it emphasizes "enterprise consciousness" rather than class consciousness. When workers control a firm, their interests are identical with management's. They no longer struggle for the betterment of workers in general or . . . of those in a particular trade or industrial sector; they think in terms of making their own workplace more profitable. In effect, workers become capitalists with capitalist problems.—*The Nation*, October 2, 1982.

Experience has shown that "enterprise consciousness" is not an imaginary danger. Despite this, Compa's forceful arguments appear to have been almost entirely ignored. The worker control movement has yet to discuss in any collective and sustained way how it can lift its own sights beyond plant-by-plant, or network-by-network, profitability toward a vision in which democratic control over work becomes a viable national and international priority. More concretely, should technical assistance organizations attempt to develop such broad-based solidarity and to combat enterprise consciousness within their frequently disconnected clients? If so, how? On these seemingly basic questions, WCM has remained mysteriously silent.

Further, a brief examination of technical assistance providers reveals a division among them concerning the longer-range aims of the movement they all support. For many, and perhaps most, democratic ownership and control are ends sufficient by themselves, so long as they become generally rather than marginally accessible. But others would combine the ideal of democracy at work with other, e.g., ecological, principles: this is crucial, to take just one case, to economic conversion groups like the Mid-Peninsula Conversion Project. Such groups would question whether it's enough to simply convert corporate-controlled nuclear missile, micro-chip, or plastic spoon factories into self-managing enterprises. Specifically, they are concerned to liberate worklife so that it supports peace rather than war-making, contributes to deep connections with the whole of life and with the entire planet, increase reliance on local and renewable energy resources, and draws on many diverse sources of satisfaction and creativity. Here, in the issue of whether democratically re-organizing production is a sufficiently full ideal—hardly a small or peripheral issue!—we have yet a third key question from which WCM appears to have turned away. So long as such conflicts remain hidden and unexpressed, how much further down that "longer road" can WCM, as a cohesive or unified movement, expect to travel?

SUMMING UP AND GOING BEYOND

To sum this all up: WCM, in 1984, is not only substantially more evolved, both quantitatively and qualitatively, than it was a decade ago, but represents an historically unique development among efforts to introduce democracy into the American workplace. It has gathered, and continues to gather, substantial strength and sophistication. Nonetheless, there is still a long and arduous road to be travelled before it exerts a stable and significant influence over this economy. The movement must confront immensely powerful external adversaries and repair internal sources of weakness and disunity. The question, in short, remains open as to how far the vision of cooperative and liberated work can take root within and recreate American worklife.

As we at *Changing Work* see it, however, this open question provides a rare opportunity for a novel kind of engaged journalism, and an exciting double role for our magazine. For not only do we plan to spread the news about WCM fully and accurately, hoping thereby to attract more and more readers to the task of liberating worklife. We have beyond this a further educational or cultural goal: to provide a medium through which the embryonic worker control movement can discover and develop its own collective voice, a place where a variety of smaller and larger experiences in changing work can be expressed and responded to, a forum which enables reflection and dialogue, where gaps and weaknesses in WCM can be explored, obstacles and pitfalls examined and strategized about, in which the lessons of both successful and unsuccessful efforts to democratize and liberate work can be shared, in which coalitions, alliances, and joint ventures of all sizes and descriptions can be initiated and supported. We hope, in short, both to reflect and to nurture the self-conscious development of this emerging movement for worker control.

Building a Marketplace Based on Values

Co-op America Would Create a Whole "Alternative Economy"

FROM *New Options* 9 (September 24 , 1984): 3

The office building is one of those awful modern concrete-and-glass structures that dominate Washington DC. The lobby is white marble, but face-
less, featureless. Even a lap dog would feel cold there. But walk into suite
number 605 and everything changes.

Seven people are arguing and laughing, and working efficiently at their
desks. Some of them are wearing suits, others shorts or blue jeans. A pop-
corn maker sits conspicuously on a shelf. Posters from co-ops line the walls.

You've walked into the offices of Co-op America, barely two years old,
which is attempting—with a minimum of fanfare—to create a national marketplace for the products of co-ops, "democratically controlled" organizations, and alternative small businesses.

Right now they're putting together their third Catalogue of products and
services, which will be mailed out next month to their already over 5,000
members. Marketing director Denise Hamler, frizzy-haired, vivacious, takes
us aside and says, "Eventually we'll bring together [products and services
from enough] groups so we can create [a relatively self-contained] economic
system responsive to our values. . . . With this kind of economic strength,
we can reach out to challenge traditional corporate values and practices."

NOT THE SEARS CATALOGUE

For $15 you can become an "individual member" of Co-op America. That
means you can order products and services through their Catalogue, "the
visualization of what we're about," says Hamler.

It is very different from the Sears catalogue. It's not glossy and it's not hundreds of pages long, but those aren't the important differences. In fact, if all goes well, someday it will be both glossy and bulky. The main difference is in who gets to sell through the catalogue.

For $50 your co-op, non-profit or small business can become an "organizational member" of Co-op America. But that's not enough to get your products into the Catalogue.

According to Paul Freundlich, the tall, personable director of Co-op America, each product or service has to meet three additional criteria. Each has to be of "reasonable cost." Each has to have national appeal. And "most important," each has to be produced by a non-profit, "democratically owned," or "independent small" business.

The Catalogue's big-ticket item is a service: Co-op America's own health and term life insurance plan. Underwritten by Consumers United Insurance Company ("the largest worker-owned insurance company in the country"), Co-op America's health insurance is inexpensive, covers your illness expenses up to $1,000,000, and covers all kinds of things not typically covered by other health plans: midwives, homeopaths, chiropractors; vasectomies and abortions; unmarried partners. . . .

Some of the Catalogue's non-service items are big tickets, too. In the Spring/Summer Catalogue, the best-selling product was Nicaraguan coffee. The biggest money-making product was a mahogany sling rocking chair made by two craft cooperatives in Honduras. Not surprisingly, the new Catalogue will have as its theme "Cooperation Among the Americas," and will feature many products made by co-ops in Central America and brought to this country by grassroots groups like Pueblo to People in Houston TX and Friends of the Third World in Fort Wayne, IN.

Like any other business, Co-op America will pull products if they're not selling well. Still, the Catalogue manages to accurately reflect the alternative culture. Of the 26 pages in the Spring/Summer Catalogue devoted to products, household goods occupy only 2½—clothing, only four. Whereas books, music, periodicals and posters occupy 11½ pages.

STILL ON TRACK

Hamler and Freundlich have been involved with co-ops seemingly forever. Freundlich was co-editor and publisher of *Communities* magazine for nine years; as a result, he knows virtually everybody who's anybody in the co-op movement. Hamler had been a regional (Ohio) and national co-op organizer, not to mention a solar home builder, organic truck farmer, and alternative newspaper editor.

But like many small business people, they felt they'd be off and running faster than they were. One internal document dated May, 1982, anticipated "a consumer membership base of 30,000 by June, 1983." (In June, 1984 it was approx. 5,000.) "Our numbers are quite low," Hamler concedes.

"Our initial direct mailing was actually quite successful," Freundlich explains. "We drew 3-4% from our best lists. The reason it took us more than a year to go out again is we just couldn't handle the numbers. [Until this spring] we were flat out concerned with getting Co-op America to a survival point. Our staff was just three people. Our health insurance had some legal problems. We didn't have a solid business plan. So we had to Take Care of Business.

"But this spring we started gearing up for another direct mail campaign. We're testing 70,000 names at the beginning of November. And we're planning a rollout on that of half a million pieces in February." With even a 2.5% response rate, that means 14,000 new members by June, 1985.

"What's most remarkable is we're still on track," Hamler says. "The path has certainly [turned out to be] a complex one. But we're still on it."

THE VISION

"With our Spring '85 Catalogue, if we have 20,000 members, we can begin to think about a four-color insert," says Freundlich. "We *know* we can sell some additional products if we have four colors."

"Like clothes where the colors are knockouts," says Hamler.

"We want to expand our products and services," continues Freundlich. "For example, I'd like to have a comprehensive educational package. [And] we should have our own credit card, a 'Co-op Ameri-Card,' for purchases among our members. . . ."

"We're talking with People's Express," says Hamler. "We've talked with the Mondragon co-op network, in Spain, about selling their refrigerators. We've talked with the Self-Help Credit Union about the possibility of putting together a Co-op America Credit Union. . . .

"When we have a credit union, when we have [some of these other things], we'll be a lot closer to having an economic system that is self-contained, unified, visible."

"It is possible [for 1960s people] to live by [their] old values," says Freundlich. "That's what Co-op America is saying. We don't have to look at our years of struggle and say: we wasted our time. . . .

"The audience we're going to with our direct mail doesn't necessarily believe it's possible to live according to those old values. We're putting it together for them. In a very *practical* way, we're drawing a little circle around environmental, political, spiritual [products and services] and saying: it all fits together. . . ."

It was hard leaving suite number 605 and taking the elevator back down to that white marble lobby.

Co-op America, 2100 "M" St. N.W., #605, Washington, DC 20063.

Hidden Costs of Housing

by Tom Bender

FROM *Rain* 10:3 (March/April 1984): 12–17

Tom Bender's offhand mention in our October/November 1983 issue that we could reduce housing costs by 90% raised many eyebrows. Possible? A pipe dream? We asked for more details, which follow. We learned also that these ideas had already won a $15,000 top award in California's Affordable Housing Competition two years ago.

Let's get some action on this, and more of this kind of rethinking of how we do things!—TK

Most home purchases are financed. Yet few buyers could tell you what their total purchase cost will be by the time their house is paid for. They don't know because they don't want to face the fact that they may have to spend all their next 10 years' income just to pay the finance charges.

What makes up our housing expenditures? Let's look first at the financial costs that add up over a person's 50-year "housing lifetime" with our present patterns (see Figure 1). These costs add up to quite a bundle out of our pockets, and the labor and materials cost of constructing the house is only a small piece of the overall cost. As we look at the separate categories of expenditures, we need to make a distinction between economic and financial costs, realize the pivotal role that durability plays in housing "costs," and see how housing scarcity masks a basic cost difference between new and used housing.

Reprinted by permission of the author.

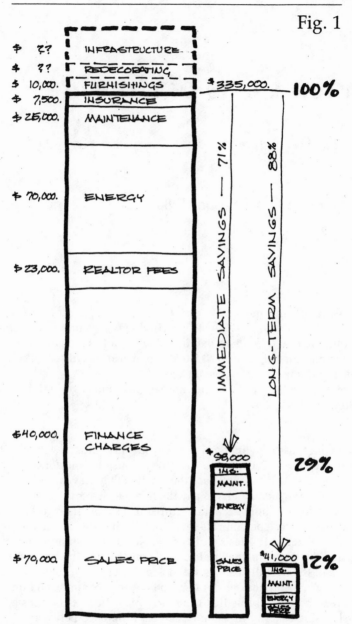

Fig. 1

$?? INFRASTRUCTURE
$?? REDECORATING
$ 10,000. FURNISHINGS
$ 7,500. INSURANCE
$ 25,000. MAINTENANCE
$ 70,000. ENERGY
$ 23,000. REALTOR FEES
$ 40,000. FINANCE CHARGES
$ 70,000. SALES PRICE

$335,000. 100%

IMMEDIATE SAVINGS — 71%

LONG-TERM SAVINGS — 88%

$98,000
INS.
MAINT.
ENERGY
SALES PRICE

29%

$41,000 12%
INS.
MAINT.
ENERGY
SALES FEES

LIFETIME COSTS OF HOUSING

Tom Bender

ECONOMIC vs. MONETARY COSTS

Making a distinction between the economic and monetary dimensions of housing is essential to seeing how decisions affecting the flow of work and money have interacted to build up today's excessive costs. The economic cost of a house consists of the work, materials, energy, and land employed in its construction. Once the house is built, that economic cost has been fully paid. If built correctly, the house has no further economic cost to its next several centuries of users, except for maintenance and operation. The economic costs deal with all the *real*, objective, and physical costs of a project—no matter who incurs them. By contrast, monetary costs stem from the rules a society sets up for distributing the benefits of economic work. Interest rates, tax laws, loan maturities, government subsidies, and the prices that different trades and professions can convince others their time is worth all alter monetary costs. As a result, they alter the final price that must be paid for economic work, who has to pay it, and who profits from it.

Monetary structures often obscure the real economic work and come to seem like some immutable natural law. In reality, they are constantly changing public policies that help shape the nature of a society—the equality or inequality of wealth, the concentration of economic and political power, and the ends to which society puts its efforts. They can, and frequently do, add a great burden on top of economic costs. Only by separating out the underlying real economics can we see the true effect of each policy affecting housing and understand how to alter such effects.

DURABILITY

Once we can penetrate the barrier that financial thinking has put between us and understanding economic costs, we can examine the actual productivity of our various housing expenditures. Construction costs, for example, are largely unavoidable economic costs, and they appear irreducible. But what is important is not just the cost, but the number of years of housing we get from that cost. The longer a building lasts, the smaller are the economic costs per year or per generation. Durability of construction is the key to economic productivity of housing.

Houses built to last 400 or 500 years can shelter 15 or more generations under their roofs before needing replacement. Each generation then has to replace only one-fifteenth of its housing, and expenditures on housing are 90% less than what they would be if new homes had to be built for each generation. Housing that lasts 400 years costs only a fraction more to build. In addition to dramatically lowering economic costs, its long life makes feasible the generosity of design that separates our shabby "low-cost" housing from ample, comfortable, and livable homes.

During the "Dark Ages" in Europe, people built solid and comfortable houses, which are still in use today. Not having to replace their homes freed the labor and materials to build their soaring and beautiful cathedrals.

Those Gothic cathedrals have already served more than 24 generations in their 800 years of use. Although the initial effort of their construction was great, their cost per generation has been far less than our shabbiest construction today, and they stand as a powerful challenge to our tradition of "economic" thinking.

Although durable construction costs somewhat more initially, it costs *much* less in the long run. Clay tile, slate, lead, and a few other roofing materials, for example, have a several-hundred year life, compared to 20 years for standard asphalt shingles. The initial cost of a tile roof is about two and one-half times that of asphalt shingles. But the repeated replacement necessary for the shingle roof boosts its economic cost over 200 years to *four* times that of clay tile. Over 300 years, shingles would cost six times as much as tile, and over 400 years, eight times as much as the lifetime roof! Actually *increasing* our economic expenditures on construction is to our advantage where it increases the durability and therefore the long-term economic benefit of the building.

The value of housing durability means more than just "build to last." It shows the importance of looking at how we *lose* as well as how we build housing. War, fires, changes in land-use patterns, tax policies that result in neglect and abandonment of housing are as important "loss-makers" as is poor construction. And the savings involved in reuse of housing underscores the high economic burden of additional housing required by population growth and relocation.

SCARCITY

From an economic viewpoint, there is a fundamental difference between the cost of new and older housing. For an older house, the economic cost has been largely paid, and what remains is only the cost of operation and maintenance needed to keep it habitable and comfortable. For a new house the economic cost is the full cost of construction. The price of used houses should therefore be far less than for new ones, and this has been true when there has been a surplus rather than a scarcity of housing available. Today, however, the opposite is true, with the monetary price of used houses paralleling that of new ones because of a combination of real and artificial scarcity.

Real scarcity arises from a growing population and the natural shortages of preferable climate and living conditions. Artificial scarcity stems largely from institutional pressures on the housing market—from finance structures and government monetary and tax policies. The situation is similar to that in the oil industry. When supplies are plentiful compared to demand, a buyer's market exists, and the price tends to fall toward the real economic costs of producing the oil. In a seller's market, where demand is greater than what is being produced, the sellers can soak the market for all it will bear. In such situations, prices have no relation to the actual costs of existing oil or housing supplies. They are limited only by the cost of available alternatives—alternative energy sources and conservation on the one hand and the economic cost of new housing on the other.

Although both economic and monetary costs are usually affected by pressures on the housing market, they are differently susceptible to the influence of public policies. Population growth, for example, may cause protracted housing shortages, resulting in scarcity prices. Such price increases are *monetary*, not economic, and can be reversed through proper expansion of the housing supply. Public policies can assist this expansion of housing supply.

As the housing supply expands, it shifts toward a dominance of new housing, raising the average economic cost of the housing supply. These increased costs are real *economic* costs, and they take a generation to be absorbed and eliminated. Public policies can have little impact on this process, other than to create a housing surplus to ensure that prices drop as economic costs are absorbed. Population growth also interacts with limited factors of favorable location, climate, scenic and cultural conditions, thereby

PURCHASE COSTS OF HOUSING

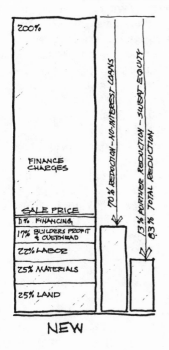

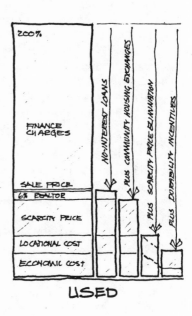

generating more competition for housing and increases in the monetary cost of housing in such locations. Such increases are generally permanent and largely irreversible.

Our building industry hasn't been able to prevent or eliminate housing scarcities, largely because of government tax and monetary policies and the nature of our financing structures. Most other major industries have become concentrated in a few firms that have their own consumer-finance divisions and that finance their growth and operations internally through retained profits. In contrast, the housing industry has remained decentralized and dependent upon bank-mortgage financing, which bears the brunt of government monetary policies. Monetary policies that rely on manipulation of interest rates to control the economy have little effect upon internally financed industries. They do, however, have a disproportionate impact on the housing industry, causing periodic massive curtailments of its output. When the money is available, the industry doesn't have the capacity to meet the demand, and when it has the capacity, people can't get mortgage money.

Keeping these ideas in mind, let's now look at how we can reduce—or *avoid the need for*—each of our expenditures for housing.

1. Eliminating finance costs: no-interest revolving loan funds. *A no-interest state-wide revolving loan fund for housing can, in one stroke, reduce the total purchase cost of a home by 65% to 75%.*

Finance costs are by far the biggest single factor in what consumers pay for housing, amounting to 65% to 80% of the actual price paid. The average house is bought and sold, mortgaged and remortgaged, every eight years. Instead of being free to its users after a century of use, the house costs its new occupants several times as much as the original sales price, and has cost its users 10 to 12 times its total economic cost in continued finance charges over that period.

Our present home-financing concepts are an outdated and unaffordable legacy from a time of low interest rates, few mortgages, and a housing market dominated by existing housing and low prices. These low prices and interest rates meant that the surcharge of finance payments were also not large. But with today's population growth, scarcity housing prices, dominance of new housing on the market, and high interest rates, the impact of finance charges upon housing costs has become unbearable. Yesterday's justifications have become unworkable in today's conditions.

Today virtually all housing is bought with mortgage money, and everyone ends up paying an immense financing surcharge. We do not all need mortgage money at the same time. So what really takes place is an equal loan of the same money back and forth, from one of us to another, as we each have need of it. For a necessity that virtually everyone "purchases," housing mortgage loans can and should be treated like the true economic trade of time and energy they are—without a massive finance charge. It is absurd that each and every one of us should have to pay an added financing "tax" of up to 10 *years* of our labor and income. That outdated concept *triples* the cost we must pay for housing.

The numerous special-interest loan-subsidy programs for veterans, the elderly, low-income households, farmers, and others are clear testimony that our conventional financing concepts are not considered workable today. Most of those programs, however, consist of a continued outflow of our tax dollars to finance institutions to underwrite their lending fees, which buyers cannot afford. Such programs do not reduce the actual costs, but only alter which pocket pays for it.

Operating in the normal money market has also meant that home mortgages have had to compete with other investments whose high profits from exploitation of people and resources set exorbitant expectations of return on investment. The result is that we, and our housing expenditures, have been pulled into a similarly exploitative relationship. Removal of housing finance from that market is necessary to permit humane and sound housing decisions to be made.

A no-interest revolving loan fund recognizes that social and economic productivity, not short-term financial "rate-of-return," are the essential measures of the use of our housing dollars. Resources shifted into extremely durable ways of meeting basic needs produce an unusually high level of social and economic value. Conversion of home financing to nonprofit public operation, as occurs with public streets, highways, water supplies, and utilities that serve everyone, means both immense cost savings to everyone and a much more effective use of our dollars. Removal of finance charges from housing expenditures would also allow building costs to more closely reflect economic productivity of more durable housing by eliminating interest surcharges on their higher initial costs.

A revolving loan fund should operate on a state-wide basis to provide no-interest home financing for all state residents. It should be tax-funded rather than bond-based, as its intention is not to secure cheaper finance money for home buyers through the state's borrowing power, but to remove the home-purchasing market from the high-profit finance industry.

Such funds would involve large sums of money and require several years to build up. With a massive initial backlog of new housing demand and outstanding loans on existing housing purchases, loans would at first be restricted to new construction, and later extended to all other housing purchases. Because of the cost savings to buyers, the initial emphasis on new construction would shift purchases into new housing to expand the housing supply. As housing vacancies eventually developed, the fund would be self-regulating—prices of existing houses would drop closer to their economic cost, it would become cheaper for most people to buy existing houses rather than to build new houses, and less use would be made of the fund. Loan repayments would be kept as close to those of conventional mortgages as feasible within household budget guidelines. Because of the lack of interest charges, repayment would occur in one-half to one-third the usual time, making the funds available more quickly for other loans.

The function of the fund would be that of an *exchange* mechanism, where all state residents exchange their time/energy/money as they each establish their housing equity. Being a revolving fund, the same dollars would be used again and again to finance many housing purchases. The initial taxpayer "sacrifice" would thus be minimal compared to the benefits gained, particularly since the fund, by eliminating interest charges, would radically lower *everyone's* cost of housing purchase.

Two of the largest reductions possible in housing costs could be accomplished through this mechanism. It would remove one of our most expensive basic necessities from massive, unnecessary finance charges. It would make possible the stable and high level of housing production needed to eliminate housing scarcity and scarcity prices. And it would also eliminate the drastic impact of federal monetary policies upon the state's housing industry by removing its mortgage financing from the finance market so heavily burdened by federal monetary controls.

2. Reducing energy operating costs: conservation. *Inexpensive conservation can reduce energy expenditures by 75%.*

The second largest hunk of housing dollars goes to energy operating costs. Over a 50-year period, this can easily amount to $50,000–$75,000. An extra economic cost of a few thousand dollars for superinsulation could result in a 90% reduction in heating costs, and the new generation of small-size fluorescent lights and more efficient appliances could similarly reduce energy costs in these areas by 75%. Along with more durable construction, these are prime examples of increased first cost of construction providing major savings over the life of the house. It also underscores the importance of dealing with financing costs, which put a massive penalty charge on such sensible first-cost alternatives.

3. Extending economic productivity: durability incentives. *Increasing the durability of housing construction and renovation to an anticipated life of 400 years would generate a five- to ten-fold increase in the economic productivity of our resources put into housing. It would correspondingly reduce the economic cost of housing by an equivalent 80% to 90%.*

The benefits of housing durability are great, but not quickly obtainable. Their consideration is essential, however, in a period when substantial expansion of our housing stock is occurring and when durability has not been a central feature of our housing tradition. We must make proper investments now if we are to reap the eventual massive benefits of durability. Durability incentives can reduce maintenance and repair costs, stretch the useful life of the economic work that went into the original construction of a house, and reduce insurance expenditures.

• *Economic,* rather than monetary, analysis should be the basis of all housing-policy analysis. Financial analysis, through the "future-discount-ing" of high interest rates, leads to ignoring the all real benefits occurring more than 10 or 20 years in the future, leading frequently to short-sighted decisions with greater long-term maintenance and replacement costs.

• Eliminate tax and mortgage subsidies that encourage investor-owned rental housing and its attendant financial-based, short-term-biased decisions.

• Encourage use of materials, construction methods, and detailing that contribute to durability of housing through research and publicity of their benefits, code requirements, and financing and insurance premiums that reflect their economic contributions.

• Where possible, eliminate or minimize housing finance charges, which magnify the additional cost of durable construction. (See discussion on revolving loan funds.)

• Minimize the impact of factors such as neglect, fire, demolition, or earthquakes, which cause premature loss of housing, through preventive programs, codes, and ordinances.

• Generate a housing surplus to allow housing prices to move away from scarcity levels down toward the actual economic cost of the housing. A revolving loan fund can accomplish this expansion in housing supply.

4. Reduction in selling costs: community housing exchanges. *Virtual elimination of realtor's fees, through establishment of community housing exchanges, could realize lifetime savings in housing expenditures amounting to 25% to 50% of the sale price of a home.*

Every home sold through a realtor diverts an average of 6% of the sale price from the homeowner's pockets. With houses being bought and sold on the average of every eight years, homeowners pay an average of six realtor's fees during their lifetime. And if the money saved from paying the realtor's fees was applied to reducing the mortgage on the house purchased, it could save two to three times its amount in interest charges.

The need for realtors or other professional services has generally escaped close scrutiny; we can reduce or eliminate the need for many such sources by using standardized documents, new technologies, or public education.

Multiple-listing services (MLS) have been set up in most communities by realtors to simplify access for themselves and their clients to information on properties available for sale. The seller fills out a card with detailed information such as lot size, number and size of rooms, kind of heating, tax assessment, mortgage situation, and amount of insulation. The realtor sends the card, along with a Polaroid picture [of the house for inclusion] in the computer-prepared booklet containing the pictures and information on *all* the houses for sale in the community, broken down by location, price bracket, number of bedrooms, and so on. The cost of a MLS is minuscule compared to the fees charged by realtors. A normal charge to a realtor is $65 a month for the service, plus a $25 charge for each listing sold.

The technology of multiple-listing services makes most of the services that realtors perform in the housing market unnecessary. A nonprofit MLS operated as a *community housing exchange* could make such listing booklets available to prospective buyers in libraries, post offices, shopping centers, employment services, personnel offices of businesses, in banks, and on newsstands. Simple guidebooks could advise both buyers and sellers what to look for, how to evaluate a house, and how to make a fair deal. They could also include necessary standard forms for contracts, earnest money, escrow, and land contracts.

People would still be able to go to realtors for any special assistance or services they wanted. But for the vast majority of sales, a community housing exchange could perform the job for about one-thousandth the cost of listing with a realtor.

5. Construction labor/owner-building. Owner-building provides a reduction in the *economic* cost of housing only where it makes use of human resources that would otherwise not be taken advantage of, as with sweatequity housing grants as part of public housing programs. Is does provide *financial* savings to the owner-builder when it avoids finance charges or taxes, as well as providing social and personal benefits.

6. Infrastructure: Reducing water, sewer, road, police, commuting, and other costs. Our patterns of housing location, design, and use substantially affect our community costs for utilities, roads, parks, and police, as well as our commuting costs. Alternate sanitation, water and energy conservation, solid waste reduction in the home, and working at home can reduce the costs of off-site development, commuting, and community services, but these savings are beyond the scope of this overview.

This overview has focused on ownership costs of houses, but similar costs and savings are possible in other sectors of the housing market. Additionally, in the rental market, separation of economic and financial analysis has developed the logic for change in mortgage regulations that would give renters ownership equity for the portion of their rent that now goes to an investor's mortgage payments—50% or more of most rental payments.

The changes we've discussed make possible immediate reductions of 75% in the cost of housing purchase and ownership, and eventual long-term savings of up to 90% in the overall cost of housing for generations to come. These changes are likely to improve, rather than sacrifice, comfort or quality, and would release vast amounts of resources and money for other social needs. At the same time, they forcefully document the value of rethinking our social institutions and economic processes to remove the encrustations of financial policies and practices that have crippled and debilitated our basic economic systems.

Housing has taken a vital leadership role in realigning our energy thinking and policies for a new era. It can fulfill a similarly vital role in the revitalization of our economic system and its reorientation toward fulfilling a greater destiny for our society.

The Male Enemy, the Left Enemy

An Excerpt from "Hard Ground: Jewish Identity, Racism, and Anti-Semitism"

by Elly Bulkin

FROM *New Women's Times* 10:4 (April 1984): 7−12

This section is an excerpt from "Hard Ground: Jewish Identity, Racism, and Anti-Semitism" which will be published, along with essays by Minnie Bruce Pratt and Barbara Smith, in Yours in Struggle: Three Feminist Perspectives on Anti-Semitism and Racism (Long Haul Press, P.O. Box 592, Van Brunt Station, Brooklyn, NY 11215; $7.95 plus 90¢ p/h).

The Cold War and the anti-Communist witch hunts of the late Forties and early Fifties devastated the progressive community in ways that scarred subsequent years of activism. As Anne Braden, a white Southern woman with decades of anti-racist work behind her, has said, "The new [Civil Rights] Movement developed with no direct links to its predecessor movements. Without doubt, it was impoverished by that fact."[1] I believe that in many ways the women's movement shares that lack of connection, that impoverishment. It might be more accurate to say that even where direct links with past struggles exist, the tendency has all too often been not to see them, not to acknowledge them or, in some instances, to acknowledge them only for the sake of angrily denying their existence. The practical effect of such responses on feminist opposition to anti-Semitism and racism has been significant.

In some parts of the women's movement, it is anathema for women to claim a tradition which involves men as well as women. In others, radical politics which are not an integral part of the women's movement are not seen as containing value, or men are not seen as anything but oppressors. In "Sisterhood—And My Brothers," Rima Shore raises one challenge to these assumptions:

> As the politics of identity play an increasing role in our community, I find my-self baffled at conflicting claims on my loyalty. We are being urged, and urging each other, to acknowledge and to reclaim the cultures from which we have emerged. . . . Am I to value the culture from which my family came while dismissing the family itself? Do I seek to identify with Jews in the abstract, but not with the brothers I have loved all my life?[2]

Outside of a family context, these questions are equally pertinent: Am I to value the "culture from which my family came while dismissing" anything men in that family have done? "Do I seek to identify with Jews in the abstract," but not identify with Jewish men who, on a personal and political level, might very well enrage me with their woman-hatred, their homophobia? Women of color confront parallel questions. For women of both groups, the answers inform our most basic analysis of racism and anti-Semitism, and affect our first steps in formulating opposition to these oppressions.

That woman-hating is the primary oppression, the one which most fully explains other oppressions is the fundamental message of much influential and widely-known feminist theory—particularly the school of thought known as "radical feminism." As with any politics based on a hierarchy of oppressions, the resulting schema implies that oppressions which are less than "primary" are of subordinate importance and political urgency. While an understanding of men as oppressors of women is an absolutely essential and major part of any analysis, an approach which, like much radical feminist theory, concentrates almost solely on sexism can skew the overall picture.

Thus far, objections to such formulations and their practical impact have been made primarily in relation to racism. The political beliefs of the Combahee River Collective, for example, challenge the validity of any theory based on the concept of a "primary oppression":

> We believe that sexual politics under patriarchy is as pervasive in black women's lives as are the politics of class and race. We also often find it difficult to separate race from class from sex oppression because in our lives they are most often

experienced simultaneously. We know that there is such a thing as racial-sexual oppression which is neither solely racial nor solely sexual, e.g., the history of rape of black women by white men as a weapon of political repression.
    Although we are feminists and lesbians, we feel solidarity with progressive black men. . . . We struggle together with black men against racism, while we also struggle with black men about sexism.[3]

In "An Open Letter to Mary Daly," Audre Lorde comments more directly on radical feminist theory:

The oppression of women knows no ethnic nor racial boundaries, true, but that does not mean it is identical within these boundaries. Nor do the reservoirs of our ancient power know these boundaries, either. To deal with one without even alluding to the other is to distort our commonality as well as our difference. For then beyond sisterhood, is still racism.[4]

Kalpana Ram is likewise strongly critical of a white Western radical feminist theory which locates women's oppression solely within "the patriarchal psychology of the male," without reference to "the complex interactions between patriarchal and non-partriarchal social forces which have shaped the position of women in Third World societies."[5]
    Prior to discussing sexual violence in the lives of the Dalit and Adivisi women of India, Ram writes about radical feminism:

A feminist analysis should be capable of theoretically incorporating a recognition that there is a real intermeshing of these different forms of oppression, and that women located at the intersection of these forms have more than one struggle on their hands.[6]

Ram's comments have implications too for the way in which radical feminist theory subsumes Jew-hating beneath woman-hating. Daly's *Gyn/Ecology*, for instance, insufficiently incorporates an understanding of racism into its analysis and fails to take account of the full lives of women of color. Daly's writing also effectively reduces the power of anti-Semitism *in itself* as a motivating force in the attempted annihilation of the Jewish people. Speaking of the Nazis, Daly points out that,

although their victims—mental patients and Jews—were of both sexes, all were cast in the victim role modeled on that of the victims of patriarchal gynocide, which is the root and paradigm for genocide;[7]

men could thereby rationalize the killing of other men *if* the victim was first forced into a powerless, and therefore, feminized, role. Might we at least consider the possibility that the Nazis *began* with a deep loathing of their victims, initially saw them as defective and sub-human, and *therefore* cast them into "the victim role"? Or the possibility that, in relation to the Jews, the Nazis' Jew-hating meshed with their woman-hating so that the feminized victim role seemed the "appropriate" one for Jewish men?

In the conclusion to this section of *Gyn/Ecology*, Daly writes:

> The Holocaust of the Jews in Nazi Germany was a reality of indescribable horror. Precisely for this reason we should not *settle* for an analysis which fails to go to the roots of the evil of genocide. The deepest meanings of the banality of evil are *lost* in the kind of research which *shrinks/localizes perspectives on oppression* so that they can be *contained strictly within ethnic and "religious group"* dimensions. The sado-rituals of patriarchy are perpetually perpetrated. Their plane/domain is the entire planet. The paradigm and context for genocide is trite, everyday, banalized gynocide. (my emphasis)[8]

I hardly think that it "shrinks/localizes perspectives on oppression" to contend that the "context" for the Holocaust is not gynocide, but "trite, everyday, banalized" anti-Semitism: specifically the German variety which goes back to Martin Luther and earlier, constituted a major strain in German political life from the late 18th century on, and was codified into German law after Hitler took power. What are the implications for acknowledging Jewish oppression as a significant and dangerous issue in times less extreme than the Nazi era if *even* the Holocaust is seen as inadequately described by the repeated statements of Nazi leaders and generations of political theorists before them which express loathing of Jews simply because we are Jews?

My comments here on *Gyn/Ecology* are less important than the fact that Daly's discussion of the Holocaust, published in 1978, has, to my knowledge, not been criticized by the many reviewers and feminist authors who have written about the book. While working in 1980 on "Racism and Writing: Some Implications for White Feminist Critics," which contained an examination of racist assumptions in *Gyn/Ecology*, I privately noted the objections I've just raised, but chose not to include them in my article. Both Daly's analysis and the lack of critical attention it received underscore the fact that in the writing of those years the issue of anti-Semitism was raised far less frequently among feminists, Jewish and non-Jewish, than it is now.

Unfortunately, the radical feminist assumptions of Daly's work continue to be found in a considerable amount of writing by white feminists. Such theory has been accepted by some women *as a given*, so that neither its assumptions nor its implications are subject to examination and possible reconsideration. In a 1982 review of Sylvia Plath's collected poems, for example, Mary Kurtzman notes:

> As so many modern women writers remind us, we are Jews in a Nazi world. (Some critics are outraged that Sylvia would feel as oppressed as a Jew. Not only are half of all Jews women, but as Daly, Rich, Barry, Chernin, Dworkin, and the rest of the feminists have shown, *men's violence against women is the ultimate in violence*.) (my emphasis)[9]

The Holocaust is here reduced to a convenient metaphor. Plath's very real oppression as a wife and a mother, as a woman poet trying to make it in a man's world, is thereby portrayed as equivalent, at least, to that suffered by "Jews in a Nazi world." The accuracy of such a comparison does not need to be explored: a certain kind of white feminist theory has already assured us that the "ultimate" oppression is men's violence against women. It will, no doubt, be good news for the massacred Indian, the lynched Black, the gassed Jew, the A-bombed Japanese to know that they have suffered something less than "the ultimate in violence."

Both the assumption that violence against women is the ultimate in violence and the subsequent devaluation of violence against males of oppressed groups are fundamental even to the radical feminist theory propounded by Andrea Dworkin, a Jewish feminist who has spoken and written about the dangers of anti-Semitism.[10] In *Pornography: Men Possessing Women*, Dworkin analyzes the situation of Jewish women in particular and then broadens her comments to include Blacks and other groups of people. Writing about "the concentration camp woman, a Jew," Dworkin says:

> It is her existence that has defined contemporary mass sexuality, given it its distinctly and unabashedly mass-sadistic character. The Germans had her, had the power to make her. And it must be said that the male of a racially despised group suffers because he has been kept from having her, from having the power to make her. He may mourn less what has happened to her than that he did not have the power to do it. When he takes back his manhood, he takes her back, and on her he avenges himself: through rape, prostitution, and forced pregnancy; through despising her, his contempt expressed in art and politics and pleasure. This avenging—the reclamation of masculinity—is evident among Jewish and black males, though it is no way limited to them.[11]

Dworkin simply assures us that these men "*may* mourn less what has happened to . . . [Jewish women] than that they did not have the power to do it" (my emphasis). Dworkin's statement is surrounded by what we know to be true—"The Germans had her"; by supposition presented as fact—"The male of the racially despised group suffers because he has been kept from having her"; and by what we know to be true of some Jewish men in "normal" times—the victimization of Jewish women through "rape, prostitution, and forced pregnancy. . . ." Is this sufficient to convince us that countless Jewish men felt no anguish for the pain, the very survival of their mothers, their wives, their daughters, their lovers, their female comrades, but felt only sexual jealousy of the Nazis who had the power to rape them? When she says that Jewish male inmates "want the power to make her," Dworkin is speaking of desire not only for sex but for rape. Doesn't this characterization of *all* Jewish male inmates deserve to be supported by something stronger than conjecture?

Dworkin's reference to Black males suggests that she would argue in much the same way about their view of Black women, *even* in situations in which Black people have suffered most deeply from white barbarism. As a feminist who has counseled rape victims, has spoken with and found shelter for battered women, and who, like women all over the world, know women among those I love who have been raped and abused by men, I have no illusions about the physical danger to women of the male-female power dynamic in this or other societies. But I fear for the practice which emerges from a theory which, in the attempt to object loudly and strenuously and justifiably to woman-hating, skims lightly over other oppressions.

It is quite different, as Melanie Kaye/Kantrowitz has done, to find heroes in those Jewish women who fought against the Nazis in ghettos or concentration camps, or, as Paula Gunn Allen has done, to celebrate a tradition of spiritually powerful Indian women. Neither negates the women- or dyke-hating within the oppressed group *itself*.[12] Neither diminishes the level of violence visited upon all Jews, all Native Americans, regardless of sex, by those who consider them less-than-human and therefore more-than-expendable. Neither denies that, as victims, the women in these groups suffer additionally *as women* at the hands of the male of the dominant race, the dominant religion. And certainly the complexity of identities, of oppressions, gets addressed in Elana Dykewomon's yet unanswered question—how to say:

> . . . I am a lesbian and I am a jew, and I am fighting back. Without giving any encouragement to jewish men, without making them feel like they still have a claim and a right to you, without denying them in such a way that it causes you to be self-hating.
> That question.[13]

"That question" is critical, and not just for those who share Dykewomon's separatist politics. As a feminist, as a lesbian, I know that I do not want to assert my Jewish identity, to oppose a range of oppressions, in a way that encourages any men to feel like "they still have a claim and a right" to me. But I will support a politics that mourns all of the Jews locked in Soviet prison, all of the Palestinians massacred at Sabra and Shatila—regardless of sex—even though such politics are shared by men whose sexism and homophobia I have also to confront.

The focus on woman-hating in radical feminist theory represents a necessary and valuable attempt, too often marred by white and Western solipsism (view that the self is the only reality), to grasp the global meaning of women's oppression. Yet this theory has also helped create such an atmosphere of hostility to the men on the left and men working in progressive causes that they end up looking practically indistinguishable from the men of the right. The equation of left with right has become something of a radical feminist stock in trade. In the middle Seventies, I heard a well-known lesbian-feminist say offhandedly at a workshop that the male left is the same as the male right. Her point was not simply that rampant sexism exists among men of all political perspectives or that woman-hating is totally unacceptable from men with otherwise progressive politics (both positions I share), but that left and right are the same in the sense that one is no more positive than the other. This ideology has persisted through the Seventies and on into the Eighties. Dworkin, for instance, one of the most vocal anti-leftists among radical feminist theorists, uses "left" as a pejorative term, sometimes accurate, sometimes not, to describe some of those men whose woman-hating is a matter of public record. In *Right-wing Women*, she manages to mention no more than a half-dozen male leftists, but goes on for pages about "the left."

The "boys of the Sixties" have a well-documented record of sexist actions and words. Marge Piercy's "The Grand Coolie Damn" is only one of many essays describing the dynamic between white "Movement" women and men in the late Sixties.[14] Although the women's movement has had an impact on a huge number of women and some men since then, sexism within the left is still alive and kicking—and women are still being kicked. But the fight against sexism is not helped by presenting a skewed picture. That Dworkin quotes two male leftists, one white, one Black, who oppose abortion does not mean that the left *per se* opposes abortion, any more than a couple of well-chosen examples of *virulent* anti-Semitism or racism within the women's movement would *prove* that the movement as a whole maintains such values.[15] Dworkin is not deterred from making generalizations by events which contradict her views: the presence of women and men from *some* left groups at pro-choice demonstrations against President Carter's Secretary of Health, Education, and Welfare Joseph Califano, and their presence at the protest in Cherry Hill, New Jersey at the National Right-to-Life Convention; the membership of a number of left groups in the Reproductive Rights National Network; the stated pro-choice position of many single or multi-issue left or progressive groups. "Men do not have principles or political agendas not congruent with the sex they want," Dworkin writes about "the left."[16] And, if, as she assures us, they are *all* like that, feminists are wrong-headed to seek alliances in that quarter.

Within parts of the women's community, the male enemy/left enemy formulation serves as a handy deterrent to women's stepping out of line and considering issues in ways which involve serious political criticism of radical feminist theory. When I discussed the racism in *Gyn/Ecology* in *Sinister Wisdom 13*, for example, I received letters which accused me of "male modes of thinking" and suggested that I had "left sympathies."[17] My failing, as far as I could tell, was that I *assumed* that the racism affecting men—the Asian men victimized by Western stereotypes and U.S. bombs, the Afro-American man randomly shot because of his color, not his sex—was both dreadful in itself *and* an inherent part of the racism which affects women of color on a day-to-day basis. But, tossed out like rotten tomatoes to splatter all but the edges of my argument, the terms "male" and "left" were clearly meant to obliterate any validity in what I had written.

Such responses have, in fact, silenced me, and, I suspect, other women.

In 1981, when *Sinister Wisdom* published an excerpt from *Pornography*, I objected strongly to Dworkin's distortions of the left. The inaccurate picture she presented undercut the possibility of effective organizing against the right wing in this country. I was angry enough to write, but I chose to send the letter to the editors as a personal correspondence, not for publication. I was not willing, as Chrystos has written at the beginning of an article about lesbian separatism, "to declare . . . [my] purity and credentials—number of years a lesbian, number of women loved, sufferings encountered as a result of, etc.,"[18] or to offer any analogous declaration in order to avoid having my argument consigned to the scrap heap of work by those who are clearly anti-woman pawns of the male left.

My caution was not misplaced. After reading a copy of that letter, a co-worker who strongly supported Dworkin's work and was well aware of my feminist activities over the years suddenly asked me what I thought of the recent charges of sexual harrassment made by several women in Boston against leftist professor Sidney Peck. I was a bit astounded, since I had never considered believing anybody but the women. But the implication was clear: making anything short of a blanket condemnation of the left makes one immediately suspect; criticizing someone who has so consistently equated the male enemy with the left enemy raises grave suspicions.

At the center of much feminist anti-leftism rests the familiar hierarchy of oppressions with sexism/gynephobia sitting unchallenged at its pinnacle. In practical political terms, this theoretical tenet implies that the pain of sexism justifies dismissing the left and seeing it as a monolithic political movement in which woman-hating and homophobia are constants. Ironically, that part of the left which sees class at the pinnacle of *its* hierarchy dismisses the women's movement wholesale for classism and for the failure to share a particular left political schema. In both instances, "other" oppressions tend to slide through the cracks.

The history of the women's movement, for instance, is certainly as replete with racism and classism and Jew-hating as the history of the left is replete, in addition to these biases, with sexism. Yet within those spheres of the women's movement which are overwhelmingly white and lesbian, largely middle-class in background or current lifestyle, heavily populated by women whose own *central* experience of oppression has been sexual, one movement is damned for its sexism and the other accepted with its flaws and the belief that work will continue to be done on its own prejudices. I fully support continued strenuous criticism of the left—by feminists who define themselves as leftists and by those who do not—both for acts of individual oppression by men against women and for group failures to take strong, active, consistent pro-woman stands based on political principle, not on opportunism. But I distinguish such responsible criticism from the kind of knee-jerk anti-leftism which can play into the hands of the right-wing powers that control this country.

Too often the feminist movement has developed in theoretical and activist isolation from work that men—or women working in groups with men—are doing. What effect does theory which sees the world in dichotomized terms—good women vs. bad men—have on the fight against Jewish oppression and racism? At one level, I think that such theory can discourage some women even from *learning* about issues which have been central concerns of the left, concerns which are central as well to groups of Jews, people of color, and others who might not define themselves as leftists: apartheid, the Israeli-Palestinian conflict, police brutality, U.S. policy in Central America. On another level, I think that it can discourage some women from *learning* about mixed groups which are combatting racism and anti-Semitism: the National Anti-Klan Network, New Jewish Agenda, the Southern Poverty Law Center, and other organizations. Additionally, it can discourage some women from *considering* participating in demonstrations organized by groups or coalitions which include men, whether these demonstrations are against the closing of Sydenham Hospital in Harlem, against the Israeli invasion of Lebanon, or against the not guilty verdict in the Greensboro shooting by the Nazis and the Klan. What gets categorized—and dismissed—as the "left" includes any number of mixed groups whose politics can be called left or progressive or radical. While major political differences might exist between these groups and any number of women's organizations, as well as between individuals in each group, the differences do not cancel out the fact that on the right-to-left spectrum of U.S. politics, where power is clearly in the hands of the right, women's interests are far better served by politics that fall definitively on the left of that spectrum. Reagan administration policies have illustrated this all too painfully.

I am assuming here that each woman needs to decide where and how to be most politically effective. As someone who has worked almost entirely in all women's groups, I am well aware of the impact that such groups can have, both within the women's/lesbian community and as a visible feminist presence in progressive coalitions. But I do not believe it is harder for me to cope with the sexism I encounter at a demonstration, meeting, or conference attended by men than it is for a woman of color to cope with the racism of an all-woman's group or demonstration, or for a poor or working-class woman to cope with the classism or Jewish women to cope with the anti-Semitism at any such gathering. Yet I have spoken to a number of white women who could not consider working in organizations with men, but who *assume*, for example, the positive value of women of color participating in groups that would require them to work closely with white women. Again, the implication that sexism is more painful, more damaging, and more central affects political theories, expectations, and actions.

While one prevalent strain of anti-leftism within the women's movement results from a critique of sexism, another strain results from a critique of Jewish oppression. Within the women's movement, the latter represents a more recent public development, and is the consequence of the growing amount of discussion, writing, and activism on the part of Jewish women regarding anti-Semitism. Some Jewish women who support the anti-leftism emerging from this concern with anti-Semitism might also see sexism as the primary oppression. Others might have long defined their politics in terms of a *simultaneity* of oppression. Still others, in the course of working out the ramifications of their own Jewish identities, seem to be in some process of rethinking and rejecting a radical feminist theory which gives insufficient weight to Jewish oppression (as to racism).

Regardless of the history of each woman's perspective on the left, it is unlikely that she has remained unaffected by the anti-leftism of so much feminist writing. She might also have been influenced by the early anti-Communism and more recent anti-leftism expressed in parts of the Jewish establishment, which has itself been motivated by genuine concern about left anti-Semitism, together, in some cases, with the desire to keep as much distance as possible from unpopular, government-investigated, and/or radical politics.

Whatever the political background and motivation of individuals, a consequence of such anti-leftism in the women's movement has already been felt. A number of statements have been made which, in their opposition to Jewish oppression, present the left as a bloc and totally ignore the existence of a Jewish left which is quite different from the New Left. In a letter to *off our backs* protesting its publication of Women Against Imperialism's anti-Jewish statement, Bat Deborah comments: "Left-wing politics, *exactly like* right-wing politics, has *always* been rabidly anti-Semitic. . . ." (my emphasis).[19] Her statement ignores the organizing against anti-Semitism by Jewish socialist movements in Europe and by Jewish socialists in this country: those who began the *Jewish Daily Forward* in 1897; those who established the Workmen's Circle in 1892 and made it a national organization in 1900; those who formed "the first American branch of the [Jewish Labor] Bund . . . in 1900."[20] Her statement also excludes Jewish-identified radicals from the left, including, for instance, those Jews who, as Communist Party members during the Popular Front period of the middle-to-late-Thirties, supported a law which would make illegal "the propagation of anti-Semitism"[21] and militantly opposed Nazism.

Outside of the Jewish left, a "radical" ideology which has been hostile to religion and many forms of ethnic identification has intersected with societally prevalent anti-Jewish attitudes. Historically, left political analysis has tended to portray class or, in some cases, race and imperialism, as primary. Within this framework, the oppression of Jews *as Jews* gets, at best, subordinated to these concerns, at times to the point of invisibility. Sometimes the argument is used that Jews who do not suffer economic or racial oppression cannot "really" be oppressed. The value of being strongly Jewish-identified is challenged, and common anti-Jewish stereotypes are incorporated into a particular left analysis. Communist Party (CP) policies, for instance, changed dramatically, so that the CP moved directly from the Popular Front period to support of the 1939 Nazi-Soviet non-aggression pact; many members of the CP did not know, while others chose not to see, the tremendous extent of Soviet repression of Jews. More recently, a John Brown Anti-Klan Committee pamphlet makes no mention of Jews as targets of Klan hatred and violence; although *Big Mama Rag* has "both written and spoken" to Committee members about "their very obvious omission . . . they have never responded."[22] A woman from a left group maintains at a public forum that the onus for the anti-Semitism of progressives is on "the Jewish community" itself because it is, she says, racist and reactionary. She apparently thinks it quite acceptable to blame Jews for the oppression *they* suffer and to make general statements about the entire Jewish community based on the politics and actions of some of its members. The All-African People's Revolutionary Party distributes an anti-Zionist leaflet depicting Jews as arch-capitalists, arch-imperialists, arch-racists:

> It was Jewish mercantile capital which financed the voyages of Columbus and da Gama. It was Jewish capital which financed slavery and the slave trade. It was Jewish capital which financed the invasion and colonization of Africa, the Middle East and the Western Mediterranean.[23]

As with the women's movement, a number of such examples do not illustrate that the left as a whole—or all its adherents—maintain anti-Jewish attitudes or would be unwilling to condemn their expression. Certainly anti-Semitism on the left is no more excusable than that on the right. But it does not benefit Jewish history and our understanding of Jewish oppression to paint the left as uniformly anti-Jewish and to ignore that part of the left which, in both Europe and the United States, has been created out of a "consciousness of uniquely Jewish needs and dilemmas."[24]

Some of the complexity of this situation is suggested in "That's Funny, You Don't Look Anti-Semitic: Perspective on the American Left," published in the 1977 anthology of the Chutzpah Collective, a group that is part of the Jewish left. Steven Lubet and Jeffrey (Shaye) Mallow write:

> In this article we refer to a Left with an apparent majority which is hostile to the Jews. We must point out, however, that we ourselves are leftists. . . . Some individual leftists have . . . expressed to us their disgust at the anti-Semitic attitudes of many "progressive" organizations. Thus, we are not referring to our allies and potential allies when we excoriate "the Left" in this article, rather, we hope that our analysis will help others speak out more clearly against the anti-Semites.[25]

Still, given the presence of anti-Semitism on the left, it is relatively easy to understand why such distinctions are not necessarily made in critiques of left anti-Semitism, as, for instance, analogous distinctions are not necessarily made by women of color in critique of white feminist racism. As Irena Klepfisz has written in an excellent article, "Resisting and Surviving America":

> There is a danger, I believe, from the Left as well, and this includes the Jewish Left—especially those in the Jewish Left who are embarrassed about being Jewish. Who will only say that Jews are guilty of this or that. Who never express any pride or love or affection or attachment to their Jewishness. Who only declare their Jewishness after making an anti-Semitic statement, as if ending such a statement with "Well, I'm Jewish" makes it all right, acceptable. That too enrages and frightens me. Those of the Left, Jew and non-Jew alike, seem to believe what the Right has always maintained—that Jews run the world and are, therefore, most responsible for its ills. The casualness, the indifference with which the Left accepts this anti-Semitic stance enrages me. It is usually subtle, often taking the form of anti-Semitism by *omission*. Its form is to show or speak about Jews *only* as oppressors, never as anything else. That is anti-Semitic.[26]

I am in fundamental agreement with the main points of this statement: that the serious danger of anti-Semitism can come from the left as well as the right; that some Jews within the left contribute to this danger. And over the past weekend I attended two events at which at least a dozen leftists identified themselves as Jewish just before making some vigorously anti-Jewish statement. But Klepfisz' comments are so sweeping that they seem to reflect a far different attitude toward it from that of Lubet and Mallow, one which implies that the left is both monolithic and bad.

At least as troublesome for me is the implication that "the Jewish Left" is the same as "Jews in the Left." Since Klepfisz has written elsewhere about the role of the Jewish Left in the Warsaw Ghetto resistance and spoken at events organized by sectors of today's Jewish Left, this equation seems inadvertent. Still, the reader of her critique is very likely to come away without knowing that a Jewish left presently exists and that it should not be confused with Jews who identify with segments of the sectarian or independent left which are anti-Jewish.

I don't think that those of us who are Jewish need to identify as part of the Jewish left to find something positive in the knowledge that it does, indeed, exist, and that it is, among other things, concerned in a major way with Jewish oppression. We do not have to embrace the left to benefit from knowing that independent left or progressive Jewish groups do exist that are also committed to fighting racism, supporting women's and lesbian and gay rights, favoring affirmative action, backing Israeli and Palestinian self-determination, opposing military and trade assistance to South Africa, and combatting the arms race, U.S. militarism and intervention in the Third World. And it is valuable to know, even when we might not be in agreement, that, among other periodicals, we can read *genesis 2*, "an independent voice for Jewish renewal," publishing since 1970; *Israel & Palestine*, since 1971 "an independent monthly providing free expression for all those who did not share the official positions of the Israeli Establishment and the Palestinian Establishment, as reflected in the PLO Charter"; *Jewish Currents*, pro-Israel, non-Zionist magazine that has been publishing independently since 1956; *New Outlook*, "dedicated to the search for peace in the Middle East and to cooperation and development of all the area's people"; and *shmate*, a new "journal of progressive Jewish thought."[27]

The dismissal of the left, the paucity of information about the Jewish left in many sectors of the women's movement, does not assist any of us in seeking to criticize Jewish oppression and racism in ways which recognize the uniqueness and danger of each. As those of us who are white attempt to combat racism, we have much to learn from the ways in which some left groups have already done so. Similarly, the commitment within the Jewish left to oppose anti-Semitism and racism in a responsible way that diminishes neither can provide those of us who are Jewish with models which can be adapted to the political circumstances in which each of us finds herself, even where we think that a group has not adequately reached its political goal or is lacking in committed opposition to sexism or homophobia or other oppressions.

Working outside of a framework in which the words and actions of those in the Jewish left can be scrutinized for what can be learned from them, Jewish feminists run the risk of neglecting valuable models which are not specifically feminist. A consequence is a certain amount of "re-inventing the wheel" which tends, I think, to affect the women's movement in a number of areas: the belief that something totally new has been developed when a similar version, relevant to a feminist context, has long been in existence, but outside the women's movement. Certainly, Jewish feminists bring to politics an unprecedented commitment to issues affecting us directly as Jews, as women, and, for many of us, as lesbians. But the dismissal of the Jewish left means that this political foundation has a far shakier base than is necessary.

The dominant society would have us believe that racism and anti-Semitism are oppressions to be pitted against one another, that opposition to one precludes serious opposition to the other, that Jews and people of color should be at each other's throats—and that Jews of color don't even exist. We cannot afford to dismiss any potentially useful models of ways to reject these destructive dichotomies and move beyond them to creative political action.

Notes

1. Anne Braden, "A View from the Fringes," *Southern Exposure*, Vol. IX, No. 1 (Spring 1981), p. 71.

2. Rima Shore, "Sisterhood—And My Brothers," *Conditions: Eight* (1982), pp. 98–99.

3. Combahee River Collective, "A Black Feminist Statement," *Capitalist Patriarchy and the Case for Socialist Feminism*, ed. Zillah R. Eisenstein (New York: Monthly Review Press, 1979), pp. 365–366.

4. Audre Lorde, "An Open Letter to Mary Daly," *This Bridge Called My Back: Writings by Radical Women of Color*, ed. Cherrie Moraga and Gloria Anzaldúa (Watertown, MA: Persephone Press, 1981; reprinted and distributed by Kitchen Table: Women of Color Press, 1984), p. 97.

5. Kalpana Ram, "Sexual Violence in India: A Critique of Some Feminist Writings on the Third World," *bitches, witches & dykes* (May 1981), p. 13.

6. Ram, p. 13.

7. Mary Daly, *Gyn/Ecology: The Metaethics of Radical Feminism* (Boston: Beacon Press, 1978), p. 298.

8. Daly, pp. 311–312.

9. Mary Kurtzman, "Demystifying Plath," *New Women's Times Feminist Review* (July–August 1982), p. 20.

10. See Jil Clark, "Andrea Dworkin on Her Writing, the Holocaust, Biological Determinism, Pornography, and S&M," *Gay Community News* (July 19, 1980), p. 10; and Dworkin, *Right-wing Women* (New York: Perigree, 1983), pp. 107–146.

11. Dworkin, *Pornography: Men Possessing Women* (New York: Perigee, 1981), pp. 144, 145.

12. Melanie Kaye/Kantrowitz, "Some Notes on Jewish Lesbian Identity," *Nice Jewish Girls: A Lesbian Anthology*, ed. Evelyn Torton Beck (Watertown, MA: Persephone Press, 1982; reprinted and distributed by The Crossing Press, 1984), pp. 28–44; Paula Gunn Allen, "Beloved Women: Lesbians in American Indian Cultures," *Conditions: Seven* (1981), pp. 67–87.

13. Elana Dykewomon, "The Fourth Daughter's Four Hundred Questions," *Nice Jewish Girls*, p. 159.

14. Marge Piercy, "The Grand Coolie Damn," *Sisterhood is Powerful: An Anthology of Writings from the Women's Liberation Movement*, ed. Robin Morgan (New York: Vintage, 1970), pp. 421–438.

15. Dworkin quotes Jesse Jackson and Jim Douglass, a "male pacifist" in *Right-wing Women*, pp. 74, 99.

16. Dworkin, *Right-wing Women*, p. 104.

17. Elly Bulkin, "Racism and Writing: Some Implications for White Lesbian Critics," *Sinister Wisdom 13* (Spring 1980), pp. 3–22; See published replies by H. Patricia Hynes, *Sinister Wisdom 15* (Fall, 1980), pp. 105–109; Louise Mullaley, Marguerite Fentin, and Andree Collard, *Sinister Wisdom 16* (Spring 1981), pp. 90–93.

18. Chrystos, "Nidishenök (Sisters)," *Maenad*, Vol. 2, No. 2 (Winter 1981), p. 23.

19. Bat Deborah, *off our backs* (Oct. 1982), p. 30.

20. Nora Levin, *While Messiah Slept: Jewish Socialist Movements, 1871–1917* (New York: Schocken Books, 1977), p. 166.

21. Arthur Liebman, *Jews and the Left* (New York: John Wiley & Sons, 1979), p. 506.

22. Deb Luger, "Anti-Semitism is Alive & Thriving in Denver, Colorado and Throughout the US," *Big Mama Rag* (February 1984), p. 11.

23. All African Peoples Revolutionary Party, *Israel Commits Mass Murder of Palestinian & African Peoples*, pamphlet (Washington, D.C.)

24. Levin, p. ix.

25. Steven Lubet and Jeffrey (Shaye) Mallow, "That's Funny, You Don't Look Anti-Semitic: Perspective on the American Left," *Chutzpah: A Jewish Liberation Anthology* (San Francisco: New Glide Publications, 1977), p. 52.

26. Irena Klepfisz, "Resisting and Surviving America," *Nice Jewish Girls*, p. 107.

27. *genesis 2*, 99 Bishop Allen Drive, Cambridge, MA 02139; *Israel & Palestine*, Boite Postale 130–10, 75463 Paris, France; I&P quotation is from Louis Marton, "Why I&P?" *Israel & Palestine*, No. 100, (October–November 1983), p. 2; *Jewish Currents*, 22 E. 17 St., NY, NY 10003; *New Outlook*, 2 Karl Netter St., Tel-Aviv 65202, Israel; *shmate*, Box 4228, Berkeley, CA 94704.

What in the Name of God?

by Bo Lozoff

FROM *The Sun: A Magazine of Ideas* 99 (February 1984): 4–5

NO NEW IS GOOD NEW

Creeping steadily toward my forties, I find myself in a peculiar position. On one hand, I'm part and parcel of the "New Age": I'm chairman of the Hanuman Foundation, director of the Prison-Ashram Project, have studied with a lot of swamis, teachers, and masters, have taught meditation and yoga for a decade, performed many years of disciplines and diets, lived in ashrams, communes, forests and school buses, gone crazy and gone sane, worn long hair, short hair, no hair . . . get the picture? I certainly sound like a "New Age" person to me! And this isn't the part where I amuse you with my re-entry into society as a successful stockbroker; no, I'm still out here in the bush, threading my way through the mysteries. If anything, I appreciate more than ever the richness of the mystical, and indescribable. It's at the center of everything I do.

But, on the other hand, I find a few things bugging me as the years roll by. For one thing, the term "New Age" sounds ridiculous and arrogant, as if we're the first people to reach for wholeness, or the hippest people to ever walk the Earth. It embarrasses me. We're not "on the verge" of anything; there's nothing new going on. We're all just doing what we can, like men and women have done throughout history. Maybe a few years ago the words "New Age" seemed useful to help us get together and to encourage parts of us which were fragile or embryonic, but now the very same words serve only to separate and condescend. We don't need a rallying banner to set us apart from anyone else; we can't afford it, if what we're after is *real* wholeness. By calling something new, we not only belittle the spiritual awareness of people in the past, but we also splinter ourselves in present-day society rather than contribute to the whole. And worse still, any such banner tends to lump together a lot of people and activities that may not really belong together; it becomes a convenient label for profiteers, megalomaniacs and mad-dogmatics who have discovered how to use space-age communications and computers to manipulate people toward their own ends. In the name of wholeness, such "New Age" hustlers have led us into more painful, fragmented partialness time and again, which brings me to my second gripe.

GULLIBLE'S TRAVELS

Hands down, the clearest ethic of the "New Age" has been to appreciate the diversity of all paths to the One, which of course, sounds one-derful. It's the stuff of non-judging, openness, tolerance, harmony; right on. But how long have we been distrusting our own gut feelings in the guise of "not judging?" The ethic is great, but our *attachment* to the ethic has created the largest, wealthiest pool of consumer suckers in history. We're P. T. Barnum's wildest fantasies come true: consumers who not only believe everything somebody might claim about their teaching or their product, but who don't blame anybody when things go wrong! ("Well, it was terrible for me, but I'm sure it's just perfect for some people.") After all, who are we to judge, right?

Wrong! We've been throwing out the baby with the bathwater. To avoid being judgemental, we have set aside our own much-needed skills of discrimination. We have allowed a high-powered marketplace of growth-oriented teachers, schools, and products to thrive for years without ever being challenged or critiqued. The pure and impure have succeeded equally well because we have copped out on our responsibility to evaluate or distinguish between them. Even the book and movie reviews in the new-age publications are generally in glowing, "uplifting" terms. Doesn't a book ever stink? Isn't that worth mentioning? How about all the tender, worshipful testimonials that appeared after Baba Muktananda's death? I never saw a word about the anguished letter from one of Muktananda's close disciples, a swami, who chronicled his master's sexual impurities with girls as young as fifteen. This letter circulated to various new-age "leaders" but of course wasn't suitable for the new-age press. What kind of wholeness are we shooting for, anyway?

Openness to others is wonderful, but it's only *half*-openness. We also need to be open to our own honest feelings. Why do we forget that our hunches and instincts come from God, too? Our own consciences—that deepest sense of right and wrong—may be our closest touch-point to God within us. Sure it's subtle, very tricky, to weed out our true gut feelings from our busy judgemental thoughts, but it's a required course. Ramakrishna, a great saint, taught that it's just as necessary to develop and use keen discrimination as it is to give up judging. Discrimination *is* wisdom; we can't get anywhere without it. And we certainly can't wait until we're enlightened before we share our opinions with each other.

Once I lay awake all night in a motel room with paper-thin walls, listening to the amorous passions of a famous swami having noisy sex with one of his followers. The swami was supposedly celibate, preached chastity, and made many public statements about the purity of his own lifestyle. As bizarre as this sounds, I was so true to my new-age ethic that I convinced myself for three years that maybe he was teaching her a profound *pranayam* (breathing technique), although every fiber of my being really knew what was going on. Finally the young lady left him, in despair and anguish over the hypocrisy in which she allowed herself to become a pawn. (I'm withholding his name here because this happened a dozen years ago, and I'd like to think he can change as radically as most of us have in that time.) But how unworthy, how separate from God, must I have felt, to have denied my own senses so fully!

QUACK QUACK

There's an old saying: "If it looks like a duck, walks like a duck, and smells like a duck, then maybe it's a duck." At some point we have to begin calling things as we see them, realizing that of course we'll turn out to be mistaken sometimes, but that's okay as long as we don't pretend to be infallible. Jesus encouraged us to be trusting, but he also said to be as clever as foxes. Meher Baba said that following a false teacher is like letting a madman sit on your throat with a razor. The Buddha told us not to accept teachings based on what other people say, or on what the teacher claims or promises, or on the enthusiasm of other followers, but rather solely on the basis of our own gut feelings, our own personal experiences.

I'm not talking about being cynical or closed-minded. But we've got to appreciate that the "New Age" is not immune to corruption, sophisticated fundamentalism, empire-building, or sincere delusion. In any age, a variety of appealing fads will be taking place alongside genuine spiritual evolution. The decision to surrender to a teaching or teacher is not one to be taken lightly. I'm definitely not suggesting that we only look for things that feel "good" or which we can understand; not at all. Feeling "right" is very different from feeling "good." Often the very best teachings are those which rip us apart, force us into our pain and weaknesses, and push us past our rigid models of how holy people should look or act, or what our spiritual journey should be like. Make no mistake about it, I deeply honor the painful parts. But as Mike Harper, an inmate at Georgia State Prison, wrote recently:

> My mind is open, my Spirit seeking light, but not so gullible as to embrace any and every philosophy stumbled across. Not every light you see is the coming of dawn; it may be just some bum firing up his stogie."

BHAGWAN ROLLS-ROYCE

Making our own best guesses, from as quiet an inner place as we can find, requires a lot of courage. It's a lot easier to let a teacher or friends or the "New Age" define things for us. One of the most hopeful and courageous decisions I've heard about lately is that the organizers of a "Unity in Yoga" conference in Portland, Oregon, declined to invite Bhagwan Rajneesh's people to make presentations at the conference. Good for them! Rajneesh's arrogant, opulent scene in Oregon looks, walks, and smells so much like a duck it's almost quacking, and it's inspiring to see a group of tolerant yoga people get up the guts to say, "We don't want to be aligned with you." What does Rajneesh's empire have to do with yoga? His disciples publicly denounce the frightened people of Antelope, Oregon, as "stupid, ignorant, small-minded bigots." They pride themselves in the *Rajneesh Times*, their newspaper, as being "as ruthless" as anyone who may oppose them. They've taken over the politics, economy, and school board of a small town, and brag to reporters that "we like to live like kings and queens; we're going to make a lot of money." Rajneesh's chief spokeswoman, Ma Anand Sheela, described the people of Antelope as "indolent old people doing nothing but marking time until they die." And Sheela herself is the head of a new religion, Rajneeshism. That's a religious viewpoint of ordinary people? Yoga means unity, togetherness, a yoking of our energies toward the One. Should the world accept Rajneesh as a great yogi just because he claims to be? He's obviously got a lot of spiritual power, and he's a brilliant writer; maybe he's even a philosopher-king. But "Bhagwan" means "God." And in my heart I know that God doesn't round up a few thousand followers and then say, in effect, "Screw the rest." A Guru loves us all.

Bo will give a talk on some of the questions raised in this essay Friday, January 27, at 8 p.m. in the Carolina Union, University of North Caorlina, Chapel Hill.

An interview with Bo and his wife Sita appeared in Issue 73 of THE SUN. For nearly 10 years they have run the Prison-Ashram Project, part of Ram Dass' Hanuman Foundation, which helps prisoners interested in spiritual growth (Route 1, Box 201, Durham, N.C. 27705).—Ed.

The Big Party

by Noel Weyrich

FROM *Philadelphia City Paper: The New Voice of Philadelphia*
(October 19–November 2, 1984): 1, 4–5, 19

*Art Rosenblum has personally invited 300,000 people from around the
world to a big party to celebrate nuclear disarmament.*

Fifty-six-year-old Art Rosenblum has spent a lot of time lately sitting on his
living room floor in Germantown with his wife, Judy, wrapping up tight
little bundles of dollar-sized handbills featuring a picture of their five-year-
old daughter. So far, they have mailed out 300,000 of them to people all over
the world.

More than just an extremely proud father, the tall, thin, goateed Rosenblum is the founder and master of ceremonies, such as it is, of the "Big
Party '84," described on those thousands of pink and green "invitations" as
a week-long celebration to be held "in every town and city in the world"
during United Nations Disarmament Week, October 24–30.

What's the occasion? Only to "CELEBRATE THE TRANSFORMATION
(and disarmament) OF THE WORLD." Wishful thinking? Perhaps. But according to Dr. Robert Muller of the United Nations, one of several highly-
respected leaders who have lent their names to the Big Party's letterhead,
the party should be thrown "every year until it succeeds."

Rosenblum has no illusions that 1984 will be that year, but he has plenty
of evidence that the invitations, which look much like 84-dollar bills drawn
by Robert Crumb (of 'Keep On Truckin' fame), are being distributed for

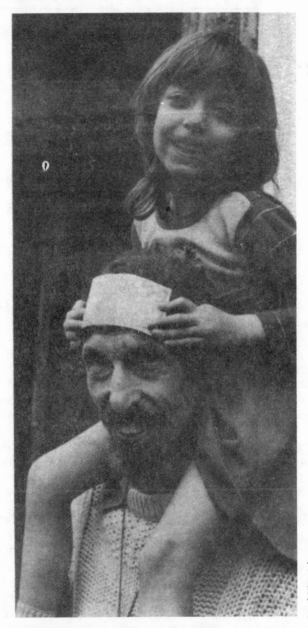

Art Rosenblum's daughter Serendipity is the Little Sister—
as opposed to Big Brother—on the Big Party invitation.
That's one of the invites, on Art's forehead.

more than just their obvious amusement value. Big Parties (which will more likely be small gatherings) are slated for Boston, Chicago, Seattle, Dubuque, Fort Wayne, Boulder, Santa Fe, Vancouver, Sao Paulo, even Aukland, New Zealand. In Philadelphia, several will be held in conjunction with a weekend workshop to be given by futurist psychotherapist Jean Huston. Additionally, Rosenblum is sure there will be dozens of other places around town and around the world where people will be gathering to share some good times and a few thoughts about disarmament.

Thinking, says Rosenblum, is what it's all about. The veteran peace activist and guiding light of the Aquarian Research Foundation (ARF), which he runs out of his home, maintains that "the arms race will end only with a sudden flip in world thinking, just like the Vietnam War, where all of a sudden almost nobody was for it.

"So rather than protest, which doesn't seem to work, or elect new officials, which also doesn't seem to work, we're just going to celebrate the belief that it's already happened."

Printed on the back of each invite is the true story of a picnic held in New York's Hudson Valley in 1979 to celebrate the belief that a nearby nuclear plant would never be completed. Cost overruns soon thereafter caused the plant to be cancelled.

"Our thoughts create our reality far more than we realize," the story admonishes. "Prepare for the Big Party to celebrate the disarmament of the world!"

For 25 dollars a set, Rosenblum has mailed Big Party kits to places as far away as South Africa, Malaysia, and Australia. The kits include 200 invitations, a Nuclear War Prevention Manual, and a subscription to the ARF newsletter, all of which are printed on a big old offset press sitting where most families might put the dining room table.

Each kit also includes a copy of *The Hundredth Monkey*, a tiny paperback anti-war tract which contains in its first few pages a simply-written story much more inspiring than that of the anti-nuke picnic.

Some 30 years ago, scientists arrived on the tiny Japanese island of Koshima, bringing sweet potatoes with them to feed the monkeys they had come to study.

A particular young monkey soon discovered the potatoes tasted better when washed in a nearby stream. Other young monkeys were quick to follow her example, though most elders continued to eat their potatoes *au naturel*.

Suddenly one day, after they had been there nearly five years, the scientists discovered that every monkey in the colony had begun washing its potatoes. At the same time, monkeys on other islands miles away also took up the practice. The scientists could only theorize that, in general, after a "new awareness" gains a certain critical number of adherents, perhaps in this case it was 100, that awareness begins suddenly to jump from mind to mind, even across great distances.

In the simplest terms possible, then, the Big Party is the start of the search for the 100th anti-nuclear monkey.

> Let's dare ask for what we really want even if it looks crazy. All we want is a whole new age where all the people love one another.
> But that might be easier than peace in a world of hate.
>
> —*ARF Newsletter credo*

To better understand what the Big Party is and what it may mean, it's probably necessary to better understand Art Rosenblum. It isn't a simple task. In conversation, his speech is clear and almost unnervingly deliberate: an elaborately-detailed shaggy-dog tale might ramble on without discernible direction until its last moment, when the upshot is revealed and the significance of each convolution at last becomes clear. Transfixed all the while by Rosenblum's intense, unwavering gaze and his inscrutibly even temperament, a listener is nonetheless distinctly aware (because he's been

THE HUNDREDTH MONKEY THEORY

Thirty years ago, scientists arrived on a tiny Japanese island, bringing sweet potatoes with them to feed the monkeys they had come to study.

One young monkey soon discovered the potatoes tasted better when washed in a nearby stream. A few followed her lead, but most continued eating them "au naturel."

Then suddenly one day, five years later, all the monkeys on the island were washing their potatoes. At the same time, monkeys on other islands miles away also took up the practice. The moral? New awareness reaches a critical mass when there are enough adherents, when that "hundredth monkey" to adopt a new idea triggers the chain reaction that turns a good idea into a universal one.

Art Rosenblum's Big Party is part of the search for the one-hundredth anti-nuclear monkey.

warned) that he is hearing only what Rosenblum feels he is "ready" to accept.

But if comprehending Art Rosenblum is difficult, admiring him is easy. He describes himself as a writer, inventor, electronics buff, printer, mechanic, airplane pilot and networker for the alternatives movement. His self-published *Natural Birth Control Book* is in its sixth edition, with 100,000 copies published over the past 13 years. The monthly ARF Newsletter, an informal typewritten update on his various researches in the fields of human potential, goes out to hundreds of paying subscribers all over the country. ARF also sells, for donations, taped talks by some of Art and Judy's favorite people, including Ram Dass, Daniel Berrigan and futurist Barbara Hubbard.

More important, however, is the unique pacifist odyssey Rosenblum's life has consisted of. Buoyed by the same relentless optimism and Gandhi-like belief in humanity that the Big Party represents, he has always stepped to his own drummer, whether society was keeping up or not. During the prosperous years of the Eisenhower and Kennedy administrations, when a young man with a measured IQ of 170 might be expected to go far, he did indeed go far—to Paraguay, where he worked as a mechanic on a primitive religious commune. In the early 60s, he spent a few years in one of America's very few successful communes. Soon after, he joined the anti-war movement full-time when it was in its infancy, even though he was nearly 40. Before the war ended, he had become dedicated to investigating "alternative lifestyles," years before the expression was a cliche.

In each instance, Rosenblum has been at the cutting edge of every new movement within his basic pacifist ideology, becoming an active member of each movement years before they came to the general public's attention. There are those who claim to see the future, but Art Rosenblum always seems to be living it.

> I have a bad memory, and, like other people with the same problem, I have to figure things out in order to survive. When I was young I would forget how to tie my shoes. So I have to think creatively because I can't always remember how something should be done.

Arthur Rosenblum was born in 1927 in the Bronx to a lawyer father who ran a ladies garment business and an artist mother who, at 85, continues to paint today, donating her works to peace groups.

In order to avoid college, the young Rosenblum decided to enlist in the peacetime army in 1945, hoping to learn radiometry. He was rejected after admitting that he hated regimentation and would probably go AWOL first chance he got. Recalling the Allied firebombing of Dresden, he told the recruiter that "any country that had to be fought for by organized murder isn't worth protecting."

So he went to college.

One day during college I was fiddling with an old motorcycle and someone dumped a bucket of water on me for making too much noise. I was furious. I went into the garage where he kept his car, deciding to do something to it, when I thought of Gandhi. I took a rag and shined up the car, instead of doing it any harm. When the owner saw what I had done, he was dumbstruck. From that time on, we were friends. . . . Today, when our daughter, Serendipity, does something we don't like, we just hug her until she behaves. Sometimes she'll behave if we just suggest she needs a hug.

In the late 40s, Rosenblum dropped out of Hiram College in Ohio to join the Bruderhof, a Christian Hutterite commune of 600 pacifists in a remote area of Paraguay. Before he left America, he managed to round up four tons of heavy machinery desperately needed by the isolated community, and then took it on the ship with him, even though he had no money.

"I just trusted that if I told people about the community, they would help," he recalls.

Though Jewish, and an atheist at the time, he stayed with the Hutterites for 15 years.

When I joined the Bruderhof, I asked them if their hope was that similar communities would grow all over the world. They said no, that they believed only in the coming of God's kingdom on Earth, though they couldn't really define what that meant. Over time, I came to realize that God's kingdom simply means a kingdom of love, a world where everybody loves one another. That's the real purpose of the arms race. It's not meant to destroy us, it's meant to put us against a wall and tell us we can't go any further this way. We have to be transformed, or else.

The Bruderhof moved to a spot near Kingston, N.Y. in 1962 and after much soul-searching, Rosenblum left the community three years later, convinced that the restrictions the leaders placed on sexual and personal behavior were simply un-Christian. Later that year, he went to his first anti-war rally in Washington, a modest affair of about 30,000 protesters.

"I saw this woman there with a guitar who told me she had come because she was 'anti-kill,'" he says, recounting the memory with uncommon animation. "She told me, 'I don't want to be killed and I don't think other people want to be killed.' Later I found out it was Joan Baez! The most famous folk singer in the country and I hadn't even recognized her!"

Rosenblum soon moved to another Christian pacifist community, Reba Place, near Chicago, overtly committed to sexual and personal freedom. He also worked part-time for the radical Students for a Democratic Society (SDS), dedicating to the peace movement the printing skills he had picked up during a brief period in the employ of IT&T.

"The community became upset with me because I was spending so much time at SDS," he says. "I thought they should have been helping SDS end the war, but they couldn't understand how I could work for a communist organization and still be a Christian. Of course, I never thought to ask them why they had let me live there while I was working for a capitalist organization—IT&T!"

Convinced of the importance of ending the Vietnam War, he decided to leave the Reba Place community and work full time for SDS. He was 39 at the time.

> One evening while at an SDS National Council meeting, I found myself seated on the floor in a circle with 30 other people in a room lit only by candles. Someone suggested we should each speak for two minutes about what we'd like the world to be like in the future. I was amazed by what came out. All of us seemed to be in agreement with every single desire expressed in that circle. In all my years of communal living, I had never seen such complete unity so easily arrived at. Later, I realized that the basic longings of all human beings must be exactly the same. We have these longings because they are a picture of the future, a clear vision of the new humanity that is to come for all of us.

Rather than accede to a leadership post within SDS, Rosenblum decided instead to help remedy a problem facing the burgeoning radical movement in almost every city in the country—printers were refusing to publish their literature.

He bought a car and traveled from one town to another, as far west as Iowa, using his knowledge of printing to purchase (or, in some cases, to simply wheedle a donation of) second-hand presses and other print machinery for communes and other New Left groups. One such operation he helped set up, the local Resistance Press, is still in existence today as a feminist cooperative, the Omega Press on Spring Garden Street.

He spent nearly two years as a traveling radical press consultant, accepting as payment only room and board and, upon leaving, $50 to get to his next destination. Years later he would read somewhere that those two years saw an "unexplainable" blossoming of the underground press movement in the eastern U.S.

> On a couple of occasions during that time I met women that I wanted to marry who were interested in me. But both wanted me to stop that work, and I said, Look, I'm the only one in the country willing to do this. If I don't do it, the war may last even one day longer, and that means that somebody has to die if I'm going to get married.

Rosenblum met a lot of people during those years on the road. In talking to them, he recalls he was struck that they didn't want so much a change in government or a revolution, but "a whole new age of love."

"We don't ask for it because we don't think it's possible," he remembers thinking. "But if we don't ask, it will never be possible. Somebody's got to ask."

In 1969, he wrote an article in a widely-circulated underground magazine saying he was interested in starting a foundation sponsoring research into the new age. It drew a response from a Philadelphia woman (now long since married and gone) who knew of a house in Germantown that could be rented for cheap. The offset press was moved into the dining room and ARF was born.

> I laugh when people say the 60s failed. On the contrary, out of the 60s people learned how to live together. It was a tremendous learning experience. In the 1950s, there was only one co-op community in the country. In the 60s, many started, many failed, many are still going. I have one listing of over 125 of them, and that's only a fraction of the true number.

Over the past 15 years, Rosenblum's research has led him into almost every imaginable form of "fringe" science and psychology. He looked into laetrile in Mexico, where he found a doctor discouraged about its future. He met with Jim Jones, the cult leader who would years later lead 600 of his followers to mass suicide in Guyana. (Years before the mass suicide, Rosenblum wrote an article expressing doubt about Jones' claimed spiritual powers.) He did est, Lifespring and Silva Mind Control, and dutifully reported the results in his newsletter with his typical frankness. (Lifespring convinced him he wanted to take flying lessons. He spent four days with Werner Erhard and concluded his time had been wasted.)

In 1974 the Running Press of Philadelphia published a compendium of his newsletters as a trade paperback named *Unpopular Science*. A glance at the index in the book (which is now unfortunately out of print) reveals the breadth of Rosenblum's interests: acupuncture, astral travel, biofeedback, clairvoyance, healing energies, executive ESP, mental birth control, psychic dentistry, plant telepathy, psychokinesis, and sex after death.

Art married Judy, 36, in 1976, after they had known each other for less than a month. Their interest in disarmament did not develop, however, until soon after Serendipity was born in 1979. Since positive thinking had long been a way of life for both of them (Judy had practiced mental programming to find a husband during the month before she met Art), the Big Party idea came quite naturally.

> Most times, kids misbehave because they want attention. We hug Serendipity when she misbehaves so she gets more attention than she asked for. It's the same thing when a government does something out of insecurity like threaten the use of weapons. We have to find a way to make them secure.

It is a quiet Wednesday morning at the little stone rowhouse at 5620 Morton Street and Art is on the floor again, stapling and stamping the last issue of the ARF newsletter before the Big Party. Judy is upstairs in one of the bedrooms, running off a last-minute insert on a xerox machine. Another bedroom has a hand-cranked addressing machine in it.

The issue (no. 136) reports that the Reagan campaign has promised to consider endorsing the party. No reply has been received from Mondale, but it seems likely that the names of Pete Seeger, Daniel Berrigan and Dick

Gregory as endorsers on the Big Party letterhead has made both politicians somewhat squeamish.

Another story points out that since nearly half of the latest edition of the *Natural Birth Control Book* is dedicated to such matters as extended orgasm, child-rearing and communal living, a new name, perhaps the *Natural Earth Control Book*, seems in order.

The mail arrives, bringing a check for $10 from a Jewish youth group in Elberon, N.J. They want 1,000 invitations for a party (invitations cost a penny apiece). Another letter asks to cancel an order for 10,000 but includes a $100 donation anyway. The writer is an est graduate who is wary of backing out of commitments.

After two years of planning and printing up over a quarter of a million invitations, the Big Party is about to be thrown, which only begs the question, "What next?"

"Disarming America and Russia isn't enough," Rosenblum says. "There are dictators making these things secretly. But if the world population would begin to expect the disarmanent of the world, the leaders would have to go along. So we don't need changes in government systems, we need people having parties all the time celebrating the transformation of the world."

And Art Rosenblum will be printing the invitations.

What would you say today if someone offered you a chance to make a lot of money in the slave trade? Well, the time will soon come when scientists who are asked to build weapons by the government will say, I can't do that! My colleagues wouldn't go along with it, my wife would leave me, the public would think I'm nuts! You simply can't ask me to build weapons!

POSTSCRIPT

Barbara Deming

by Minnie Bruce Pratt

FROM *Gay Community News* 12:7 (August 25/September 1, 1984): 6, 8

Barbara Deming died early on the morning of August 2 on Sugar Loaf Key, Florida at the home she shared with Jane Gapen, her lover of many years.

Barbara strove for truth all her life. She sometimes told the story of herself as a young woman in her twenties, when she, in the privacy of room and journal, had written the words, "I am a lesbian; I must face this truth." Several days later, rereading her journal, she became afraid that someone else might see it. She cut the sentence out of the page and threw it away.

Moving around her room half an hour later, she glanced down and saw her words glaring up at her from the wastepaper basket and said to herself, "You can't throw truth away. If you try to throw it away, you get into worse trouble than the trouble you were trying to escape."

It was through her stubborn holding on to her own truth, turning it over and over, and joining it to the truths of others that Barbara taught so many of us.

Born in 1917, she worked for many years in an individual and personal way, writing short stories, poems, and literary essays. But after a trip to India, she began to read Gandhi. In 1959, after discovering the Committee for Nonviolent Action, she began her work as a nonviolent activist.

Over the next 20 years, Barbara expanded her understanding of the relationship between all struggles against violent domination. She visited Cuba, and during the U.S. war on that country, South and North Vietnam. She was arrested and jailed during an anti-racist, civil rights demonstration in Bir-

mingham in 1963, an interracial peace walk in Georgia in 1964, and a peace action at the Pentagon in 1967.

In late July 1983, she was arrested with 53 other women in the town of Waterloo, N.Y. They were confronted by a mob of angry townspeople, mostly men, while the women peacefully walked from Seneca Falls to the Seneca Army Depot at Romulus, to protest the U.S. deployment of cruise and Pershing missiles in Europe.

Barbara wrote about her peace and anti-racist work, as well as her own struggles as a woman and as a lesbian, in *Prison Notes* (1966, hopefully soon to be reprinted), *Revolution and Equilibrium* (1971), *We Cannot Live Without Our Lives* (1974), and *Remembering Who We Are* (1981). Selections from these works and other writings are collected in *We Are All Part of One Another* (New Society Press, 1984). Her novel, *A Humming Under My Seat—A Book of Travail*, will be published in the spring of 1985 by the Women's Press of London.

Barbara was diagnosed with cancer in February of this year. After a painful struggle that included surgery and chemotherapy, it became clear, in mid-July, that she was dying. She declared that, contrary to society's dictates, she was "not going to go off and die discreetly." Instead, summoning up a fiery energy, she spent the last two weeks settling practical matters and visiting with family and friends, on the phone and in person, talking over the love and friendship between her and them, and the fact of her death.

Besides saying goodbye, she spent time preparing to die. She called this "dancing toward death." And some nights, a group of women gathered at the house to sing and meditate with her on this dance. One night as we chanted, she stood, tightening the drawstring of her pants, (she was very thin), raised her hands and danced a little in her own elegant, angular way.

Barbara died four days later on Lammas, the day the sun was midway between the fullness of summer and the fall dying of light, a day celebrated as harvest day and a day of completion. In the way of her dying, she stood and faced death as she had faced others who stood in opposition to her, seeing both an enemy and a friend; and in the way of her dying, she faced herself, once again showing us a different way to live.

For those wishing to express love and respect for Barbara, donations to the tax-exempt fund which she helped establish are welcome: Money for Women Fund, 207 Coastal Highway, St. Augustine, FL 32084.

DIRECTORY

Changing Men: Issues in Gender, Sex and Politics
306 North Brooks
Madison, WI 53715
(608) 262-4380

3 issues per year. $12 for 4 issues to individuals; $24 supporting; $7.50 limited income; $24 to institutions. Inquire for rates beyond the U.S. Changed title from **M: Gentle Men for Gender Justice** in 1985.

Changing Work: A Magazine About Liberating Worklife
P.O. Box 5065
New Haven, CT 06525
(203) 486-4416 and (203) 389-6194

Quarterly. $10 per year.

Civil Liberties
American Civil Liberties Union
132 West 43rd Street
New York, NY 10036
(212) 944-9800

Quarterly. Membership rates begin at $20.

Connexions: An International Women's Quarterly
People's Translation Service
4228 Telegraph Avenue
Oakland, CA 94609
(415) 654-6725

Published every 3 months. $12 per year to individuals; $24 to institutions. Inquire for rates beyond the U.S.

Crime and Social Justice
Institute for the Study of Militarism and Economic Crisis
P.O. Box 40601
San Francisco, CA 94140
(415) 550-1703

2 issues per year. $12 per year to individuals; $25 to institutions. Add $2 per year beyond the U.S.

East West Journal
Kushi Foundation
17 Station Street, Box 1200
Brookline, MA 02147
(617) 232-1000

Monthly. $18 per year. Inquire for rates beyond the U.S.

Environmental Action
1346 Connecticut Avenue, NW, #731
Washington, DC 20036
(202) 833-1845

6 issues per year. Available with membership
to EA: $18 the first year; $20 thereafter.

The Feminist Connection
P.O. Box 429
Madison, WI 53701
(608) 238-3338

Suspended publication in 1985.

Fifth Estate
5928 Second Avenue
Detroit, MI 48202
(313) 831-6800

Quarterly. $5 per year to individuals; $7 beyond the U.S.; $10 to institutions. An addi-
tional $1 pays for half subscription for a
prisoner.

**Gay Community News: The News-
weekly for Lesbians and Gay Males**
167 Tremont Street
Boston, MA 02111
(617) 426-4469

50 issues per year. $29 per year. Add 50 per-
cent beyond the U.S.

**The Guardian: Independent Radical
Newsweekly**
Institute for Independent Social
Journalism
33 West 17th Street
New York, NY 10011
(212) 691-0404

46 issues per year. $27.50 per year; $5 to prisoners. Add $11 postage beyond the U.S.

Health/PAC Bulletin
Health Policy Advisory Center
17 Murray Street
New York, NY 10007
(212) 267-8890

Bimonthly. $17.50 per year to individuals;
$35 to institutions.

Interracial Books for Children Bulletin
Council on Interracial Books for
Children
1841 Broadway
New York, NY 10023
(212) 757-5339

8 issues per year. $14 per year to individuals;
$20 to institutions. Write for a free catalog
listing the materials developed by the
Council.

**It's About Times: Abalone Alliance
Newspaper**
2160 Lake Street
San Francisco, CA 94121
(415) 549-1527

10 issues per year. $8 per year.

Journal of Pesticide Reform
Northwest Coalition for Alternatives to
Pesticides
P.O. Box 375
Eugene, OR 97440
(503) 344-5044

Quarterly. $12 per year to individuals; $20 to
institutions; $15 beyond the U.S.

Lucha/Struggle
The New York Circus
P.O. Box 37, Times Square Station
New York, NY 10108
(212) 316-0400

Bimonthly. $10 per year to individuals;
$20 to institutions. Add $5 postage beyond
the U.S.

M: Gentle Men for Gender Justice. See under new title **Changing Men.**

Michigan Voice: Michigan's Alternative Newspaper
5005 Lapeer Road
Burton, MI 48509
(313) 742-1230

Monthly. $12 per year.

Mother Jones
Foundation for National Progress
1886 Haymarket Square
Marion, OH 43305
(614) 383-3141

10 issues per year. $18 per year. Inquire for rates beyond the U.S.

Multinational Monitor
P.O. Box 19405
Washington, DC 20036
(202) 387-8030

Monthly. $18 per year to individuals; $25 to nonprofit institutions; $35 to business institutions. Inquire for rates beyond the U.S.

NCAP News. See under new title, **Journal of Pesticide Reform.**

New Options
P.O. Box 19324
Washington, DC 20036
(202) 822-0929

Published every 4 weeks. $25 per year in the U.S.; $32 to Canada; $39 elsewhere.

New Women's Times
804 Meigs Street
Rochester, NY 14620
(716) 271-5523

11 issues per year. $15 per year to individuals; $30 to institutions and beyond the U.S.

Northern Sun News
Northern Sun Alliance
1519 East Franklin
Minneapolis, MN 55404
(612) 874-1540

10 issues per year. $8 per year; $12 for membership.

Not Man Apart
Friends of the Earth
1045 Sansome Street
San Francisco, CA 94111
(415) 433-7373

Monthly. $18 per year to nonmembers; included in membership of $25.

Nuclear Times
298 Fifth Avenue, #512
New York, NY 10001
(212) 563-5940

10 issues per year. $15 per year. Inquire for rates beyond the U.S.

Nucleus: A Quarterly Report from the Union of Concerned Scientists
26 Church Street
Cambridge, MA 02238
(617) 547-5552

Quarterly. Sent to sponsors contributing $25 or more per year. Subtitle changed from **A Report to the Union of Concerned Scientists Sponsors** in late 1984.

Off Our Backs: A Women's News Journal
1841 Columbia Road, NW, #212
Washington, DC 20009

11 issues per year. $11 per year to individuals; $20 to institutions; free to prisoners. Inquire for rates beyond the U.S.

Philadelphia City Paper: The New Voice of Philadelphia
6381 Germantown Avenue
Philadelphia, PA 19144
(215) 848-7667

24 issues per year. $10 per year.

The Progressive
409 East Main Street
Madison, WI 53703
(608) 257-4626

Monthly. $23.50 per year to individuals; $18.50 to students; $35 to institutions; $29.50 to individuals beyond the U.S.; $41 to institutions beyond the U.S.

Rain
3116 North Williams
Portland, OR 97227
(503) 249-7218

6 issues per year. $18 per year to individuals; $7.50 to persons with incomes under $6,000; $25 to institutions. Inquire for rates beyond the U.S.

Socialist Review
3202 Adeline
Berkeley, CA 94703
(415) 547-3732

6 issues per year. $45 sustaining; $19.50 regular; $22 beyond the U.S.

Sojourner: The Women's Forum
143 Albany Avenue
Cambridge, MA 02139
(617) 661-3567

Monthly. $11 per year to individuals; $22 to institutions and beyond the U.S.

Sojourners
P.O. Box 29272
Washington, DC 20017
(202) 636-3637

11 issues per year. $15 per year; $18 surface mail beyond the U.S. Add $15 for airmail.

The Sun: A Magazine of Ideas
412 West Rosemary Street
Chapel Hill, NC 27514

Monthly. $25 per year in the U.S.; $27 to Canada and Mexico; $28 to other countries.

13th Moon: A Feminist Literary Magazine
P.O. Box 309, Cathedral Station
New York, NY 10025
(212) 678-1074

Published irregularly. $19.50 for 3 issues.

Whole Life Times: Journal for Personal and Planetary Health
18 Shepard Street
Brighton, MA 02135
(617) 783-8030

8 issues per year. $11.95 per year. Add $4 beyond the U.S.

Womanews: N.Y.C. Feminist Newspaper and Calendar of Events
P.O. Box 220, Village Station
New York, NY 10014
(212) 989-7963

Monthly. $8 per year to individuals; $15 supporting or first class mail; $20 to institutions.

INDEX

This index may be searched by name of person, organization, country, or geographical region, as well as by topic. Organization, country, and U.S. government department names are preferred to names of individual spokespeople; however, all social change organizations, publications, and activists mentioned in the text are included in the index. No entry is provided for Reagan Administration or United States President as their presence and influence—within the United States, internationally, and within foreign countries—can, more often than not, be presumed.

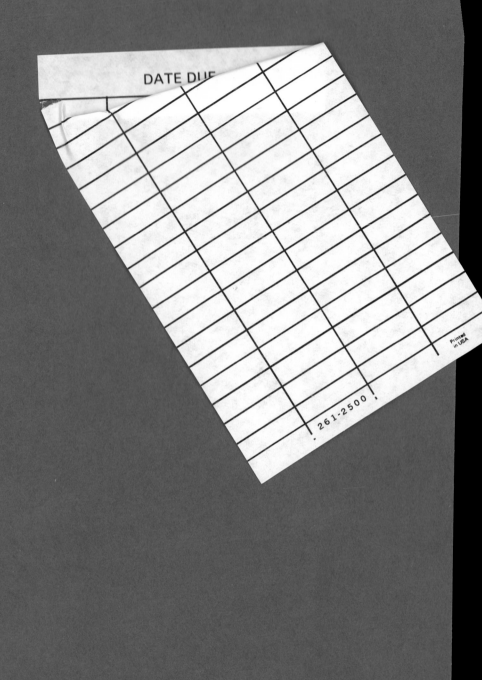

DATE DUE

261-2500

Printed
in USA